FORD BRONCO
4 X 4 PERFORMANCE PORTFOLIO
1966-1977

Compiled by R M Clarke

ISBN 1 85520 4746

BROOKLANDS BOOKS LTD.
P.O. BOX 146, COBHAM,
SURREY, KT11 1LG. UK
sales@brooklands-books.com

Brooklands Books

MOTORING

ROAD TEST SERIES

Abarth Gold Portfolio 1950-1971
AC Ace & Aceca 1953-1983
Alfa Romeo Giulietta Gold Portfolio 1954-1965
Alfa Romeo Giulia Coupés 1963-1976
Alfa Romeo Giulia Coupés Gold Port. 1963-1976
Alfa Romeo Spider 1966-1990
Alfa Romeo Alfasud 1972-1984
Alfa Romeo Alfetta Gold Portfolio 1972-1987
Alvis Gold Portfolio 1919-1967
AMX & Javelin Gold Portfolio 1968-1974
Armstrong Siddeley Gold Portfolio 1945-1960
Aston Martin Gold Portfolio 1948-1971
Aston Martin Gold Portfolio 1972-1985
Aston Martin Gold Portfolio 1985-1995
Audi Quattro Gold Portfolio 1980-1991
Audi Quattro Takes On The Competition
Austin-Healey 100 & 100/6 Gold Port. 1952-1959
Austin-Healey 3000 Ultimate Portfolio 1959-1967
Austin-Healey Sprite Gold Portfolio 1958-1971
Bentley & Rolls-Royce Portfolio 1990-2002
Berkeley Sportscars Limited Edition
BMW 6 & 8 Cyl. Cars Limited Edition 1935-1960
BMW 1600 Collection No. 1 1966-1981
BMW 2002 Gold Portfolio 1968-1976
BMW 6 Cylinder Coupés & Saloons Gold P. 1969-1976
BMW 316, 318, 320 (4 cyl.) Gold Port. 1975-1990
BMW 320, 323, 325 (6 cyl.) Gold Port. 1977-1990
BMW 3 Series Gold Portfolio 1991-1997
BMW 5 Series Gold Portfolio 1981-1987
BMW 5 Series Gold Portfolio 1988-1995
BMW 6 Series Ultimate Portfolio 1976-1989
BMW 7 Series Performance Portfolio 1977-1986
BMW 7 Series Performance Portfolio 1986-1993
BMW 8 Series Limited Edition
BMW Alpina Performance Portfolio 1967-1987
BMW Alpina Performance Portfolio 1988-1998
BMW Z3, M Coupe & M Roadster Gold Port. 1996-02
Borgward Isabella Limited Edition
Bricklin Gold Portfolio 1974-1975
Bristol Cars Portfolio
Buick Performance Portfolio 1947-1962
Buick Muscle Portfolio 1963-1973
Buick Riviera Performance Portfolio 1963-1978
Cadillac Automobiles 1949-1959
Cadillac Eldorado Performance Portfolio 1967-1978
Cadillac Allante Limited Edition Extra
Checker Limited Edition
Chevrolet 1955-1957
Impala & SS Muscle Portfolio 1958-1972
Corvair Performance Portfolio 1959-1969
El Camino & SS Muscle Portfolio 1959-1987
Chevy II & Nova SS Muscle Portfolio 1962-1974
Chevelle & SS Muscle Portfolio 1964-1972
Caprice Limited Edition 1965-1976
Chevy Blazer 1969-1981
Camaro Muscle Portfolio 1967-1973
Camaro Performance Portfolio 1993-2000
Chevrolet Corvette Gold Portfolio 1953-1962
Chevrolet Corvette Sting Ray Gold Port. 1963-1967
Chevrolet Corvette Gold Portfolio 1968-1977
High Performance Corvettes 1983-1989
Chrysler 300 Gold Portfolio 1955-1970
Valiant 1960-1962
PT Cruiser Performance Portfolio
Citroen Traction Avant Gold Portfolio 1934-1957
Citroen 2CV Ultimate Portfolio 1948-1990
Citroen DS & ID 1955-1975
Citroen DS & ID Gold Portfolio 1955-1975
Citroen SM Limited Edition Extra 1970-1975
Shelby Cobra Gold Portfolio 1962-1969
Crosley & Crosley Specials Limited Edition
Cunningham Automobiles 1951-1955
Datsun Roadsters Performance Portfolio 1960-71
Datsun 240Z & 260Z Gold Portfolio 1970-1978
DeLorean Gold Portfolio 1977-1995
De Soto Limited Edition 1952-1960
Dodge Limited Edition 1949-1959
Dodge Dart Limited Edition Extra 1960-1976
Dodge Muscle Portfolio 1964-1971
Charger Muscle Portfolio 1966-1974
Dodge Viper Performance Portfolio 1990-1998
ERA Gold Portfolio 1934-1994
Facel Vega Limited Edition Extra 1954-1964
Ferrari Limited Edition 1947-1957
Ferrari Limited Edition 1958-1963
Ferrari Dino Limited Edition Extra 1965-1974
Ferrari Dino 308 & Mondial Gold Portfolio 1974-1985
Ferrari 328 348 Mondial Ultimate Portfolio 1986-94
Fiat 600 & 850 Gold Portfolio 1955-1972
Fiat Dino Limited Edition
Fiat Pininfarina 124 & 2000 Spider 1968-1985
Fiat X1/9 Gold Portfolio 1973-1989
Fiat Abarth Performance Portfolio 1972-1987
Ford Consul, Zephyr, Zodiac Mk. I & II 1950-1962
Ford Zephyr, Zodiac, Executive Mk. III & IV 1962-1971
Ford Cortina 1600E & GT 1967-1970
High Performance Capris Gold Portfolio 1969-1987
Capri Muscle Portfolio 1974-1987
High Performance Fiestas 1979-1991
Ford Escort RS & Mexico Limited Edition 1970-1979
High Performance Escorts Mk. I 1968-1974
High Performance Escorts Mk. II 1975-1980
High Performance Escorts 1980-1985
High Performance Escorts 1985-1990
High Perf. Sierras & Merkurs Gold Port. 1983-1990
Ford Thunderbird Performance Portfolio 1955-1957
Ford Thunderbird Performance Portfolio 1958-1963
Ford Thunderbird Performance Portfolio 1964-1976
Ford Automobiles 1949-1959
Ford Fairlane Performance Portfolio 1955-1970
Ford Ranchero Muscle Portfolio 1957-1979
Edsel Limited Edition 1957-1960
Ford Galaxie & LTD Gold Portfolio 1960-1976
Falcon Performance Portfolio 1960-1970
Ford GT40 Gold Portfolio 1964-1987
Ford Bronco 4x4 Performance Portfolio 1966-1977
Ford Bronco 1978-1988
Shelby Mustang Ultimate Portfolio 1965-1970
Mustang Muscle Portfolio 1967-1973
High Performance Mustang IIs 1974-1978
Mustang 5.0L Muscle Portfolio 1982-1993
Mustang 5.0L Takes On The Competition
Goggomobil Limited Edition
Holden 1948-1962
Honda S500 • S600 • S800 Limited Edition 1962-1970
Honda CRX 1983-1987
International Scout Gold Portfolio 1961-1980
Isetta Gold Portfolio 1953-1964
ISO & Bizzarrini Gold Portfolio 1962-1974
Jaguar and SS Gold Portfolio 1931-1951
Jaguar C-Type & D-Type Gold Portfolio 1951-1960
Jaguar XK120, 140, 150 Gold Portfolio 1948-1960
Jaguar Mk. VII, VIII, IX, X, 420 Gold Port. 1950-1970
Jaguar Mk. 1 & Mk. 2 Gold Portfolio 1955-1969
Jaguar E-Type Gold Portfolio 1961-1971
Jaguar E-Type V-12 1971-1975
Jaguar S-Type & 420 Limited Edition 1963-1968
Jaguar XJ12, XJ5.3, V12 Gold Portfolio 1972-1990
Jaguar XJ6 Series I & II Gold Portfolio 1968-1979
Jaguar XJ6 Series III Perf. Portfolio 1979-1986
Jaguar XJ6 Gold Portfolio 1986-1994
Jaguar XJS Gold Portfolio 1975-1988
Jaguar XJ-S V12 Ultimate Portfolio 1988-1996
Jaguar XK8 Limited Edition
Jeep CJ-5 & CJ-7 4x4 Perf. Portfolio 1976-1986
Jeep Wagoneer Performance Portfolio 1963-1991
Jeep J-Series Pickups 1970-1982
Jeepster & Commando Limited Edition 1967-1973
Jeep Cherokee & Comanche Pickups P. P. 1984-91
Jeep Wrangler 4x4 Performance Portfolio 1987-99
Jeep Cherokee & Grand Cherokee 4x4 P. P. 1992-98
Jensen - Healey Limited Edition 1972-1976
Lagonda Gold Portfolio 1919-1964
Lancia Aurelia & Flaminia Gold Portfolio 1950-1970
Lancia Fulvia Gold Portfolio 1963-1976
Lancia Beta Gold Portfolio 1972-1984
Lancia Stratos 1972-1985
Lancia Delta & integrale Ultimate Portfolio
Land Rover Series I 1948-1958
Land Rover Series II & IIa 1958-1971
Land Rover Series III 4x4 Perf. Portfolio 1971-1985
Land Rover 90 110 Defender Gold Portfolio 1983-1994
Land Rover Discovery Perf. Port. 1989-2000
Fifty Years of Selling Land Rover
Lamboghini Performance Portfolio 1964-1976
Lamboghini Performance Portfolio 1977-1989
Lamboghini Diablo Performance Portfolio 1990-2001
Lincoln Gold Portfolio 1949-1960
Lincoln Continental Performance Portfolio 1961-1969
Lincoln Continental 1969-1976
Lotus Sports Racers Portfolio - covering 1951-1965
Lotus Seven Gold Portfolio 1957-1973
Lotus Elite Limited Edition 1957-1964
Lotus Elan Ultimate Portfolio 1962-1974
Lotus Elan & SE 1989-1992
Lotus Europa Gold Portfolio 1966-1975
Lotus Elite & Eclat 1974-1982
Marcos Coupés & Spyders Gold Portfolio 1960-1997
Maserati Cars Performance Portfolio 1957-1970
Maserati Cars Performance Portfolio 1971-1982
Maserati Cars Performance Portfolio 1982-1998
Matra Limited Edition 1965-1983
Mazda Miata MX-5 Performance Portfolio 1989-1997
Mazda Miata MX-5 Takes On The Competition
Mazda RX-7 Gold Portfolio 1978-1991
McLaren F1 • GTR • LM Sportscar Perf. Portfolio
Mercedes 190 & 300 SL 1954-1963
Mercedes G-Wagen 1981-1994
Mercedes S & 600 1965-1972
Mercedes S Class 1972-1979
Mercedes S Class Limited Edition Extra 1980-1991
Mercedes 230 • 250 • 280SL Gold Portfolio 1963-1971
Mercedes SLs & SLCs Gold Portfolio 1971-1989
Mercedes SLs Performance Portfolio 1989-1994
Mercedes 190 Limited Edition Extra 1983-1993
Mercedes CLK & SLK Limited Edition
Mercury Comet & Cyclone Limited Edition 1960-1970
Cougar Muscle Portfolio 1967-1973
Messerschmitt Gold Portfolio 1954-1964
MG Gold Portfolio 1929-1939
MG TA & TC Gold Portfolio 1936-1949
MG TD & TF Gold Portfolio 1949-1955
MGA & Twin Cam Gold Portfolio 1955-1962
MG Midget Gold Portfolio 1961-1979
MGB Roadsters 1962-1980
MGB MGC & V8 Gold Portfolio 1962-1980
MGB GT 1965-1980
MGC & MGB GT V8 Limited Edition
MG Y-Type & Magnette ZA/ZB Limited Edition
MGF Limited Edition
Mini Gold Portfolio 1959-1969
Mini Gold Portfolio 1969-1980
Mini Gold Portfolio 1981-1997
High Performance Minis Gold Portfolio 1960-1973
Mini Cooper Gold Portfolio 1961-1971
Mini Moke Gold Portfolio 1964-1994
Starion & Conquest Performance Portfolio 1982-90
Mitsubishi 3000GT & Dodge Stealth P.P. 1990-99
Morgan Three-Wheeler Gold Portfolio 1910-1952
Morgan Plus 4 & Four 4 Gold Portfolio 1936-1967
Morgan Cars Portfolio 1968-2001
Morris Minor Collection No. 1 1948-1980
Nash & Nash-Healey Limited Edition 1949-1957
Nash-Austin Metropolitan Gold Portfolio 1954-1962
Nissan Skyliner GT-R Limited Edition Extra 1989-02
NSU Ro80 Limited Edition
NSX Performance Portfolio 1989-1999
Oldsmobile Automobiles 1955-1963
Oldsmobile Muscle Portfolio 1964-1971
Cutlass & 4-4-2 Muscle Portfolio 1964-1974
Opel GT Gold Portfolio 1968-1973
Opel Manta Limited Edition 1970-1975
Packard Gold Portfolio 1946-1958
Pantera Ultimate Portfolio 1970-1995
Panther Gold Portfolio 1972-1990
Plymouth Limited Edition 1950-1960
Plymouth Fury Limited Edition Extra 1956-1976
Barracuda Muscle Portfolio 1964-1974
Plymouth Muscle Portfolio 1964-1971
Pontiac Limited Edition 1949-1960
GTO Muscle Portfolio 1964-1974
Firebird & Trans-Am Muscle Portfolio 1967-1972
Firebird & Trans-Am Muscle Portfolio 1973-1981
High Performance Firebirds 1982-1988
Firebird & Trans Am Performance Portfolio 1993-2000
Pontiac Fiero Performance Portfolio 1984-1988
Porsche 356 Gold Portfolio 1953-1965
Porsche 912 Limited Edition
Porsche 911 1965-1969
Porsche 911 1970-1972
Porsche 911 1973-1977
Porsche 911 SC & Turbo Gold Portfolio 1978-1983
Porsche 911 Carrera & Turbo Gold Port. 1984-1989
Porsche 911 Gold Portfolio 1990-1997
Porsche 911 Takes On The Competition 1990-1997
Porsche 914 Ultimate Portfolio
Porsche 924 Gold Portfolio 1975-1988
Porsche 928 Performance Portfolio 1977-1994
Porsche 928 Takes On The Competition
Porsche 944 Ultimate Portfolio
Porsche 968 Limited Edition Extra
Railton & Brough Superior Gold Portfolio 1933-1950
Range Rover Gold Portfolio 1970-1985
Range Rover Gold Portfolio 1985-1995
Range Rover Performance Portfolio 1995-2001
Range Rover Takes on the Competition
Renault Alpine Gold Portfolio 1958-1994
Riley Gold Portfolio 1924-1939
Rolls-Royce Silver Clould & Bentley S Ultimate Port.
Rolls-Royce Silver Shadow Ultimate Portfolio 1965-80
Rolls-Royce & Bentley Gold Portfolio 1980-1989
Rover P4 1949-1959
Rover 2000 & 2200 1963-1977
Studebaker Gold Portfolio 1947-1966
Studebaker Hawks & Larks 1956-1963
Avanti Limited Edition Extra 1962-1991
Subaru Impreza Turbo Limited Edition Extra 1994-2001
Sunbeam Tiger & Alpine Ultimate Port. 1959-1967
Suzuki SJ Gold Portfolio 1971-1997
Vitara, Sidekick & Geo Tracker Perf. Port. 1988-1997
Toyota Land Cruiser Gold Portfolio 1956-1987
Toyota Land Cruiser 1988-1997
Toyota Supra Performance Portfolio 1982-1998
Toyota MR2 Gold Portfolio 1984-1997
Toyota MR2 Takes On The Competition
Triumph TR2 & TR3 Gold Portfolio 1952-1961
Triumph TR4, TR5, TR250 1961-1968
Triumph TR6 Gold Portfolio 1969-1976
Triumph Herald 1959-1971
Triumph Vitesse 1962-1971
Triumph Spitfire Gold Portfolio 1962-1980
Triumph 2000, 2.5, 2500 1963-1977
Triumph GT6 Gold Portfolio 1966-1974
Triumph Stag Gold Portfolio 1970-1977
Triumph Dolomite Sprint Limited Edition
TVR Gold Portfolio 1959-1986
TVR Performance Portfolio 1986-1994
TVR Performance Portfolio 1995-2000
VW Beetle Gold Portfolio 1935-1967
VW Beetle Gold Portfolio 1968-1991
VW Karmann Ghia 1955-1982
VW Bus, Camper, Van Perf. Portfolio 1954-1967
VW Bus, Camper, Van Perf. Portfolio 1968-1979
VW Bus, Camper, Van Perf. Portfolio 1979-1991
VW Scirocco 1974-1981
Volvo PV444 & PV544 Perf. Portfolio 1945-1965
Volvo 120 Amazon Ultimate Portfolio
Volvo 1800 Gold Portfolio 1960-1973
Volvo 140 & 160 Series Gold Portfolio 1966-1975
Forty Years of Selling Volvo

CAR AND DRIVER SERIES

Car and Driver on BMW 1957-1977
Car and Driver on Corvette 1978-1982
Car and Driver on Corvette 1983-1988
C and D on Datsun Z 1600 & 2000 1966-1984
Car and Driver on Ferrari 1955-1962
Car and Driver on Ferrari 1963-1975
Car and Driver on Ferrari 1976-1983
Car and Driver on Mopar 1956-1967
Car and Driver on Mustang 1964-1973
Car and Driver on Pontiac 1961-1975
Car and Driver on Porsche 1955-1962
Car and Driver on Porsche 1963-1970
Car and Driver on Porsche 1970-1976
Car and Driver on Porsche 1977-1981
Car and Driver on Porsche 1982-1986

RACING & THE LAND SPEED RECORD

The Land Speed Record 1898-1919
The Land Speed Record 1920-1929
The Land Speed Record 1930-1939
The Land Speed Record 1940-1962
The Land Speed Record 1963-1999
The Land Speed Record 1898-1999 - Hard Bound
Can-Am Racing 1966-1969
Can-Am Racing 1970-1974
Can-Am Racing Cars 1966-1974
The Carrera Panamericana Mexico - 1950-1954
Le Mans - The Bentley & Alfa Years - 1923-1939
Le Mans - The Jaguar Years - 1949-1957
Le Mans - The Ferrari Years - 1958-1965
Le Mans - The Ford & Matra Years - 1966-1974
Le Mans - The Porsche Years - 1975-1982
Le Mans - The Porsche & Jaguar Years - 1983-91
Le Mans - The Porsche & Peugeot Years - 1992-99
Le Mans - 1923-1999 - Hard Bound
Mille Miglia - The Alfa & Ferrari Years - 1927-1951
Mille Miglia - The Ferrari & Mercedes Years - 1952-57
Targa Florio - The Post War Years - 1948-1973 - H.B.
Targa Florio - The Porsche & Ferrari Years - 1955-1964
Targa Florio - The Porsche Years - 1965-1973

ROAD & TRACK 'PORTFOLIO' SERIES

Road & Track BMW M Series Portfolio 1979-2002
R & T BMW Z3, M Coupe & M Roadster Port. 1996-02
R & T Camaro & Firebird Portfolio 1993-2002
Road & Track Corvette Portfolio 1997-2002
Road & Track Dodge Viper Portfolio 1992-2002
Road & Track Ferrari V-12 Portfolio 1992-2002
Road & Track Ferrari F355 & 360 Portfolio 1995-02
R & T Jaguar XJ-S - XK8 - XKR Portfolio 1975-2003
R & T Mercedes SL - SLK - CLK Portfolio 1990-03
Road & Track MX-5 Miata Portfolio 1989-2002
Road & Track Mustang Portfolio 1994-2002
Road & Track Nissan 300ZX & 350Z Portfolio 1984-03
Road & Track Porsche 928 Portfolio 1977-1994
Road & Track Porsche 911 Portfolio 1990-1997

ROAD & TRACK 'ON' SERIES

Road & Track on Aston Martin 1962-1990
Road & Track on Audi & Auto Union 1952-1980
Road & Track on Audi & Auto Union 1980-1986
Road & Track on Austin Healey 1953-1970
Road & Track on BMW Cars 1966-1974
Road & Track on BMW Cars 1975-1978
Road & Track on BMW Cars 1979-1983
R & T on Cobra, Shelby & Ford GT40 1962-1992
Road & Track on Corvette 1953-1967
Road & Track on Corvette 1968-1982
Road & Track on Corvette 1982-1986
Road & Track on Corvette 1986-1990
Road & Track on Ferrari 1975-1981
Road & Track on Ferrari 1981-1984
Road & Track on Ferrari 1984-1988
Road & Track on Fiat Sports Cars 1968-1987
Road & Track on Jaguar 1950-1960
Road & Track on Jaguar 1961-1968
Road & Track on Jaguar 1968-1974
Road & Track on Jaguar 1974-1982
Road & Track on Jaguar 1983-1989
Road & Track on Lamborghini 1964-1985
Road & Track on Mercedes 1952-1962
Road & Track on Mercedes 1963-1970
Road & Track on Mercedes 1971-1979
Road & Track on MG Sports Cars 1949-1961
Road & Track on MG Sports Cars 1962-1980
Road & Track on Pontiac 1960-1983
Road & Track on Porsche 1951-1967
Road & Track on Porsche 1968-1971
Road & Track on Porsche 1972-1975
Road & Track on Porsche 1975-1978
Road & Track on Porsche 1979-1982
Road & Track on Porsche 1985-1988
R & T on Rolls Royce & Bentley 1950-1965
R & T on Rolls Royce & Bentley 1966-1984
Road & Track on Saab 1972-1992
R & T on Toyota Sports & GT Cars 1966-1984
R & T on Triumph Sports Cars 1967-1974
R & T on Triumph Sports Cars 1974-1982
Road & Track on Volkswagen 1951-1968
Road & Track on Volkswagen 1968-1978
Road & Track on Volkswagen 1978-1985
Road & Track on Volvo 1957-1974
Road & Track on Volvo 1977-1994

ROAD & TRACK BY AUTHOR

Road & Track - Henry Manney at Large & Abroad
Road & Track - Best of PS
Road & Track - Peter Egan "At Large"
Road & Track - Peter Egan Side Glances 1983-92
Road & Track - Peter Egan Side Glances 1992-97
Road & Track - Peter Egan Side Glances 1998-02

PRACTICAL CLASSICS SERIES

PC on Land Rover Restoration
PC on Midget/Sprite Restoration
PC on MGB Restoration
PC on Sunbeam Rapier Restoration
PC on Triumph Herald/Vitesse

HOT ROD 'ENGINE' SERIES

Chevy 265 & 283
Chevy 302 & 327
Chevy 396 & 427
Chevy 454 thru 512
Chrysler Hemi
Chrysler 273, 318, 340 & 360
Chrysler 361, 383, 400, 413, 426 & 440
Ford 289, 302, Boss 302 & 351W
Ford 351C & Boss 351

RESTORATION & GUIDE SERIES

BMW 2002 - A Comprehensive Guide
BMW '02 Restoration Guide
Classic Camaro Restoration
Chevrolet High Performance Tips & Techniques
Chevy-GMC Pickup Repair
Engine Swapping Tips & Techniques
Land Rover Restoration Portfolio
Lotus Elan Restoration Guide
MG 'T' Series Restoration Guide
MGA Restoration Guide
Mustang Restoration Tips & Techniques
Practical Gas Flow
Restoring Sprites & Midgets an Enthusiast's Guide
SU Carburetters Tuning Tips & Techniques
The Great Classic Muscle Cars Compared

MILITARY VEHICLES

Complete WW2 Military Jeep Manual
Dodge WW2 Military Portfolio 1940-1945
German Military Equipment WW2
Hail To The Jeep
Combat Land Rover Portfolio No. 1
Land Rover Military Portfolio
Military & Civilian Amphibians 1940-1990
Off Road Jeeps Civilian & Military 1944-1971
US Military Vehicles 1941-1945
US Army Military Vehicles WW2-TM9-2800
VW Kubelwagen Military Portfolio 1940-1990
WW2 Allied Vehicles Military Portfolio 1939-1945
WW2 Jeep Military Portfolio 1941-1945

MOTORCYCLES

To see our range of over 60 titles visit www.brooklands-books.com

30/10Z3

CONTENTS

ACKNOWLEDGEMENTS

These early Broncos continue to attract an enthusiastic following, so when stocks of our original 100-page Road Test book ran out, we decided to see what else we could find about the vehicle in our archives. We found quite a lot more and, as a quick glance at the index of this book will show, we have included it in this new and expanded volume.

The material here is reproduced with the kind permission of the leading motoring magazines and we are indebted to them for their understanding and generosity. So our thanks for the features in this book go to *Auto Topics, Car Craft, Car Life, Car and Driver, Custom Car, Four Wheeler, Four Wheeler Drive Book, 4-Wheel Drive, 4-Wheel Driver, 4-Wheel & Off-Road, Motor Trend, Off-Road Australia, Off-Road Fun Cars, Open Road, Popular Science, PV4* and *Used 4x4 Buyers' Guide*.

R.M. Clarke

There isn't any doubt that the Bronco was a major milestone in the history of sport-utility vehicles. Before its introduction in August 1965, the sport-utility market was really the domain of just two specialist manufacturers - International Harvester and Jeep. Ford was the first of the majors to try its hand and although the Bronco was in many ways a blatant copy of IH's Scout, it immediately established the Dearborn company as a major player in the market.

The first Broncos came only with a 105bhp, 170 cubic inch six, but from March 1966 a 200bhp 289 V8 was made optional, and thus became the first V8 engine in a sport-utility vehicle. The V8 option switched to the 302 motor in 1968 and then from 1973 a 200ci six replaced the 170ci type. Lastly, the 302 V8 was standardised from 1975.

Ford learned a lot as the sport-utility market developed around the Bronco. The original three models - roadster, wagon and pick-up - had interchangeable body sections so that one could easily be converted to the other. This idea had been pioneered by the Scout, but by 1971 the market had changed and only pick-up and wagon derivatives were on offer. Two years later, the pick-up also disappeared, leaving the final Broncos as wagons with optional Sport (intermediate) and Ranger (high-line) levels.

For 1978, the Bronco was redesigned on Ford's 104-inch wheelbase truck platform, and became a rather different vehicle. The cheeky, bobtailed original has nevertheless retained a place in the affections of 4x4 enthusiasts and I am sure that the articles in this book will appeal to them enormously.

James Taylor

Bronco

New Bronco with bolt-on steel cab rides high, wide, and handsome on Dearborn test track.

FORD MOTOR COMPANY has a new star on the horizon for off-the-road fans. It's called the Bronco and comes in a number of forms—from open sportster to a fully closed, 4-passenger wagon. Or you can have it as a pickup. Optional steel tops make up the difference, with either bench or buckets up front and an optional 2-passenger seat for the rear.

This inexpensive utility car should easily be competitive with other recreational vehicles. But the Bronco goes most one better. Its 6 cylinder, 170-inch engine puts out 105 hp. This lets it cruise easily at legal speeds and top 80 mph, or claw its way over rugged terrain at a snail's pace in 4wd.

The Bronco comes only as a 4wd vehicle with a 3-speed column shift and 2-speed transfer case (that includes neutral position for operation of power take-off or winch).

DRIVING THE BRONCO

We road tested prototype Broncos and climbed steep grades, bounced over rough ground, and hit slightly over 80 mph on Ford's test track. They're quite comfortable to drive either on or off the pavement. Long lists of options, heavy-duty suspension, and even a snowplow make the new Bronco an extremely adaptable vehicle. With a potential 70,000-unit market by 1970, Ford isn't overlooking the off-road enthusiast. Their new horse hits the shoe on the nail.   /MT

Special carburetor and fuel pump ensure Bronco a constant fuel supply at any body angle.

Very functional interior leaves room for options like Mustang buckets in place of standard bench seat. Trans is all-synchro.

Lockable steel top adds versatility. Transfer case includes 4-wheel drive and neutral for running optional power take-off.

The Roadster Model

Ford's New Go-Anywhere Vehicle

The Station Wagon

The Short-Roof Pickup

BRONCO

Ford

An entirely new line of Ford four-wheel-drive utility vehicles called the Bronco will lead the parade of 1966 Ford Division products.

Donald N. Frey, Ford Motor Company vice president and Ford Division general manager, said it is "not mere coincidence that the Ford Mustang has been joined by a Ford Bronco."

"The Bronco and the Mustang both respond to the voice of modern, active Americans," Mr. Frey said. "These Americans on the go—men and women who seek adventure as well as practical transportation—helped 'design' the Bronco for us and we are building it for them."

"We talked to outdoors adventurers who enjoy exploring the remote wilderness," he explained, "and they told us the kind of features they desired in a sportsman and utility vehicle."

We were sure because of our experience in building military utility vehicles that we could give them the features they wanted, he added,

The characteristics asked for include: higher highway cruising speed; the ability to climb steeper grades; improved riding comfort; more weathertight cabs; more comfortable seats; shorter turning radius; and readily available parts and service.

The Bronco is offered in three body styles—open "roadster," short-roof pickup, and fully-enclosed delivery or station wagon.

The roadster model is the "basic" Bronco. It has no cab roof or doors and is an open sports model with a windshield which can be folded flat and secured to the hood with a spring-loaded pin. A bench seat is standard equipment and a cargo area 55.2 inches by 61 inches is provided in the car.

7

The full-length steel roof on Bronco delivery and station wagon models fully encloses the unit and offers weather-tight driver and passenger comfort. Channel-type front and rear bumpers are standard on all Bronco models. In addition to providing normal protection, Bronco bumpers are designed to be the first point of contact in both "angle of approach" and the "angle of departure" to protect chassis components and sheet metal from possible damage when operating in severe terrain.

Full doors, easy-to-operate roll-up windows and a bolt-on steel driver cab make the Bronco a weather-snug, lockable utility pickup. In warm weather, the steel top may be unbolted and removed. The full doors are compatible with the optional vinyl top so that "convertible" protection from summer showers can be combined with the convenience of roll-up windows, if desired. (The Bronco's 32.8-cubic-foot pickup box capacity is the largest for any vehicle of its type.)

Two-passenger, bench-type rear seats may be ordered in combination with front bucket seats in the Bronco delivery or station wagon (above) and two other body styles. With this arrangement, the steel bulkhead is deleted to provide rear-seat access. The spare tire, normally mounted on the bulkhead, is then mounted on the interior of the tailgate, offering protection from dust and dirt.

With the low front tunnel of the Bronco, a three-man bench seat becomes practical and is offered as standard equipment. Twin bucket seats — patterned after those in the famed Ford Mustang—are optional for maximum comfort and lateral support.

A two-passenger, bench-type rear seat also may be added in combination with the front bucket seats for four-passenger seating. With this arrangement, the steel bulkhead is deleted to provide rear seat access. The spare tire, normally mounted on the steel bulkhead, is then mounted on the tailgate, inside the vehicle and behind the rear seat.

Power Train

The Bronco is powered by a 170-cubic-inch, 105-horsepower six-cylinder engine specially adapted for rugged use in off-highway operation. Unique to the Bronco engine are a special carburetor and fuel pump for positive fuel supply under all conditions; a special oil bath air cleaner; and a large, six-quart-capacity oil pan to assure proper lubrication. The clutch housing is cast iron for protection against damage in rocky terrain.

The Bronco transmission is a manual three-speed, fully synchronized design with column-mounted selector. The synchronized low gear is of particular value since it permits shifts into low without stopping when steep grades are encountered.

The two-speed transfer case has a single, floor-mounted shift lever. In sequence from front to rear, the lever provides "4-wheel drive, low," "neutral," "2-wheel drive, high," and "4-wheel drive, high." It is not necessary to stop or declutch when shifting into or out of "4-wheel drive, high."

The transfer case, in addition to providing the 4-wheel drive compound low gear, provides "neutral" for the operation of an optional power-takeoff to power such devices as logging saws in remote locations.

"Through-drive" design is featured in the transfer case to provide direct drive to the rear wheels without engaging the gears in the transfer case when the front axle is disengaged. This provides longer gear life and quieter operation.

Constant velocity, double-cardan universal joints are used at the transfer case for both front and rear driveshafts. This type of universal joint divides the angle equally between joint members and permits a higher mounting position for the transfer case for maximum ground clearance at the center of the vehicle as well as greater durability, quieter operation and smoother power flow to the axles.

Two rear axles are offered on the Bronco — a standard axle of 2,780 pounds' capacity, and an optional axle of 3,300 pounds' capacity. Both are available with optional limited-slip differential for maximum traction.

Brakes are of the proven Ford passenger car and truck design. Front drums are 11-inch diameter by 2 inches in width with rear drums 10 inches in diameter by 2½ inches wide. These oversized brakes provide the Bronco driver with easier stopping and lighter pedal effort on severe grades.

A steel bulkhead separates the cargo compartment from the driver and passenger compartment. Half-doors are optional.

A vinyl top is optionally available for the Bronco roadster to provide weather protection, enclosing the cargo area as well as the front compartment.

Adding full doors with easy-to-operate roll-up windows and a bolt-on steel driver's cab to the Bronco roadster, make the vehicle into a weather-snug lockable utility pickup. In warm weather, the steel top may be unbolted and removed.

The full doors are compatible with both the vinyl and steel tops to provide "convertible" protection from summer showers and convenient roll-up windows if desired.

A full-length steel roof turns the Bronco into a fully-enclosed delivery vehicle or station wagon. This all-steel structure is bolted to the body sides and windshield. Large fixed windows in the sides and rear lift-gate provide excellent visibility.

In this form, the Bronco is completely lockable for safe storage of tools or luggage. The rear-lift-gate opens easily with one hand and is supported by two sturdy, self-locking arms that hold it in the open position for added ventilation if desired.

Chassis Features

The Bronco front suspension is a unique design which combines extreme ruggedness with complete anti-dive characteristics — even under panic-stop conditions.

This is achieved through a tubular beam axle located by forged steel radius rods and track bar. Because the radius rods transmit the braking and driving force and the track bar maintains axle alignment, coil springs may be utilized for optimum riding comfort. Front shock absorbers are mounted to the radius arm for maximum control.

A new 37-degree-turn front axle is used on the Bronco to provide minimum turning circle diameter. Even with its 92-inch wheelbase for added riding comfort and stability, a Bronco can be turned in a 34-foot circle, curb to curb.

The rear springs of the Bronco are semi-eliptic leaf design, featuring Ford's exclusive taper-leaf configuration for minimum harshnes. Optional heavy-duty, single-stage springs also are available for maximum loads. Rear shock absorbers—like the front shock absorbers featuring constant viscosity fluid—are mounted outboard.

The Bronco frame is of box section construction through its entire length, as are front and rear cross members. Eight rubber cushions effectively insulate the Bronco body from chassis and road noise.

In addition to offering added protection to front-end components in rocky terrain, the Bronco anti-dive front suspension is important for plowing snow. Anti-dive keeps the plow from digging into the road surface but still insures a thorough cleaning job.

A large 14-gallon fuel tank mounted in a protected area between the frame side members behind the rear axle is standard with an 11-gallon tank mounted under the driver's seat optional. Filler pipes for both tanks are conveniently located on the left side of the body, and a selector valve under the driver's seat permits easy change-over when one tank runs dry. A switch under the dash panel changes the fuel gage reading from one tank to the other to permit the operator to check exactly how much fuel is in each tank.

Channel-type front and rear bumpers are standard on all Bronco models. In addition to providing normal protection, these bumpers are designed to be the first point of contact in both the "angle of approach" and the "angle of departure" to protect the chassis components and sheet metal from possible damage when operating in severe terrain. ∎

It's a BRONCO, Buster!

Ford's New Off-Road Runabout
Is a Do-it-Yourself Rodeo

IN MUCH THE same manner as it did with the Mustang, Ford Motor Co. has squinted at market research data, poked a tentative finger into the breeze and plunged headlong into a ripening market. This one buys 4-wheel-drive utility vehicles, largely for recreation, a domain until now pretty much that of the Jeep and the IH Scout, along with England's Land-Rover and a smattering of Japanese offerings. Now, however, there's a Bronco by Ford.

There may be some question about why the nation's No. 2 car builder should produce such an off-road, 4wd vehicle as the Bronco. This type of vehicle accounted for something less than 35,000 sales last year, the bulk of that in Scouts and Jeeps. But Ford has been watching the big picture, seeing a market which has grown from 11,000 in 1960 to triple that last year

and projects that to a potential of 70,-000 annually in five more years. To a company that can sell nearly half a million copies of a new model during its first year of production (Falcon and Mustang), a market potential of 70,000 still must seem small potatoes.

"Actually," says one FoMoCo executive, "we're interested in anything that has to do with transportation. We've even looked at motorcycles, too, but that doesn't necessarily mean that we'll be building them." There has been rapid growth in the off-road recreational field, a natural adjunct to the Affluent Society's increasing prosperity and leisure time. That is what switched Ford from a looker to a doer.

The Bronco bears a close resemblance to the IH Scout—so close, in fact, that one Fordman even characterized it as a "Chinese copy." But there are great differences between the

two—and other 4wd utility vehicles—in mechanical design. Unlike the others, the Bronco comes only as a 4wd vehicle; no 2-wheel-drive version is offered, as yet. A somewhat more obvious difference is that the Bronco, alone among the field, has coil springs suspending the body at the front axle (although some Jeep trucks use torsion bars with independent front suspension).

Power for the Bronco is delivered by Ford's familiar 7-main-bearing, 170-cu. in. Six, rated at 105 bhp and modified slightly to better cope with off-road distresses. For more positive fuel supply under really rugged conditions, a different single-barrel carburetor and heavier duty fuel pump are used. An oil bath air cleaner is a necessity for deserts and dusty back trails, and a 6-qt. oil pan provides an extra measure of lubrication for hard lugging operations. A cast-iron housing shields the 9.375-in. clutch and an optional skid plate is available to assist in that chore. Ford's all-synchromesh 3-speed manual transmission, with ratios of 3.41 low, 1.86 second, and 1.00:1 high, is

10

Ford Bronco

operated via a steering-column mounted lever.

The heart of this vehicle's goat-ability, however, lies in the 2-speed transfer case behind the transmission. Controlled by a single, floor-mounted lever, this gear case determines the mode of operation and even includes a "neutral" for running stationary equipment via the power take-off. The arrangement is called "through-drive," disengaging completely the driven gears from the drive-shaft gear when rear-wheel-drive is selected, which cuts down gear noise and wear.

Function selection is straight-line, with 4wd in low range at the far forward notch and neutral in the next spot toward the rear. Declutching for the shift from 4wd mode in high range, at the most rearward notch, to rear wheel only in high range, one notch forward, is unnecessary. Use of constant velocity, double-Cardan universal joints for both drive-shafts from the transfer case provides a further benefit. The case can be located higher in the chassis, improving ground clearance in the critical mid-section of the vehicle, since the joints equalize the required angularity. While such joints are somewhat more expensive, they also are more durable and smoother in operation.

Since both the Bronco and the Scout have 15-in. tires as standard, effective gearing works out to be closely comparable. The Scout's slightly "longer" low gear (ignoring the amount of torque available in the first place) is compensated for in stump pulling contests by a shorter final drive ratio—4.27:1 to Bronco's 4.11. Ford isn't really losing here either since a 4.57:1 final drive is an option. Both vehicles have identical ratios in the transfer cases, 2.46:1 multiplication for low range and direct in high. The greater grip of the 7.35-15 tires on a standard Bronco would give it something of an edge, as would the obviously more powerful standard engine. However, at its torque peak the Bronco's Six generates only a mere 3.3 lb./ft. more than the Scout's "half-a-V-8" Four.

There is little about the Bronco structure that is either novel or notable. Like the Scout, it seems excessively heavy for its size—no doubt in anticipation of extreme mistreatment. The body is sturdy, heavy gauge, all-welded; a veritable coal car of a structure reinforced by the deep tunnel between front seats. The tunnel spreads out to form the rear cargo bed. The body sits atop a rigid frame which, like its front and rear crossmembers, is full-length, box-section steel. Eight rubber cushions insulate against chassis and road noise. The hood is broad and flat and about as easy to raise as a similarly sized chunk of lead.

The running gear is the Bronco's long suit. Here, Ford engineers have spent some time and thought in the effort to do the job better, drawing upon their experiences with such things as the "twin I-beam" front ends on their pickup trucks. With front wheels that are going to be used as driving wheels, Ford predictably avoids the independent suspension of the swing-arm pickup. Instead, a tubular beam axle is used and stout, forged, radius arms extend back to near the transmission crossmember, serving to take braking and driving forces. A tubular track bar extends between left frame rail and right axle extremity to locate the axle. Freed of all duties save that of cushioning, springs can thus be coils. These mount atop a stamped arch bolted ahead of the axle as a cap for the radius rods.

Ford engineers make much of the "complete anti-dive" incorporated in this front suspension, pointing out its obvious advantage when the Bronco is pushing a snowplow attachment. The radius rods transfer the braking torque from the axle to a point almost mid-way down the chassis, rather than pulling down the front end through the usual spring or control arm arrangement. The radius rods also carry the lower mounting for the shock absorbers. And, as a further advantage, coil springs allow the front wheels to turn sharper angles, to 37°, for a tight, 34-ft. turning circle.

LOCKED INTO low range, 4-wheel drive, Ford's Bronco growls its way through the rough mountainside brush even where solid ground is rare.

WORM'S EYE view reveals coil-suspended front axle located by radius arms running back toward center of stout chassis side-rails.

The rear suspension is straightforward Hotchkiss, utilizing taper-leaf semi-elliptic springs to reduce harshness. Optional heavy-duty springs are available for maximum loads, as is a 3300-lb. axle to replace the standard one of 2780 lb. capacity. Limited slip differentials are options for all axles, front and rear. Somewhat generous brake capacity is provided from 11-in. drums in front, 10 in. at the rear, with 2 in. and 2.5 in. widths, respectively. Easier stopping and lighter pedal pressures on severe grades were the criteria in specifying oversize brakes.

In keeping with the back-to-nature nature of the beast, Ford has made provision for extra fuel capacity. In addition to the 14-gal. tank mounted between the rear frame rails, there is available an optional auxiliary tank of 11 gal. Filler pipes for both are located high on the left side of the vehicle and a selector valve is positioned under the driver's seat; a toggle switch on the underside of the dash panel changes fuel level readings from one tank to the other.

Initially, there will be three versions of the Bronco. The basic Roadster comes as an open car without roof or side doors. Cut-down "half-doors" are fitted to improve the appearance and a full-length vinyl top is available at extra cost for weather protection. The windshield folds flat atop the hood for the ultimate in open-air motoring. In the basic model, a steel bulkhead separates the cargo compartment behind a full-width bench seat.

A short-roof Sports Utility pickup version is equipped with bolt-on steel driver's cab and full depth doors containing roll-up windows and frames. The vinyl top can still be used once the short-top cab is removed. For the third version, there is a full-length steel roof which bolts to windshield and body sides, converting the Bronco into a station-wagon type of vehicle. Fixed windows are located in the sides and in the rear lift gate on this top, which makes the car fully lockable for safe storage of tools or valuables.

Although the bench front seat is standard, an option provides for installation of Mustang-like front bucket seats for greater comfort and support during off-road driving. With the buckets, the steel bulkhead—as well as the spare tire bracket normally attached to it—are removed to permit access to an optional rear bench seat. In this arrangement, the spare is then relocated on the inside of the tailgate. This, however, is only the beginning of the Bronco variations.

As might be expected from the Mustang-maker, this new vehicle has a great deal of custom tailoring which can be specified. Bronco options include many items of a dress-up nature in addition to the expected components for heavy duty use. A "custom equip-

4WD UTILITY VEHICLES

	Bronco	Scout	Jeep	Land-Rover (long w.b.)
Wheelbase, in.	92.0	100.0	81.0	88.0 (109.0)
Length	152.1	154.0	135.5	142.4 (175.0)
Height	69.2	68.0	69.5	77.5 (81.0)
Width	68.8	68.6	71.7	64.0 (64.0)
Track	57.0	55.1	48.4	51.5 (51.5)
Turning circle, ft.	33.6	38.0	n.s.	38.0 (45.0)
Box length, in.	55.2	60.0	39.75	43.0 (72.7)
Wheelhouse width	40.0	37.5	36.0	36.3 (36.3)
Tailgate width	56.0	39.0	36.0	n.s.
Min. ground clearance	6.6	9.3	n.s.	8.0 (9.7)
Tires, std.	7.35-15	6.00-16	6.00-16	6.00-16 (7.50-16)
Engine, type/displ.	6/170	4/152	4/134	4/140
Bhp @ rpm	105 @ 4400	93.4 @ 4400	75 @ 4000	77 @ 4250
Torque @ rpm	146 @ 2400	142.7 @ 2400	114 @ 2000	124 @ 2500
Bore & stroke	3.50 x 2.94	3.88 x 3.22	3.12 x 4.37	3.56 x 3 5
Compression ratio	8.4:1	8.19:1	7.4:1	7.0:1
Fuel capacity	14.0	11.0	10.5	10.0 (16.0)
Curb weight	3107	3000	2274	2900 (3294)
Gross vehicle weight	3900	3900	3750	n.s.
Axle capacity, std., front	2500	2000	2000	n.s.
Rear	2780	2300	2500	n.s.
Brakes, front	11 x 2	9 x 1.75	9 x n.s.	n.s.
Rear	10 x 2.5	9 x 2	9 x n.s.	n.s.
Transmission ratios, first	3.41	3.339	3.339	2.99
Second	1.86	1.85	1.55	2.04
Third	1.00	1.00	1.00	1.37
Transfer case ratios, high	1.00	1.00	1.00	1.15
Low	2.46	2.46	2.46	2.89
Final drive ratio, std.	4.11	4.27	4.27	4.70

MUSTANG BUCKET seats are for comfort in the rough. Sparse panel can be dressed up with extra gauges, accessory switches.

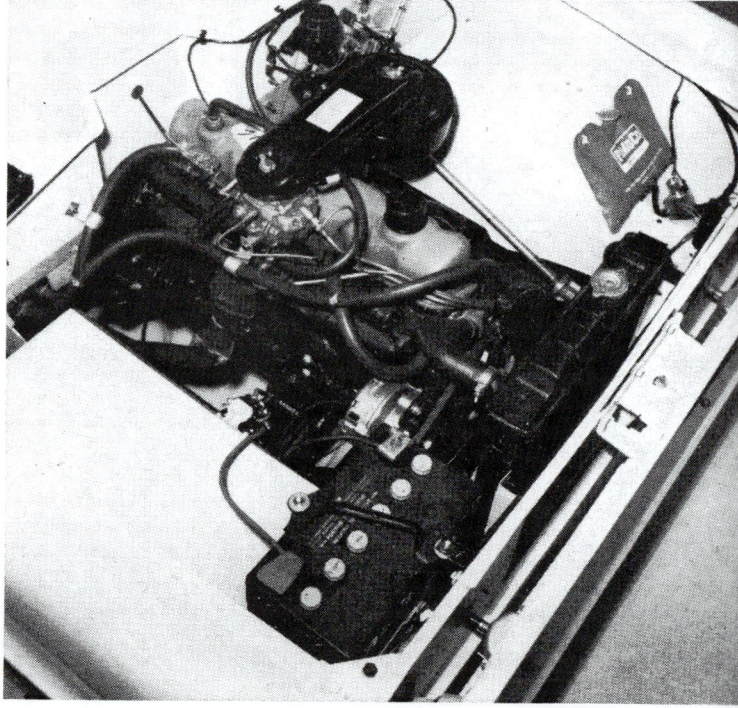

SPECIAL AIR cleaner and carburetor help adapt 170-cu. in. Six to rugged off-highway usage. A V-8 could easily slip in there.

Ford Bronco

ment package" includes, for instance, a cigarette lighter, chromed wheel covers, chromed front and rear bumpers and taillight bezels, full-width front floor mat, oil pressure gauge and ammeter, horn ring, and dual sun visors. A radio, padded dash, electric windshield washers, emergency signal flasher, chromed hand rails and a luggage rack for the full-length top are other options. Then there are the "work"

options, such as front and rear power take-offs, snow plow, tow bar, tow hooks and winch. And not overlooked is that almost forgotten vestige of past motoring, a hand throttle on the dash.

During the Bronco's coming out ceremonies, Ford General Manager Donald N. Frey characterized it "as neither a car nor a truck, but as a vehicle which combines the best of both worlds. The Bronco can serve as

a family sedan, sports roadster, snow plow, or farm and civil defense vehicle. It has been designed to go nearly anywhere and do nearly anything."

As it stands, the Bronco makes a pleasant runabout with plenty of stamina for bashing about the bush. But we can't help thinking about all the extra space going to waste under the broad hood. With Ford's demonstrated tendency toward increasing engine sizes in its smaller cars, prospects of either the 289-cu. in. V-8, or 200-cu. in. Six, under the hatch are pretty good. There are probably plenty of buyers who will plan their own conversions if the company doesn't do it, if for no other reason than because the job would be so easy. ■

SHORT-TOP cab bolts onto Bronco to make neat pickup with 32.8 cu. ft. capacity.

FULL-LENGTH top with fixed windows converts Bronco to station wagon; rear seat is optional.

BARE VEHICLE with doors and roll-up windows assures plenty of wind-in-the-face driving if the windshield is lowered and latched to the hood.

It competes with the Scout and fills the gap between Jeep and Wagoneer

Popular Science
REG. U.S. PAT. OFF. *Monthly*

Ford's Agile New **BRONCO**

By Jan P. Norbye, *Automotive Editor*

WHEN the market for rugged, go-anywhere cars had grown to 50,000 units a year, Ford had an idea for a new type of lightweight four-wheel-drive sportsman's vehicle: a car that would go like a Mustang on the road and like a Jeep in the rough. Could they invent one? They tried, and came up with a sporty and tough workhorse called the Bronco. Finding the weak spot in the Bronco-concept proved an impossible task. I tried everything I knew—and failed. CONTINUED

Passenger-car ride and sports-car handling have been built into the Mustang's new stablemate: Bronco.

It's a go-anywhere car with a Mustang spirit

Asking the "four-wheelers." The design goals for the Bronco were not laid down by Ford engineers—they were compiled from comments on existing go-anywhere cars by member of about 300 "four-wheeler" clubs all over the United States. Their total membership exceeds 10,000, and the consensus was that four-by-four sportsmen's and utility vehicles needed higher highway cruising speeds, ability to climb steeper grades, better weather sealing, more comfortable seats, improved ride comfort, and shorter turning diameters. That was what Ford set out to give them.

In addition to these requirements, James Heywood, Executive Engineer of Ford Trucks, demanded that Paul Axelrad, the Principal Vehicle Engineer for the Bronco, should make maximum use of existing Ford parts. This would not only assure ready availability of spare parts everywhere but also keep manufacturing costs down.

The engine. To power the Bronco, they chose the Econoline version of the 170-cu.-in. six, which differs from the Falcon's in having solid valve lifters instead of hydraulic one. They also worked out a special carburetor with

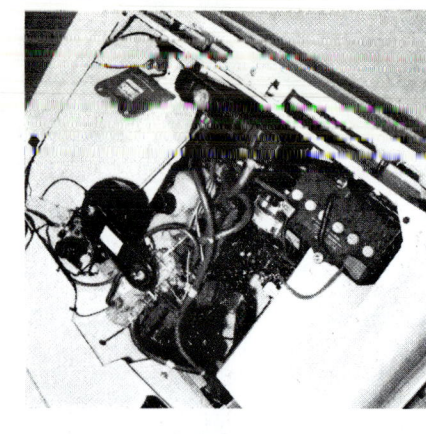

Six-cylinder 170-cu.-in Econoline engine puts out 105 hp. at 4,400 r.p.m., with 146 lb.-ft. of torque at 2,400 r.p.m. No power options exist now, but compartment is big enough for a V-8.

Bronco steers as easily as some large passenger cars, despite four-wheel drive—and steering is free of wheel kick, vibrations, and rattles. Body lean on hard cornering is remarkably slight.

I stopped in foot-deep mud and let the Bronco sink in, only to drive out as if the mud were a pool of water. I ran it up a 45-degree grass slope, slippery with morning dew, and the Bronco climbed it in third gear, low range, with four-wheel drive. I put it through some hard cornering on a road course, and the Bronco behaved like a real sports car. I drove it at top speed—about 85 m.p.h.—down the straight, and the ride was better than in many taxicabs, the directional stability excellent, the noise level inside the vehicle quite tolerable.

Standard seat is a three-place bench, but Mustang-type bucket seats (above) are optional. Parking brake is foot-operated, controls are simple, and instruments are set in one large dial.

Front axle is firmly located by forged-steel radius rods and a track bar. Coil springs allow larger steering angles than most leaf-spring installations, and spring characteristics are better suited for passenger-vehicle needs.

floats designed to function up to a 60-degree climb or descent and a 20-degree lateral tilt. They replaced the usual dry paper filter with an oil-bath air cleaner and fitted an aircraft-type fuel pump that will deliver under all conditions. They redesigned the oil pan so it would clear the front axle and raised its capacity to six quarts.

I talked with Axelrad about the back of power options for the Bronco, but he intimated that bigger sixes and V-8s might follow, with enough customer demand. Japanese "four-wheelers" such as Nissan and Toyota have 135-hp. base models, and Ford might do well to prepare a more powerful Bronco.

A ride in the Bronco. Now come with me for a drive. Before moving off, check the transfer-case lever by pulling it fully back and moving it one notch forward. That gives rear drive, high range (all the way back gives four-wheel drive and high range). Move the steering-column gearshift into first and start off. It's just like an ordinary car. Work your way up

gear. That gives you a lot of noise and very low speed, so you change up immediately. If the ground is not too soft, you can easily start off in second. Go into third at about 20 m.p.h., and you'll feel able to pull a Sherman tank out of the Sahara. On a really steep hill, you might need second gear again, but normally you would just stay in third until you hit hard pavement again. Now change back to two-wheel drive, head for the garage, and start asking questions.

Whys and wherefores. How come it's so quiet in two-wheel drive? That's because the rear axle is coupled to the main shaft in the transfer case; thus, when the front axle is disengaged, the transfer gears are not

to third gear, speed up, find a road with some turns and some bumps. It rides better than a pickup truck, and the seats are comfortable.

Now let's try it off the road. Get second gear. Steer for this open field. Move the transfer-case lever back—you don't have to touch the clutch, just pull. There you go, all four wheels driving. The ground is too soft? The car is slowing down even with full throttle in second gear? Just engage *first*. You heard me, first gear. At speed? Yes, go ahead. First gear has synchromesh, so there's no need to stop. Got it? Yes, the car is gaining speed again, the revs are rising and you begin to wonder about shifting up again. Don't do it; there's a better way. Slow down, declutch and rev the engine, move the transfer-case lever all the way forward (through neutral, into low range with four-wheel drive).

The Bronco rolled to a stop while you were working on that, but that's just as well. All set? Start off again in first

radius arms and coil springs adapted from the Twin-I-Beam pickup-truck chassis, which gives a very good anti-dive effect.

How is it possible for a four-wheel-drive vehicle with a 92-inch wheelbase to turn inside a 34-foot circle? The outer joints in the front axle permit turning angles up to 37 degrees—a new high in rugged cars.

Why did Ford choose the front and rear axles from the four-wheel-drive F-100 as a basis for the Bronco, when the parts for the MUTT (Military Utility Tactical Transport) with all-independent suspension were also made in large numbers by Ford? The fact is that the MUTT, great as it may be in the jungle, is not very good for road use, with its small wheels, high ground clearance, and high center of gravity. The geometry of its suspension could become a danger rather than a help when going around turns on a good road. So Ford concluded that a rigid-axle chassis was likely to prove more satisfactory for the general public.

Does the Bronco have power brakes? No. The reason you needed only light pedal pressure to stop when heading down that steep hill is the size of the brake drums. The front drums are 11 inches across; the rear ones are 10 inches across. Such large drums also contribute to long lining life.

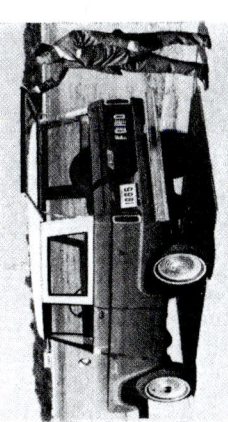

Split tailgate opens conventionally, giving access to area behind rear seat. The spare wheel is attached to the lower section.

turning. This not only cuts down gear noise but also saves transmission wear.

How did they get the drive line so smooth at low speeds? At either end of the transfer case you'll find a constant-velocity universal joint. These joints eliminate fluctuations in the rotational speed of the drive shafts and thus permit quieter operation and assure longer life of all transmission parts—plus giving the smooth feeling you mentioned. One more thing. The use of constant-velocity joints allows mounting the transfer case higher, which makes for higher ground clearance in the middle.

How did they manage to avoid nose-dive when stopping? The front suspension uses

Models and options. The Bronco pickup I tested is only one of three available body styles: the others are a wagon and a roadster. The pickup box is 61 inches wide and 55.2 inches long, with a total net volume of 32.8 cubic feet. The all-steel wagon has a Scout-style rear seat (passengers facing forward). Access to the rear seat is easy, as both front seats can be tilted forward. The roadster is the "basic" Bronco. It has no doors, but fiberglass half-doors are optional.

Like most other ruggeds, the Bronco can be supplied with power takeoffs, snow-plow mounts, tow bars and hooks, winches and trailer hitches. Ford has tried to make sure that if the Bronco will go practically anywhere, it will also be able to do practically anything.

Road Test:

FORD BRONCO

Doors have roll down windows, open wide. Ample weatherstripping around edges insures low noise level, little wind leaking. Front seat folds forward and on models without the bulkhead, rear seat entry or loading is easy.

Ford's Bronco received one of the most rousing send-offs of any new four-wheel drive rig. It debuted on television, in full color pictures in hundreds of magazines and almost every automotive writer has had his say. Since we here at FOUR WHEELER prefer to make a rather extensive examination and drive over a wide variety of terrain before making a formal report our test story is necessarily a little late.

The test required approximately two months and the types of terrain driven were comparable to anything an average four wheeler would encounter with the single exception of deep snow. We found few weak points and several which impressed the test staff as extremely good.

Some good, some bad, is the usual result of the first road test of an all new vehicle but in the case of the test Bronco there are several trail qualities we feel deserve special mention—among these are ride, comfort and economy and each will be discussed in detail later in this report.

Starting with the engine, it is no stranger to Ford enthusiasts. Bronco is powered by an updated version of the 170 cubic inch Falcon. At 3800 rpm it produces 105 horsepower; torque peaks at 2400 rpm and is rated at 158 lbs.-ft.

This powerplant has been owner tested in thousands of Falcons and in this capacity was one of the most economical engines in the compact class. As tested, the Bronco turned in a healthy 14 to 19 miles per gallon average for most types of driving. This really wasn't much of a surprise for the 170 Six has always been a rather remarkable gas miser. The test rig was outfitted with the 4.11-to-1 gearset and undoubtedly with the optional 4.57 this mileage figure will drop considerably.

Compression ratio is 9-to-1 and most experts consider this ratio a borderline case for regular fuel. Throughout the test the Bronco was fed a diet of regular and performed well although we might not be so easily convinced in some areas (like south of the border) where regular is of a poorer quality.

While this is basically the same engine as that found in Ford's compact line there are a few changes which are calculated to make it a more healthy animal on off-the-road trails. The major differences are a special carburetor and fuel pump for positive fuel supply under all conditions, a special oil bath air cleaner to keep it well lubricated in abrupt changes in trail attitudes. Beneath the engine is a rugged, cast iron skid plate which also protects the clutch housing.

Coupled to the engine is a Ford-built, three-speed, fully synchronized transmission with a column-mounted shift lever. Syncronizing low gear is an intelligent thing to do and it proved to be a big advantage in slow speed manuevers. It is extremely easy to shift into low gear even when the forward speed is just a little too fast for easy changing.

The Bronco has a two-speed transfer case with a single floor-mounted lever. For those who have driven Ford's bigger four-wheel drive outfits this will not be unusual but a single lever for front drive control and the low range will be something that many four wheelers have not yet encountered.

Starting at the front it shifts straight back with no right angles. First comes 4wd low, then neutral, 2wd high and finally 4wd high. Although there is no official allowance for it, the engineers claim that a minor modification permits the transfer case to shift into 2wd low. This is apparently a hold over from the truck line but there are few conceivable circumstances when it would be of value to either the enthusiast or competitor.

Four-wheel to two-wheel drive shifts or back will either be a delight or a constant nuisance to the driver of the Bronco. The throws of the transfer case are unbelievably short. Just a few inches and the rig is either in 4wd or 2wd high. Since it is not necessary to stop, or even slow down very much, this becomes a big advantage on the trail or when the road suddenly becomes slick from ice or water. On the other hand it is extremely easy to make a mistake and drive city streets in 4wd high. This will really not damage the rig but will cause unnecessary wear on front driving parts even if the hubs are disengaged.

Another complaint about the transfer case from the test staff was that the lever was several inches too long. From the tip of the shift lever to transfer case lever is less than an inch when the bronco is in high gear, 2wd high. This means that it is virtually impossible to shift into high gear without touching the transfer case lever—making it extremely easy to inadvertently shift into 4wd high. The concensus of opinion from those who drove the rig was that the first modification they would make would be to apply a hacksaw liberally to the shift lever. Here the agreement ended with some favoring a position just a few inches below the transmission shift lever to those who would saw it off about six inches above the floorboard.

There is one engineering quality of the Bronco's transfer case that might be overlooked if the rig is merely analyzed and not driven. Test drivers credited the rig's very low noise level at highway speeds to this individual design feature.

When in two-wheel drive the transfer case provided direct drive from the powerplant to the rear wheels without using the gears in the transfer case when the front axle is disengaged. This means that with hubs not only has the front drive shaft, differential and axle been completely disengaged, the gears in the transfer case do not turn. This results in a much longer life for the transfer case and the road test proved that the outfit runs far quieter than average at highway speeds.

Automotive test drivers are great ones for trying specific tests that prove or disprove statements by public relations men who get most of their information from spec sheets provided by the engineering departments. It stands to reason then that the drivers who were assigned to pick the Bronco up at the assembly plant could hardly wait until they were out of sight of the executives to jam on the brakes.

After reading so many words about the "superior anti-dive characteristics — even under panic stop conditions," they

Luxury items throughout the Bronco will be a welcome feature for many four wheelers. Padded dash is seldom seen and should save a lot of bumped foreheads.

Glove compartment is small and not very deep. Front windshield control locks well and securely seals against winds during high speed travel. Note weatherstripping.

just had to try it out.

Depending on how you look at these things they either accomplished a lot or proved the fact that windshields are harder than heads. What the initial drivers had forgotten was the fact that the Bronco has brakes that won't quit. On the front they are a healthy 11-inch diameter by two-inch, while the rear drums measure 10 inches diameter by 2-1/2 inches wide. Combine these large brakes with the approximate weight of 3200 lbs. and the answer is: Whoa! The problem of anti-dive had to be checked out later, for no one felt much like trying it a second time that day.

When the opinions for braking ability

were asked for there were at least two answers that it couldn't be better. And in the opinion of all those who drove the Bronco the outfit has more than ample braking whether unloaded or completely weighted down with gear for an extended camping trip.

Looking a little further into the question of why everyone was so eager to check out the anti-dive characteristics of the Bronco goes directly to claims made by the factory when the rig was first introduced. The rig has a suspension unique among back country rigs. Centering around a tubular beam axle which is firmly located by forged steel radius rods and a track bar the engineers

claimed it would virtually eliminate dive. Speaking from an engineering standpoint this is because the radius rods transmit, and to some degree absorb, the braking and driving forces while the track bar maintains axle alignment. Since these forces are scientifically accounted for, the engineers were also able to use coil springs for the front suspension and cash in big on the added benefit of comfort (or soft ride) that this type of springing can give.

While it might seem like a small detail, the front shock absorbers can now be mounted on the radius arms—providing an additional margin in comfort. Back in the back, so to speak, another small, but important device has been used to gain additional softening for the ride. Here the rear springs are of the traditional semi-elliptical leaf design, but have been manufactured in a taper-leaf configuration. This is a principle that has been utilized in both passenger cars and light trucks to provide maximum softness in a spring that must, because of the demands upon it, also be maximum in durability.

Combining the unusual configuration of the rear leaf springs and the coil springs of the front, Ford engineers have come up with an extra-ordinary paved road ride. Since the noise level is already far below average for 4wd rigs, long trips are far less fatiguing. On the trail this springing combination pays off in an extremely comfortable ride over all but the roughest of trails.

In checking out the highly touted anti-dive characteristics we found that the publicity was well grounded. In panic stops from 30 and 40 miles per hour front end dip or sway was virtually absent. Down in the speeds where a driver would want this quality, like pushing a snow plow over an asphalt driveway, the Bronco could not be made to dip at all.

Driver controls are well placed and within easy reach of even the shortest person. There is ample foot room, but one complaint of drivers was the nearness of the shift lever (shown in reverse position) and the 4wd control.

BRONCO POWERPLANT WILL BE NO STRANGER TO FORD ENTHUSIASTS; IT IS BASED ON 170- CUBIC INCH FALCON ENGINE.

At high speeds on the highway front end sway, sometimes a complaint with coil springs, was not noticeable even during cross winds of 40 to 50 miles per hour.

One Bronco feature which all of the test staff found objectionable were the front drive, free wheeling hubs and the position in which the engineers chose to mount them. First, regardless of the make of hub they stick out too far to be protected by the wheel and tire. This means in rocks or deeply rutted trails or any number of other back country hazards the hubs are vulnerable to many harsh shocks which are almost certain to damage this vital accessory.

Second, the hubs provided with the Bronco did not appear to be of the best design. The in-out control is a raised bar which is turned manually and sticks out further than the rest of the hub body. Since this device turns quite easy, it is not inconceivable that in rocks, for instance, pressure from a rock could turn the hub to the free position when the driver is in 4wd. There would be no way for the driver to know this had happened and in the event he had the limited slip differential option in front he could cause serious damage almost instantly. In any event the loss of front driving power

ENGINE
Engine: ohv Six
Bore/Stroke: 3.5 x 2.9 inches
Displacement: 170 cubic inches
Compression Ratio: 8.4-to-1
Horsepower: 105 hp at 4400 rpm
Torque: 146 lbs.-ft. at 2400 rpm
Fuel Consumption: 14-19 mpg

GENERAL
Wheelbase: 92 inches
Length: 152.) inches
Width: 68.8 inches
Height: 69.2 inches
Tread, F/R: 57.4 inches
Ground Clearance: 6.6 inches
Turning Radius: 16.8 feet
Curb Weight: 3107 lbs.

GEARING
Axle: 4.11-to-1
Transfer Case: 2.46-to-1
Transmission:
  low, 3.41; second, 1.86; high, 1; reverse NA
Overall Ratios:
  low, 14.02; second, 7.65; high, 4.11; reverse, NA
Compound Ratios:
  low, 34.49; second, 18.82; high, 10.11; reverse, NA

would handicap the driver immediately. Several accessory hubs have already been designed for the Bronco and one, with the locking lever inside the hub body, has already been approved by Ford.

Inside the Bronco are a few luxury items that four wheelers are not accustomed to. One of these, a padded dash made quite an impression on the drivers who had considerable trail experience. Most of them had small children standing up on slow-speed trails and a nose bumped on the dash panel is accepted as normal. The padded dash will not eliminate the tears from bumps on the head but it will sure make them easier to live with. The Bronco has sun visors and these are also padded.

The test rig had bucket seats which were extremely comfortable; for those who prefer, it also is available with a full length front bench seat.

The cargo compartment is large and equal to back country rigs in the Bronco class; capacity is a fat 32.1 cubic feet. Loading from the rear is a snap since the single piece, down-swinging tailgate runs the full width of the rig. The opening is 56 inches across and permits loading items the full width of the cargo compartment.

On the outfit we tested the front loading was excellent. This rig was built with the bucket seats and no bulkhead. With the bulkhead, of course, things must be lifted over if loaded from the front.

One feature of the cargo compartment that gives a little cause for concern is the method of storing the jack. While it is pretty much accepted in our sport to store the spare tire outside the rig, leaving the jack where it is available to anyone passing by is something else. In the long top, as tested, this is not so much of a problem, but in the short top or bobtail, it is something that might present too much of an invitation to some persons.

There are several other details which are minor but worth mentioning. The instrument panel has a full complement of gauges including oil pressure and ammeter. The gas tank has 14 gallons capacity but an option, which fits under the seat, raises the capacity to 25 gallons.

One feature we didn't have the opportunity to check out but felt that it should be an integral part of any back country design was the placement of the front and rear bumpers. Both these components are designed to be the point of first contact for the maximum approach or departure angle.

The most difficult part of writing a test review is summing up a vehicle in a few words. In the case of the Bronco this is not impossible but would be hard to do. The rig has much that is unique, especially in the front suspension, and many features that are seldom seen on back country rigs. It has an excellent ride, good fuel economy and power enough for nearly every type of manuever.

Yet, with all that is new about the Bronco, it did not seem strange, or even really new to us. It was more like driving a rig that seemed somehow familiar. Probably this is due to a long experience with Ford 4wd equipment in the half- and three-quarter-ton field. One thing was evident in the reactions of all the experienced trail drivers who tried their hand at the Bronco while it was being tested. The new Ford back country machine is one which an off-the-road enthusiast can easily become friends with in short order.

Top half of tailgate is full-width and opens wide for ample ventilation. Loading gear or getting something out in a hurry is easy; lock permits protecting load.

When completely opened for loading, Bronco tailgate offers more space than any other similar rig. Note bulkhead which is not standard for all versions.

BRONCO OFFERS SEVERAL FAMILIAR AND WELL PROVEN DESIGN QUALITIES PLUS MANY WHICH ARE NEW TO FOUR WHEELERS.

BRONCO Sportsman

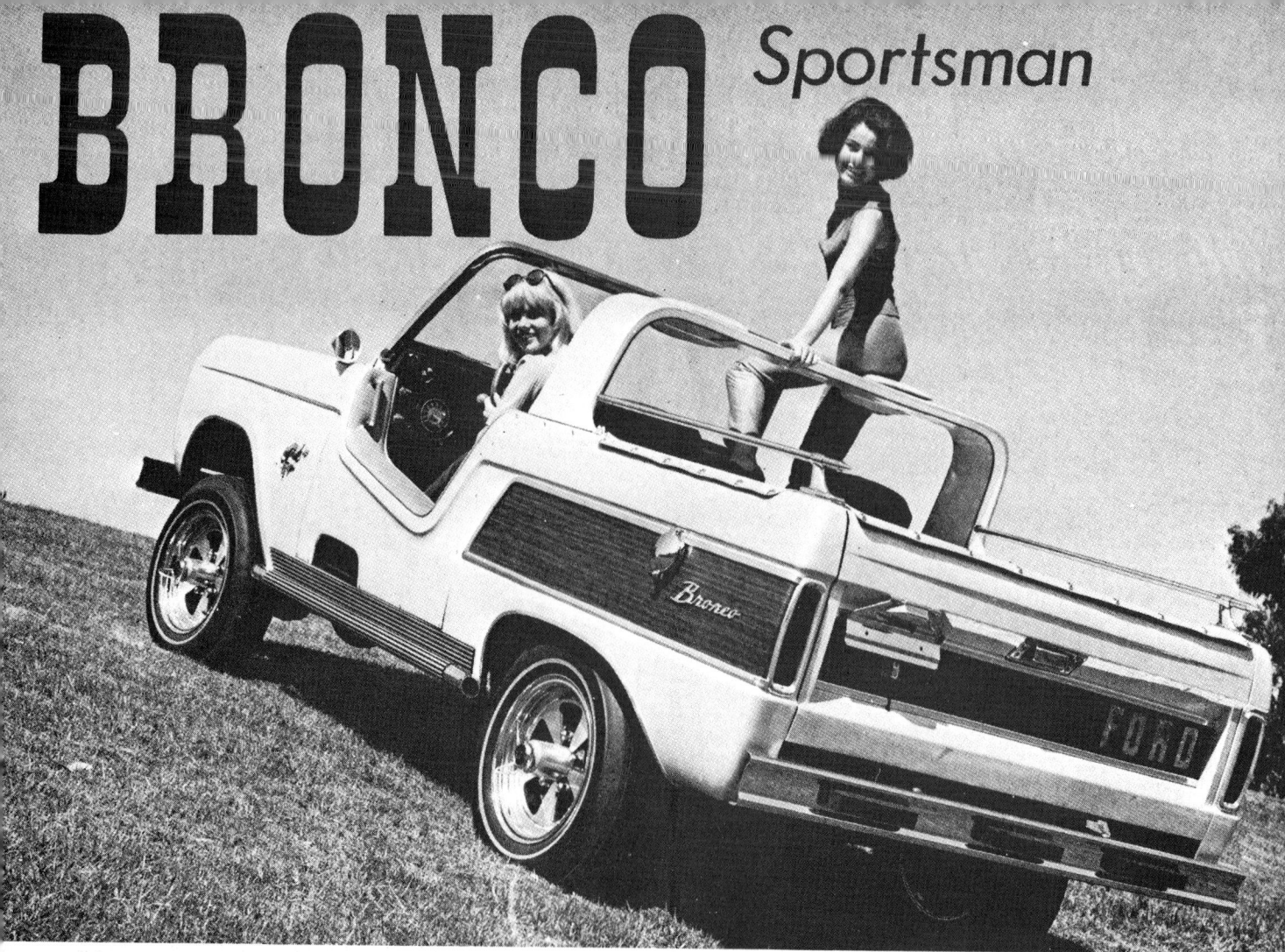

A Custom Roadster by Ford!

Bronco Sportsman, a special customized version of Ford Motor Company's new four-wheel-drive vehicle, was a recent attention getter at the 43rd International Auto Show at the Pan Pacific auditorium in Los Angeles, Calif. The utility/sports-type vehicle was designed in Ford's Styling Center in Dearborn, Mich., and the customizing was carried out by Barris Kustom, North Hollywood, Calif.

Many interior and exterior modifications have been made to the basic six-cylinder Bronco roadster to achieve a unique sporty appearance with added luxury and safety features. The exterior paint is a specially formulated golden saddle pearl, and modifications include an NHRA-approved roll bar with integral headrests, a windshield designed to coordinate with the contour of the roll bar, walnut appliques on the rear side panels and exposed chrome exhaust pipes.

The heat-shielding rocker panel behind the pipes is formed of black and white anodized aluminum. Chrome wheel lip moldings accent the machined steel alloy wheels, which are equipped witl knock-off hubs. The hood was redesigned to incorporate an air scoop for added engine cooling. Rubber "snubbers" protect the bumpers from scratches and a performance-type gas filler adds to the sportiness of the trim. Completing the exterior modifications are special racing mirrors and unique stepover door panels with a padded sill, built-in step and an assist handle.

Custom interior appointments include a walnut steering wheel and front bucket seats with russet suede bolsters and perforated leather cushions and seatbacks. The instrument panel is trimmed with suede padding and is outfitted with walnut-trimmed control knobs.

Beige loop carpeting covers the floor of both front and rear compartments, with narrow walnut strips dividing the carpet in the rear to facilitate loading and unloading. Both the front seats and the jump seats in the rear area are equipped with deluxe push-button seat belts.

A tonneau cover for rear compartment protection is designed with quick-fastening snaps. Sides of the load bed are topped with a stainless steel rail. The Bronco Sportsman will be displayed at auto shows throughout the country. ■

THE FALCON Six handles off-the-road chores easily, but takes a high rpm beating in highway cruising.

COIL SPRINGS, forged steel radius rods and a 1-in. dia. track bar locate the Bronco's front drive axle.

economical enough when a 4-wheel drive climb to a 5000-ft. mountain top is taken into consideration. The engine's 9.1:1 compression ratio required premium fuel, hence the 100-miles cost can be computed to be in the neighborhood of $2.50.

The Bronco is fine for *hombres* who don't care for horses, but who want to hit the horse trails. The Bronco can tote grub from the general store or pack the young'uns off to the schoolhouse. In a pinch the Bronco can help with the spring plowing.

But best of all about the Bronco is that West of the Pecos rodeo aura that makes a driver shout, "Eeeee-aaaaayyhhooo!" as he plows 4-wheel full tilt through a mountain stream or breaks airborne over a mountain top.   ∎

CAR LIFE ROAD TEST

ACCELERATION & COASTING

(Graph: MPH vs ELAPSED TIME IN SECONDS, showing 1st, 2nd, 3rd gears and SS ¼)

CALCULATED DATA	
Lb./bhp (test weight)	34.9
Cu. ft./ton mile	178
Mph/1000 rpm (high gear)	17.5
Engine revs/mile (60 mph)	3620
Piston travel, ft./mile	1770
Car Life wear index	63.8
Frontal area, sq. ft.	27.3
Box volume, cu. ft.	433

SPEEDOMETER ERROR	
30 mph, actual	30.5
40 mph	40.6
50 mph	50.2
60 mph	60.5
70 mph	69.6
80 mph	
90 mph	

MAINTENANCE INTERVALS	
Oil change, engine, miles	6000
transmission/differentials	6000
transfer case	6000
Oil filter change	6000
Air cleaner service mi.	6000
Chassis lubrication	6000
Wheelbearing re-packing	24,000
Universal joint service	36,000
Coolant change, mo.	24

TUNE-UP DATA	
Spark plugs	Autolite BF-82
gap, in.	0.032
Spark setting, deg./idle rpm	0/750
cent. max. adv., deg./rpm.	30/4700
vac. max. adv., deg./in. Hg.	24/19
Breaker gap, in.	0.024
cam dwell angle	35/38
arm tension, oz.	17/20
Tappet clearance, int./exh.	0/0
Fuel pump pressure, psi.	4
Radiator cap relief press., psi.	12

PERFORMANCE	
Top speed (4200), mph	74
Shifts (rpm) @ mph	
3rd to 4th ( )	
2nd to 3rd (4200)	38
1st to 2nd (4200)	27

ACCELERATION	
0-30 mph, sec.	5.8
0-40 mph	8.8
0-50 mph	14.9
0-60 mph	22.6
0-70 mph	40.5
0-80 mph	
0-90 mph	
0-100 mph	
Standing ¼-mile, sec.	21.9
speed at end, mph	59
Passing, 30-70 mph, sec.	34.7

BRAKING	
(Maximum deceleration rate achieved from 70 mph)	
1st stop, ft./sec./sec.	23
fade evident?	no
2nd stop, ft./sec./sec.	23
fade evident?	moderate

FUEL CONSUMPTION	
Test conditions, mpg.	14.15
Est. normal range, mpg.	13-16
Cruising range, miles	188-232

GRADABILITY	
4th, % grade @ mph.	
3rd	11 @ 40
2nd	19 @ 28
1st	26 @ 18

DRAG FACTOR	
Total drag @ 60 mph, lb.	184

Tilt! That's the way things go when Nash wants to get at the Bronco's 289-inch engine. Forward half of the fiberglass body is hinged at the frame front for easy access, is secured at rear with the popular "hood pins." Walt Phillips made the body and readied it for mounting.

During initial runs at Motor City Dragway, Nash cranked on a number in the 9.20 second and 150 mph brackets as he got the feel of this new drag machine. Since we have "gone to press" he has probably improved on these times. Ready to go racing, Doug is seen below in Bell fire suit.

"BRONCO BUSTER"

That's what they call this rootin' tootin' match race machine from up Michigan way! Built by Doug Nash, with a big assist from Ford's Truck Division, this 1400 pound lightweight is outfitted with a fiberglass body and full aluminum frame. Powered by an injected 289-inch Ford Bronco engine, the little fuel-burner is another wild horse in Ford's performance corral.

Ernie MacEwen gave Nash an assist in building up the little 289-incher. Equipped with a Hilborn injector, Mallory ignitor, M/T aluminum rods, Forgedtrue pistons, and complete Crane roller camshaft and assembly; the powerplant thrives on a healthy nitro-alky mix. A Moon tank delivers fuel through braided steel lines to front-mounted pump.

By BUD LANG

BRONCO BUSTER! That's Doug Nash's all-new fiberglass-bodied hauler, the wildest looking match race car to hit the scene yet. A long-time FoMoCo fan, Doug has run through a succession of ten Fords and Mercs in his brief 24 years, but this one tops them all. Based on an aluminum chassis with power by a little 289-cubic inch Ford engine, this machine is the realization of over four months frenzied labor. It was built with one purpose in mind and that was to win races and make money. After all, how else does a professional drag racer make a living? While this car is Doug's sole means of support, his earlier efforts were not. All were modified for street use except the latter three which consisted of a Super Stock Galaxie and two B/FX Comets. These machines held records

Photos by Dick Scritchfield & Ford Motor Co.

Above—Tom Smith (left) and Nash install the aluminum roll cage assembly. Unit attaches to channel frame through angle brackets at base of each leg with bolts. Team made almost entire chassis assembly of aluminum and stainless steel to keep weight down. Bronco tips scales at 1400 pounds.

Because the rear section of the straight aluminum frame rails ride above the '66 Ford rear-end, it was necessary to drop the front. This was accomplished by "kicking" the front crossmember. This action also causes Bronco to run with its tail in the air, a preferred attitude for dragging.

under NHRA and/or 1320 sanction while being campaigned, giving evidence of Nash's talent for building winning cars.

Doug related that when plans were being made for a new funny car early this year, it was decided that the car would be unlike any others running. Extensive use of aluminum would be employed, and total weight of the car would be kept to a minimum without minimizing safety. As you can see, this is just what came about; an aluminum chassis, fiberglass Bronco body, all mounted on a short 112-inch wheelbase.

With considerable assistance from Tom Smith, Doug constructed the frame and roll cage of channel and tubular aluminum. The cage assembly is designed so that it may be easily unbolted and removed. A '66 Ford rearend

is equipped with Airheart disc brakes and 4.57:1 gears, with axles and housings narrowed so the Halibrand mags and 9.00 x 15-inch Goodyears will clear the body panels. The resultant tread width at rear comes out to 57-inches. Autolite shock absorbers are positioned behind the axle housing and work with Air Lift bags encased in coil springs. A Watts linkage arrangement above the rearend controls chassis side sway.

The front axle assembly was fabricated from .049" x 1¾" stainless steel tubing with perches for top-mounted Autolite suspension shocks and split radius rods. It takes Logghe billet steel spindles and American 12-spoke magnesium racing wheels. Avon motorcycle type 18-inch rubber offers a thin profile on these rims. Mounted to the upper of two front tubular crossmembers is a P-S

Machine Products competition steering unit, which by the way, lies on its side with the pitman arm driving the right spindle, the left connected by a tie-rod. A single sway bar atop the axle stabilizes the front end.

Though everything else is precision made and plays an important role in this fantastic "truck," it's the power plant that must get the job done. Here we find that Doug has relied on the little 289 cubic inch Ford engine, an engine he is quite familiar with. The only modification to the stock displacement block, other than a good hone job, was to have it O-ringed. Bearing clearance at the rods and mains has been increased to .003" and the journals polished to increase both crank and bearing life under heavy load conditions. Supporting the

29

BRONCO BUSTER

crankshaft is a cast aluminum main support girdle.

Special racing components in the engine include three-rib forged aluminum connecting rods by Mickey Thompson and Forgedtrue pistons with Forgedtrue dykes compression and Perfect Circle oil rings, end gapped to .020". A Crane roller billet camshaft, #R298HI, operates with Crane adjustable aluminum rocker arms, lifters, dual springs and Crane custom racing valves. The intakes were opened up to 1⅞-inch while the exhausts are now 1⅝-inch. A Crane high rev kit and aluminum retainers have also been employed in this high r.p.m. engine. Though valve timing duration is a mild 298 degrees, lift is a whopping .546" at both valves. The heads were also sent to Crane Engineering in Hallandale, Florida, where they were O-ringed, milled, ported and the combustion chambers CC'd. Stock gaskets painted with Copper Coat are used to seal the heads to the block.

A Hilborn fuel injection system delivers an alky-nitro load to the cylinders where it is fired by a Mallory Mini-Mag ignition and Autolite BF603 plugs and S-7 wiring. The headers on Doug's Bronco were produced by The Hot Rod Shop in Detroit. SAE 50 Valvoline racing oil was selected to run in the engine which was built by Doug and Ernie MacEwen. Valvoline was also used on the bearings, pistons and cylinders when assembling the block while Crane Assembly Lube was used on the cam, lifters, rockers and bolt threads. These steps were taken to cut down on friction and prevent excessive heat and galling when the engine is first fired. Bill's Speed Shop in Plymouth, Michigan, took care of the balancing chore when all the parts were assembled.

Glamorizing this entire package is a two-piece fiberglass body by Walt Phillips, the forward section of which hinges forward exposing both the engine and driver's compartment. After Walt finished mounting the body, the car went to Shedlik's Paint Styling studio where Paul painted the car a wild gold and red lacquer combination.

On the strip, Nash's "Bronco Buster" is a sight to behold. What with its rakish front end, spoke wheels and bobbed pickup box, you know it's far from stock. Another point of interest is the large fiberglass front bumper. It is designed to help keep the front end down during hard, top-speed runs through the lights. Summing everything up, there is no doubt in our minds that Doug has come up with one of the fanciest match race cars yet, and in keeping with the spirit of tipping the scales lightly, he has done so with one of the smallest, more proven engines yet . . . the little 289-inch Ford. Ⓒ

Blasting off the line, Nash's Bronco gets a handful of traction early due to automatic trans. American magnesium spoke wheels give the "Bronco Buster" a real early American look. Slight forward rake to body and bumper angle are conducive to high speed handling.

Situated to the right of the Moon fuel tank is a small radiator that offers just enough cooling to allow the Bronco to make a frantic 9-second ¼-mile dash.

Everything's functional in the driver's compartment. A Jones mechanical drive tach gives true rpm readings while Covico wheel works with a P-S steering unit. Gauges are for oil, water.

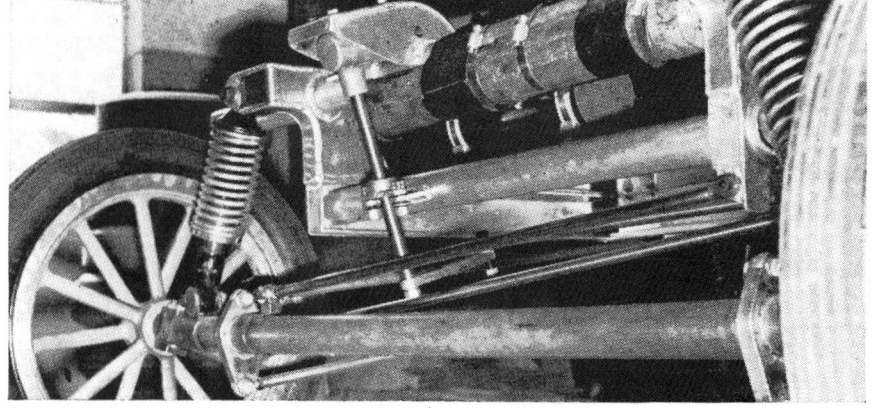
Nash decided on a stainless steel axle to keep weight down here, too. Then, like many others, he hangs bars of lead from the frame. Gets kind of confusing after a while. Kicked up front crossmember supports a P-S Machine race car steering and pair of Autolite shocks.

Stabilizing the rear-end, we find Nash installed Autolite shocks, Watts linkage and Air Lift bags. These latter units also allow "weight jacking" for improved traction off the line. Though Smith-Nash constructed the Bronco alone, Ford Truck Division gave assistance.

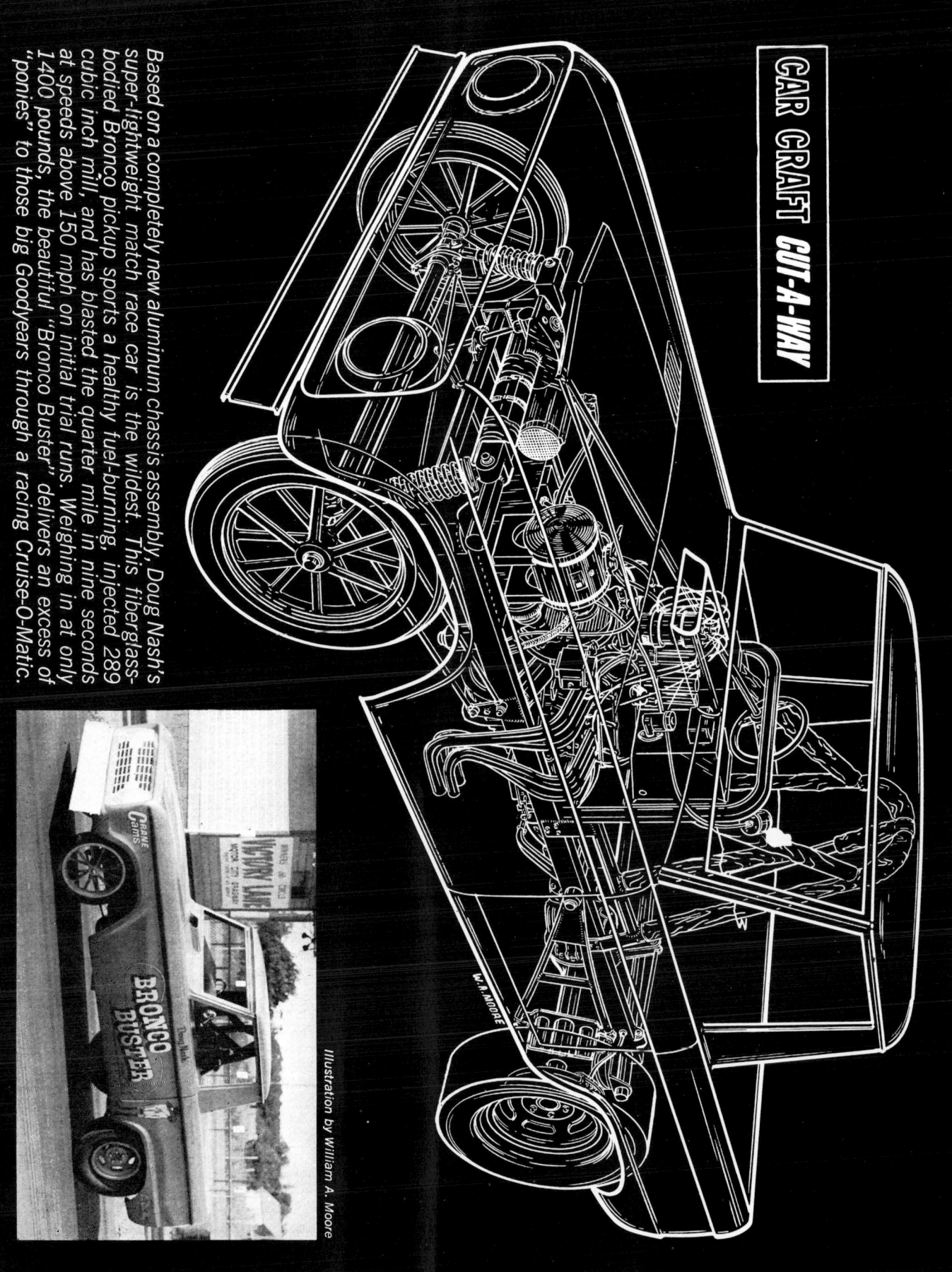

Illustration by William A. Moore

Based on a completely new aluminum chassis assembly, Doug Nash's super-lightweight match race car is the wildest. This fiberglass-bodied Bronco pickup sports a healthy fuel-burning, injected 289 cubic inch mill, and has blasted the quarter mile in nine seconds at speeds above 150 mph on initial trial runs. Weighing in at only 1400 pounds, the beautiful "Bronco Buster" delivers an excess of "ponies" to those big Goodyears through a racing Cruise-O-Matic.

31

BRONCO CAMPER

Four Wheelers who like bobtail rigs but still want a little more comfort will be interested in the two new camper units which have just been introduced for Ford's new Bronco

One, built by Open Road Campers, Inc., is a completely equipped, slide-in camper that sleeps four adults. The new camper unit also provides a fully equipped galley with formica covered top, manually operated hand pump and city water pressure outlet mounted around a white porcelain sink.

Sleeping accomodations are provided by a double bed in the cab over compartment plus pull out Gaucho beds.

Standard features include a 50 lb. plastic lined ice box, five gallon butane tank in safety sealed compartment with pressure regulator, three burner range with thermostatically controlled oven and broiler, 17 gallon FDA approved polyethelene water tank, large wardrobe closet, fiberglass insulation throughout, louvered and screened windows, 12/110 volt

Dreamer Camper Company is already experienced in the bobtail field with campers for Scout and Land Rover. New Bronco camper is shown above is now available.

combination interior lights with circuit breaker control, city water input and drainage connections, vent hood over range and butane lights in galley area.

The second of these recently introduced all-new camper units is a compact, rugged Dreamer camper This company also makes camper units for Scout and Land Rover. The Dreamer/Bronco weighs less than 800 lbs. and can be easily be removed in a few minutes either at home or in the back country. It is equipped with sleeping accomodations for four, a fiberglass galley and dining table, three burner stove, ice box, a water and electrical system, and includes ample storage and wardrobe closets.

It is constructed of tough, lightweight aircraft aluminum, with a hand finished wood paneled interior. Completely insulated with a blanket of hy-density fiberglass, the camper is comfort conditioned for hot or cold weather.

Open Road's new camper for the Bronco is a slide-in type which sleeps four adults. New camper also has fully equipped galley with formica covered top, manually operated hand pump; city water pressure outlet mounted on sink.

FORD'S BRONCO with its standard 6-cylinder engine is quite capable of unseating an unstrapped rider in somewhat less than the standard rodeo time of eight seconds. But now with an optional 200-hp, 289-cubic-inch V-8, it packs the violence of a Brahman bull.

The car we had was one of several V-8s entered in the recent 4-wheel-drive Grand Prix held in Santa Ana riverbed near Riverside, Calif. (MT, June '66). They all were beaten by a less muscular 6-cylinder Bronco primarily because 200 hp feeding into a 4:57-ratio limited-slip differential is somewhat akin to whipping water in a Waring blender. On the street one tends to stay under 50 mph even in "high" to insure returning with an engine still glued together. Off highway, however, and forgetting about the bruising business of racing for Top Eliminator in a Jeep rodeo, this Bronco is stopped by nothing short of the immovable.

Our version was what is called "Sports Utility," differing from the "Roadster" in that it had a steel cab and full doors. For further utility the "Wagon" form may be ordered with a seat and steel

AN APPEALING, PRACTICAL OFF-ROAD VEHICLE EQUIPPED AS TESTED FOR $3301. THE BRONCO'S BODY IS SUBJECT TO DINGS, BUT SUSPENSION IS NOT.

BUCKIN' BRONCO V-8

MONO-BEAM FRONT SUSPENSION WITH COILS AT EACH WHEEL IS USED. REAR SPRINGS ARE PROGRESSIVE-TYPE ELLIPTICS. TRACK IS 57.4 INCHES.

BUCKIN' BRONCO V-8

covering for rear passengers, and a vinyl soft top is alternately available. One of our wives unkindly compared our sports package to a "squashed up dump truck," but these sentiments were not shared by the amazing number of Jeep, Toyota, Land Cruiser, etc. owners who, spotting the parked Bronco, stopped short for an impromptu inspection. The elan of this off-road clan is impressive, making us regret having to finally admit that we weren't really a member, that we had to return the vehicle to its owner that Friday.

You sit high but comfortably in the Bronco, with an outstanding feature being the ready accessibility of the transfer-case control. We do feel, though, that somebody at the gear factories of each of the 4wd makers should do something to make the transfer case as civilized to shift about in as are the current light-truck transmissions used. The dash is a utilitarian one, and thus quite pleasing in appearance, and the heater is obviously designed for topless operation in Alaska. The rugged mats and pedal covers should take nearly as much abuse as uncovered steel, and are less slippery.

The highway ride is choppy due to the short wheelbase, but is reasonably well cushioned by the front-coil springing. No brake or steering boost is needed or even offered, although a steering damper could well be applied if off-road use is frequent. Turning diameter is 33.6 feet, a figure claimed to be less than any other vehicle in Bronco's class. The chassis design deserves credit; it provides an acceptable degree of creature comfort without any sacrifice in ruggedness. Our pictures prove better than words that the Bronco underpinnings are for all practical purposes indestructible.

Owner or mechanic could understandably be frightened by his first glimpse of the massive V-8 stuffed into a compartment originally designed to house a 170-cubic-inch 6. However, closer inspection reveals quite convenient accessibility to frequently serviced items. The distributor is topside at the front, only the left-rear spark plug is obstructed in any way, and that oft-buried item, the filler for the brake master cylinder, is as easy to reach as the oil intake. Lubrication and oil change intervals are Ford's standard 6 months or 6000 miles, whichever comes first under normal operating conditions.

Gasoline consumption for the V-8 can range anywhere from 15 mpg for easy highway driving to a low of 7 mpg experienced during our rough cross-country picture taking. Considering the low gearing of our test unit, this is not bad at all. A standard fuel capacity of 14 gallons is the highest in its class, and so is the warranty of 24,000 miles or 24 months. Another plus factor, of course, is Ford's network of 6400 dealerships across the country.

Optional equipment includes power take-off, a winch, heavy-duty axles and a wide assortment of dress-up accessories. Either Warn or Dana free-running front hubs are available. Stowage area is 56 inches wide and 55 inches long.
— *Don MacDonald*

PHOTOS BY PAT BROLLIER

(Above left) Ground clearance, though rated nominal 6.6 inches with standard tires, becomes phenomenal with 8.15 tires.

(Above right) Unlocking Dana hubs is 2-man job as car must be rocked slightly to free them. Item on bumper is tow bar.

(Left) Much of the confusion in this view of the engine results from anti-smog pumps and plumbing, but servicing is still easy.

(Above) The cab is roomy and well planned. Picture also illustrates common occurrence of seat belts installed backwards.

BRONCO

by EDWARD ORR

When Ford introduced the Bronco it probably received more attention across the country than any back country rig before or since. Now that the hullabaloo that accompanied Bronco's debut has died down lets take a good long look at Ford's favorite filly.

For the last year the Bronco has had the edge in the power option department, being the only vehicle with a choice of a six or eight cylinder engine. Recently Scout got into the act with a V-8 but it cannot match the Bronco for horsepower.

The optional V-8 powered FOUR WHEELER'S test vehicle and the 200 horsepower that turns on at 4400 rpm is plenty for the 3000 pound machine. Off the pavement I could break the wheels loose in almost any gear. The peak torque of 282 foot pounds shows up early, for a V-8, at 2400 rpm and gives the Bronc more lugability than would be expected from a rig of this type with a V-8.

Another interesting option tested was the combination front and rear limited slip differentials. Ford is one on the very few manufacturers that offers this, and after the test crew finished romping the Bronco it was easy to understand the controversy that surronds this idea.

On hills the LS was a wonder. The guaranteed traction and low end torque could cover a multi-

tude of driving sins. On short steep hills that other rigs had to charge to top, the Bronc just crawled over, like it had cleats.

But sand was another set of tracks. For technical reasons, that will be covered in a later article, the LS performs strangely in sand. Turns could be made if I kept my foot out of the carburetor but when the power was applied, while in the turn, the rig straightened out like someone had suddenly unhooked the steering linkage. The only way to bring it back on course was to let off on the gas. It may be that this limitation would bother only the competition minded but it is a point for the cons.

One feature that can be seen in the pictures and is sure to attract attention is the unusual rubber on the rig. Part of the test was run at the Phoenix Club's Jamboree and these tires were the talk of the camp. They are the new Gates Commandos mounted on 12 inch rims. They have a wide lug tread design that grips on hills like a set of claws and are plenty broad enough for the sandy river bottoms. Like any wide, treaded tire they sing a bit on the highway and the tire balancer turned a little pale when I drove into the shop but, in my opinion the advantages count for more, and it looks like the tire is here to stay.

When it comes to handling the Bronco is a little schizophrenic. On the highway the rig must be rated as excellent. It rolls at freeway speeds with the stability and comfort of a passenger car

The V-8 engine displaces 289 cubic inches and provides plenty of punch and surprising economy. For the competition minded, the mill offers good hop up potential.

and in spite of the 92 inch wheelbase it practically ignores cross winds. At around 65 mph there is a noticeable wind noise but considering the design of 4wds in general it would be surprising only if the noise were absent.

Off the road the Hyde side of the Bronco's personality shows its face. The rig has the shortest turning radius in the field — bar none. But cranking the steering wheel the necessary eleventeen turns to reach the lock and then back for an opposite turn can keep the driver busier than a one armed paper hanger.

In the rocks and ruts department the term "bucking Bronco" comes to mind and stays there. I am still nursing a swollen knuckle that was the result of being slapped about the head and shoulders by the steering wheel after it had torn itself from my hands. A steering stablizer would probably help a lot. It darn sure couldn't hurt.

No 4wd machine has ever pretended to the throne of economy and it might be feared the 289 cubic inch V-8 would be a gas gobbler. But it ain't so McGee. In the several thousand miles of driving that comprised the test the overall mpg figure fell between 11 and 12. If this seems on the low side, remember that the Bronc went for days at a time without ever coming out of low range. The road average climbs to a respectable 13 to 14 mpg and that includes pulling a trailer.

Now about that bounce.......Hate to disappoint you fellas, but it is not the big deal it has been made to seem. A bit of background might be helpful in understanding the problem. First an auto company does not stay in business without pleasing the public, and the softer than normal suspension of the Bronco is not something Ford dreamed up out of thin air. Plenty of people with bent backsides were pleading for an off the road rig that wouldn't keep their chiropractor in the Cadillac clan. And Bronco is Ford's answer.

The seats are comfortable, the leg and head room good, and that suspension soaks up bumps that would rattle your teeth on other rigs. But the problem is not all a result of suspension compromise. Driving skill plays a part.

The bounce, or more correctly spring wrap up, is basically a result of being in the wrong gear at the right time. What happens on a hill is the driver counts on the horses to make up for his lack of momentum and near the top power exceeds traction. Then instead of spinning, and leaving nice deep holes for the guy behind, the softer springs allow the wheel to jump and progress is slowed — to put it mildly.

There are two solutions. One, air bags and heavy duty dual shocks can be added to the front end. This insures there will be enough force to hold the wheel in contact with the ground. But there went the riding qualities. Or you can select a lower cog at the bottom of the hill and pick up a little momentum before reaching the crucial point. On the Phoenix run I learned this the hard way.

They had a one try per hill rule and I made the mistake of trying to idle up one of the tougher hills. Everybody had a good laugh as I backed down and went the four banger route. But the next time it was my turn to laugh. On the toughest hill of the run I gave the Bronc its head at the bottom and as soon as the momentum was felt to be sufficient I let off on the gas slightly. She snorted over the top with ease and I parked to watch several of the "tried and true" species of 4wds dig up the hill so badly that another course had to be cut.

On the subject of comfort, and its hard to talk about the Bronco without that subject coming up, it must be rated tops. As mentioned it takes the backache out of boondocking and is a real pleasure on the long highway hauls. Adding to the comfort angle on chilly nights is a heater that would probably cook breakfast. The thing has got three speeds, hot hotter, and "I told you to repent, you sinner".

Some of the interior features have been modified since the first model was introduced and the transfer case lever is one of them. In an earlier report the test crew complained the lever was too long, and it was. It has been shortened but retains the short throw that was so popular in that test. The top is a handsome T handle with a button on the driver's side. To switch from 2wd to 4wd the button is pressed and the lever moved an inch or so. No clutch. The button controls a locking device that prevents accidental shifts and works so well you could kick the thing out by the roots without slipping into the wrong cog.

On the minus side there were two items that bothered the drivers. One was the placement of the rearview mirror. It is glued to the windshield right at eye level and created a blind spot that is annoying, if not dangerous. The other squawk was the location of the spare tire. It bolts to the inside of the tailgate, (which rattles) and all loading must be done over or around it. The old problem of the exposed jack has been solved however. It is now tucked away beneath the spare.

The windshield folds down by simply removing a chromed knob on each side and lowering the glass to the hood. There a pin engages a lock to keep it in place. It sounds easy but I'm sure Mack Sennet would have loved to have films of someone with short arms trying to put the windshield back up. The holding ring is located in the center of the hood where it is nearly impossible to reach and there is about an inch and a half of space between the frame and the hood into which you must reach to grab the unlocking knob.

When all the tally sheets were in the Bronco earned a very respectable score. There are still a few bugs but Ford is hard at work and the future models promise many improvements. This means some things will stay and some will go.

One thing is bound to go, and its a shame. Every new vehicle introduced in the 4wd field goes through an initiation of sorts. Friendly razzing and the horse laugh while it sinks in the quicksand are all part of the game. But with Bronco it has built a strong sense of camaraderie among owners. Not since the early days of campers have I had the pleasure of other drivers waving to me simply because they were driving the same type of vehicle.

The metallic cavalry we have assembled here represents the newest wave in middle-class hip. A few years back the only guy who bought himself an off-the-road vehicle was, most likely, an oil field rigger, a forest ranger, a prospector, a Minute Man, a white hunter, or a social outcast who was just plain nuts about shunning not only pikes but every other form of paved road as well. Nowadays, it seems like every red-blooded American suburbanite wants a Jeep or one of its many offspring.

If it hasn't already happened on your block, one of these bright days you can expect a call from some Captain Virility of the Split-Level Set, inviting you over to take a look at his newest automotive acquisition. You'll rush right over, expecting to see a sleek new Lamborghini or, at the very least, a 427 Sting Ray. But what you'll find is one of these incredible monsters standing there in all its high, slab-sided glory. The suspension will be sticking out from the undercarriage, the tops of the fenders will be only slightly below your breastbone, and there'll be a cab towering so high you figure you'll get a nosebleed if you ever have to go for a ride—provided, of course, that your atrophied muscles are strong enough to vault you into the seat.

Meanwhile, old Captain Virility scrambles out of the cab and launches into a frenzied rhapsody about how *practical,* how tough, how well-made, how *honest* his new vehicle is. It's the medium he alone has discovered to transport him "back to nature." No more deceiving himself with a $5000 foreign sports car that he can't enjoy because of the traffic, and the fuzz, and the money it costs to get it serviced; from now on it's back to fundamental values—sea, sand, sky, rocks, trees—and there ain't nothin' can stop him!

Come on, neighbor. Every beach within 200 miles is now restricted to specially-authorized beach buggies, and there's a mile-long waiting list to get one of the coveted permits. If Captain Virility tries to use his proud new possession up in the mountains, he's more than likely to come home with a load of buckshot in his tail, courtesy of the farmer who owns the land he was trespassing on.

You know all this . . . and so does he. But *dammit,* you still can't help admire him, his rugged individualism—you're a little jealous of his new, Hemingway ap-

GET OFF THE ROAD!

We try several samples of the automotive world's all-purpose elixir for whatever might ail you...and they <u>all</u> work.

PHOTOGRAPHY: GARY RENAUD

proach to life. Here's this guy who spends forty hours a week listening to idle prattle about the latest socko campaign by Mary Wells, or reading the *Wall Street Journal* to find out the closing prices of pork belly futures—just like you do. And on the weekends he mows his lawn, paints his house, plays a few rounds of golf and goes to all the cocktail parties—just like you do. But—anytime he wants to—he can transform himself into a real, live adventurer. From now on, nobody's going to have the temerity to suggest that he isn't in absolute control of his own life. He's no longer restricted to traffic-clogged highways, no longer phased by rock-throwing back country roads. Suddenly his four-wheel-drive off-the-road vehicle has made him master of his own destiny. Freedom Rider!

It really doesn't matter that the damn thing's transfer case will probably rust away from disuse, and that the power-winch securely bolted to the front bumper will only be used to haul helpless saplings out of the backyard. When friend Virility goes roaring and bucking into town, even if it's just for another case of Beefeaters, poor slobs like you are bound to think wistfully of all the good times he *can* have in that lumbering little truck.

And, no matter how many niggling laws restrict its use, a four-wheel-drive vehicle is fun. Big fun. We spent a couple of weeks tearing up sand and sod around Long Island beaches and the hills behind Bridgehampton Race Circuit with five such vehicles: a long-wheelbase Land Rover, a Toyota Land Cruiser, an International Scout, a Jeep Universal, and a Ford Bronco. And we all wish we could do it more often. (Originally, we had planned to include another vehicle, the Datsun Patrol, but miffed at our treatment of their economy sedan, the RL-411 (*C/D*, May), Datsun refuses to submit any more of their vehicles for our evaluation.)

When this test was first proposed we had assumed that all four-wheel-drive vehicles are pretty much alike. How wrong we were. Off-the-road vehicles remain one of the few products for which each manufacturer has its own concept of what constitutes the ideal. Perhaps nowhere is the difference so apparent as in the prices of the five vehicles we tested. Rather than specify exactly what we wanted, we asked each of the companies to provide us with a vehicle that, in their opinion, represented the best compromise between second-car practicality and off-the-road fun. Rover was the only one to provide us with a long-wheelbase version (probably because their big six-cylinder engine is only available in the long-wheelbase model). Kaiser, on the other hand, went to the other extreme and provided us with a vitamin-packed V-6 in

their short-wheelbase version of the ubiquitous Jeep Universal. On two points, at least, all five manufacturers agreed; all the cars came through with metal hardtops and heater/defroster units. The cars which were most comfortable in the over-the-road portion of our test, the Ford Bronco and the Rover, both came equipped with radios, while the best off-the-road models, the Jeep and the Rover (again), also came with power winches. The Toyota, well-placed in both categories and probably the best value for the money, had neither a radio nor a winch.

Because the vehicles we tested were equipped with widely differing amounts of extra-cost options, it is important to note in the specifications table that the prices are "as tested," and not base prices for each model. Other specifications vary accordingly, and are not intended as a source of direct comparison. Our intention is to present some basic information and our impressions of typical examples from each of the manufacturers.

The vast differences in fittings, ride comfort and performance reflect the individual manufacturer's design emphasis rather than the foibles of a particular version. For instance, the medium-priced Jeep V-6 was far and away the most spartan, being almost devoid of instrumentation and totally lacking in sound-deadening insulation, but it also had the most comfortable seats of the bunch. At the other extreme was the Land Rover, which had the most comprehensive dashboard and loads of nifty little convenience gadgets like swing-up steps and four doors instead of just two, but its seats were not nearly as comfortable as the Jeep's. The Ford Bronco was the smoothest riding, most softly sprung member of the group, and it was the only one equipped with a coil spring suspension instead of semi-elliptic leaf springs on all four wheels. It had obviously been designed primarily for over-the-road comfort and *occasional*

off-the-road use. Had it not been for the pseudo-Mustang bucket seats the Bronco would have been, far and away, the most comfortable car. Unfortunately, the padding around the edges of the Bronco's seats is so thick that your back is supported only at the shoulder blades—the rest of you caves into an uncomfortable hunchbacked position. The Toyota had the harshest suspension and was the roughest riding of the group, but its very stiff spring rates helped make it an outstanding off-the-road performer.

In terms of acceleration, our little Jeep left the rest of the field panting in its wake. But its narrow spring leaves had so much lateral compliance that it would shift disconcertingly from side to side under any kind of side load. This, plus a chronically grabbing brake, made everyone wary of driving the little stormer in heavy traffic.

Whether a compromise between over-the-road and off-the-road usage is desirable turned out to be a different matter. The Scout had no outstanding attributes because it—more than any of the others—was designed as a compromise. The result was that no one felt very strongly about it one way or the other. Most automotive devices have some kind of personality; the Scout didn't. It was like a washing machine—a solid, utilitarian appliance that gets the job done largely unnoticed.

All of the cars were capable of keeping up with the incredible demands of driving on the Long Island Expressway, where one minute you're slogging along at four mph and the next you're caught up in a swarming phalanx of NASCAR racers who think nothing of drafting each other at 85 mph. The weakest member of our convoy was the Scout. Even though it was equipped with International's new V-8 engine, it simply lacked the acceleration to keep up. (In fairness, we should mention that this Scout was fresh off the assembly line with very few miles on it when we tested it.)

Except for the Land Rover, which had a four-speed transmission, all our test vehicles were equipped with three-speeds. None was what you would call slick shifting, and only the Bronco had a synchronized first gear (first *and* second on the four-speed Rover were unsynchronized). One fault common to all the cars was gear spacing. First and second gears were inevitably low ratio ranges, designed for maximum power application, with the high cruising gear a country mile away. This held true even for the four-speed Rover, with first being a sort of "underdrive" and second and third acting much the same as the lower two gears on the other vehicles' three-speeds.

Noise level in these cars was universally atrocious. The Ford Bronco—the most Detroit-ized of our test group—was the quietest, with the Scout a close second. The remaining three—Rover, Toyota and Jeep—are in a class by themselves. Suffice it to say that conversation is effectively drowned out, and that even thought pro-

40

Ford Bronco

International Scout

Jeep Universal

Land Rover

Toyota Land Cruiser

cesses can become confused as a result of the roaring and rattling all around you.

While none of these vehicles is in line for an award as the "world's most commodious station wagon," their off-the-road performance makes up for what they lack on the pavement. We began our off-the-road testing at the Bridgehampton Race Circuit on the end of Long Island. This windswept course is located in the midst of high, sandy dunes and proved to be an ideal testing ground for these vehicles. When we wanted loose sand it was available; as was hard sand, steep grades, thick underbrush and all the rest of the impossible conditions that a standard two-wheel drive vehicle can't handle. So we descended on Bridgehampton one bright morning and we came away different people—all of us. When our convoy was finally grouped around the administration building, our photographer mentioned that he'd like all of us to go out and search for a dramatic slope on which he could position the vehicles for a group shot. *Roar! Roar! Roar! Roar! Roar!* All five cars shot off in four-wheel-drive to find an appropriate location.

Dust clouds trailed each of the cars as they rumbled from dune to dune in search of the perfect setting. Spontaneous races broke out everywhere and it wasn't long before the photographer realized that no one was really interested in helping him out—we all just wanted to find out for ourselves what this off-the-road hang-up is all about.

It took nearly 45 minutes to get us regrouped and beaten into submission, and another 15 minutes before the beleaguered photographer found the spot he wanted. Finally, all five cars were staged on the side of THE hill. For another 15 minutes we sat patiently still while the cars were carefully (and somewhat precariously) positioned. As we stood there, waiting for the shot to be taken, challenges were hurled about like insults in a nightclub: "My Jeep will take that Rover up any hill you want to name," "The Land Cruiser will kill you both" and on and on.

When the photographer unwittingly cooperated by saying "Okay, I'm finished here. Now I'd like to get some running shots of the cars going over rough terrain," it was all over. He had given us the justification we needed for what we had been plotting all along.

The scene that followed was a Mack Sennett version of Le Mans. The drivers sprinted to their cars, and, within seconds, all five were fired up and roaring helter-skelter over every dune in sight.

It seemed that everyone felt it necessary to challenge the Land Rover, which was in the capable hands of our Technical Editor. Soon it was apparent that the only other cars that stood a chance were the Jeep and the Toyota. But, frantic as their efforts might be, the stately Land Rover couldn't be topped. The whole thing came to a halt when the Jeep, after nearly beating the

Rover up a particularly soft dune, got hung up on top of a hummock and had to be ignominiously pulled off with its winch.

All the off-the-road vehicles proved their worth in this spontaneous test procedure. The only one that was constantly left behind was the International Scout, whose engine didn't have the pulling power and kept wheezing to a halt midway up the steep dunes.

On the next day we trekked down to the deserted beaches to see if there were any marked differences on the long level stretches of very soft sand. There were. Our Toyota, which had been such a challenger at Bridgehampton, suddenly couldn't cut it. Not being what you would call a lightweight, and—because we had decided that we wanted to evaluate these cars as both off-the-road and over-the-road vehicles in the same trim—we hadn't bothered to reduce the pressure in any of the tires. *Scrunch.* The short-wheelbase Toyota bogged down. It simply sank into the sand and every time we stepped on the gas, its powerful engine would just dig us in more deeply. So out came the winch again—this time the one on the Rover. Even with their tires fully pumped up, the rest of the vehicles were able to make it through the hub-deep sand, although none but the Jeep, because of its light weight and fat tires, inspired any overwhelming confidence that you could, invariably, pull yourself out of any predicament you might get into.

Except for the International Scout, every one of these vehicles had one outstanding point. For the Jeep, it was its brute power. For the Bronco, its over-the-road comfort. For the Toyota, its outstanding performance in everything except soft sand. For the Rover, it was the ease with which it tackled any obstacle. But each vehicle except the Scout, had its faults as well. The Jeep was perched on an uncertain suspension. The Toyota was rough riding. The Bronco wasn't really designed for sustained use in rough terrain. And the Rover we tested was too expensive for most people in the market for a second car.

As we said at the outset, much of the recent demand for off-the-road vehicles comes from people who don't really need them, people who simply want something that will allow them to escape from the confines of their lives and the restrictions of a road map. After driving these cars for a couple of weeks, we can understand that philosophy. It's a great feeling to get out on an unmarked hunk of land and raise a whole lot of hell. So do yourself a favor. Get off to the outback and find out what it's all about. Go wherever you damn well please! It's guaranteed to soothe the mind, enliven the spirit, cure a multitude of nine-to-five maladies and alleviate irregularity. And there hasn't been anything like that for the last fifty years, except maybe Excedrin, which isn't nearly as much fun. **C/D**

OFF-THE-ROAD Specifications					
	Ford Bronco	International Scout	Jeep Universal	Land Rover	Toyota Land Cruiser
Wheelbase	92.0 in	100.0 in	81.0 in	109.0 in	90.0 in
Track: F	57.4 in	56.1 in	48.5 in	51.5 in	55.3 in
R	57.4 in	55.7 in	48.5 in	51.5 in	55.1 in
Ground clearance	7.8 in	7.6 in	8.0 in	9.8 in	7.9 in
Weight	3165 lbs	3615 lbs	2274 lbs	3912 lbs	3470 lbs
Turning circle	33.5 ft	44.2 ft	40.3 ft	52.5 ft	36. ft
Engine:					
Type	In-line 6	V-8	V-6	In-line 6	In-line 6
Displ.	170 cu in	266 cu in	225 cu in	160 cu in	237 cu in
Power	105 hp	155 hp	160 hp	123 hp	134 hp
0-60 Time	19.4 secs.	20.5 secs.	10.8 secs.	18.5 secs.	16.9 secs.
Price (as tested)	$2922	$3491	$3310	$4950	$3181

Land Rover has full instrumentation and ventilation flaps beneath the windshield.

Jeep's instrumentation consists of a speedometer. For fresh air you open a window.

A CLOSE LOOK AT THE '69 BRONCO

In the past 18 months Ford's Broncos have become remarkable performers at off road competitions. Within the space of a year the rugged Bronco has become the machine to beat. Most other makes are gearing their races towards this goal.

With all the national publicity on the rig in racing, we suddenly realized that very little has been published recently on how the Bronco performs for the average back country enthusiast. We called Ford and made arrangements to pick up a stock rig with the normal options a four wheeler would want plus a set of off road wide wheels and tires. It was to be nothing special, and our test was to be the type of driving any western four wheeler would do — highway, desert and mountains.

The test vehicle was delivered with a V-8 engine, Gates Commando, 11-inch tires and the Sport Bronco Package. This last option is sort of a deluxe trim feature and includes such goodies as chrome bumpers, cigarette lighter, vinyl panels, parchment floor mat, bright metals, and other touch up details. The bucket seats were also optional. The Bronco also came with a 3:50-to-1 axle ratio.

Talking with Bronco salesmen in the west, we learned that the rig we had was equipped almost identically to most of the Broncos they delivered to their customers. It was just what we

combined into a single lever with four positions: 2wd high, 4wd high, 4wd low and neutral. A push button arrangement locks the unit out of the lower gears and prevents inadvertently shifting into the lower gears while traveling.

To be quite frank, this shift lever looks so much like an automatic shift on a passenger car that we were asked on occasion: "How do you like the automatic?" From a practical standpoint, the lever is well-positioned and works well. Shifts are easy and once the driver gets into the habit of pushing the little button, he can get into low gear easily.

In the past much has been written about the Bronco's handling and ride. While there are few specific engineering improvements to point to, the 1969 Bronco gave us no reason to complain in this department. At highway speeds it held well and required virtually no correction for corners.

The test unit had a linkage shock absorber-type steering stabilizer and this probably accounts for its stable ride. Off the road handling has also been greatly smoothed out and it takes a fast speed and big rock to give the driver's hands a bad shock.

Off the road bounce by the front end has often been a Bronco owner's complaint. We tried this out on several desert hills and many miles of fast-driven trails. In our opinion, the test vehicle gave no indication of excessive reaction in this phase of the test. True, there was some bounce, but the amount was neither excessive nor more than found in comparable rigs.

By off road standards the interior of the Bronco is excellent — one of the best in the field. The interior appointments are well positioned, fit good and while everything about the appointments is attractive the materials are practical, long wearing and nearly everything will clean with a hose.

We have commented on the cargo capacity and passenger space before and it has always impressed our test people. The Bronco had bucket seats and the bench seat in back. This is ideal for transporting four people across the desert but will always leave the occupants searching for room to store their gear. With two persons aboard, the Bronco has more than ample space to store a two week supply of grub and camping gear.

One of the options we didn't ask for and wished we had, was the auxiliary gas tank. Not that the 14.5 gallon stock tank is inadequate, the test crew's dislikes coming into civilization for fuel. If we were asked the three most important options for the Bronco would be the auxiliary tank, the 3.50 gear set and wide tires.

Add these options to the engineering refinements over the years and the Bronco is a far superior machine than it was before. It is common knowledge that it can do better than hold its own in competition. Our test showed that the 1969 can do better than hold its own for the requirements of back country drivers.

44

BRUSH BUSTING BRONCO FROM NORTH OF THE BORDER

Canadian readers often write in and accuse us of not being partial to north of the border rigs. Well, it's a misconception!

In our opinion, the fellow who said that Texans were taciturn didn't really know Canadians. It has taken them seven years to send in their first car story and we are printing it here. Now before you get the idea that we are running this feature simply because it is the first car story we've had from Canada we'd suggest you read on. There is going to be a few surprises for the fellows who simply bolt on speed accessories.

The rig is a 1967 Bronco V-8, wagon style and it now has 30,000 miles on the odometer. The modifier is a high school teacher named Homer Rogers and we're going to tell you about the 4wd rig just as he told us, in one, two, three order. These are the modifications he has made:

1. A Hurst syncro-loc floor shift was installed.

2. A Smith's 0-8000, 270 degree tach was installed along with an AM-FM radio.

3. A set of traction bars were fastened securely to the heavy duty positraction rear axle assembly extending midway up the vehicle — about to the center of the auxiliary gas tank.

4. A viscous fan assembly was modified to fit behind the heavy duty radiator.

5. A Delta Kit Mark 10 capacitive discharge kit was assembled and installed, permitting 6500 rpm with increased mileage, plug life and never an ignition falter.

6. The center skid plate was extended to protect the two-inch dual exhausts and stock mufflers from damage.

7. Beneath every wheel well opening, 16 gauge steel was formed to completely fill in above the wheel for gravel and rock protection of the underbody. The metal was under-coated before installing.

8. The rear bumper was moved out about four inches and is removable from the frame-mounted trailer hitch plates.

9. A 2-1/2-inch diameter heavy wall stainless front bumper was installed along with a quarter-inch front skid plate, both to protect the hydraulic steering stabilizer and steering arms.

10. In the engine department the following items were added:

(a) An eight quart oil pan, fully baffled with swing gates and windage tray, was constructed and cadmium plated before installing. The drain plug is a 3-1/2 inch barrel drain for really fast drains and the wiping out of the pan at each oil change. The oil pump pickup tube was modified from the original 7/16-inch ID pipe to 11/16-inch ID pipe — complete with swinging pickup from a Chrysler Hemi (426). The pan has an oil temperature fitting located on one side.

(b) A Ford hi-performance camshaft and solid lifters was installed. The cam is a C30-Z-6250-C camshaft for the 271 horsepower 289 cid.

(c) A "Vari-Cam" camshaft sprocket was also installed.

(d) A Cobra aluminum hi-rise intake

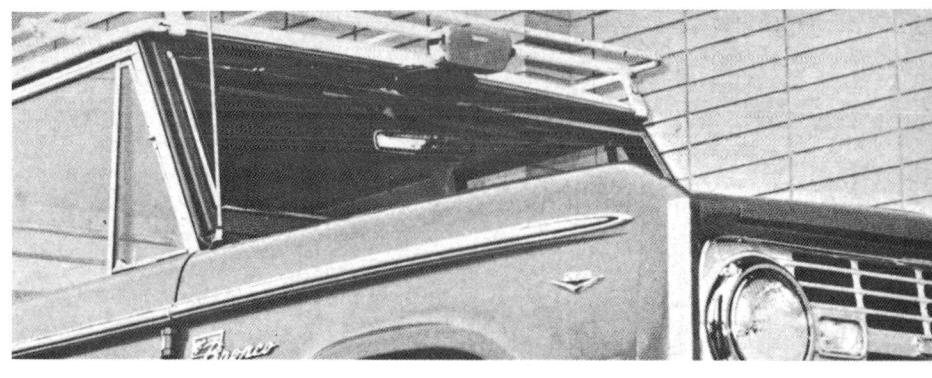

manifold and a center float, 600 cubic foot per minute Holley four-barrel carburetor was fitted.

(e) The distributor advance curve was modified as was the Carburetor jetting on a dyno.

(f) A home-made aluminum air filter can was fabricated to hold a washable polyurethane air filter element which will admit hot air when the engine is cold and cold outside air when the engine heats up to working temperature.

(g) Because of the relaxed smog laws in the wilds of Canada a continuous duty bilge blower was installed. This pulls air directly from the engine crankcase through a baffled rocker cover. Two restrictive breather caps were installed on the other rocker cover to admit air to the crankcase. A partial vacuum is always present in the engine crankcase because of this set up. So all blowby, water and fumes are immediately removed keeping the engine interior spotless.

11. A hood lock was installed.

12. The front seat was modified to "pullmanize" completely flat resulting in a sleeping bed six feet, six inches long and 50 inches wide.

13. Two interior lights were installed along with full carpets and underfelt.

14. Many other *trivial* (editor's emphasis) modifications were made — full instrumentation, vacuum gauge, oil temperature, clock, etc. The transfer case shift quadrant was modified to give a low gear in two-wheel drive — very handy in slow traffic conditions.

The Bronco was ordered with 3.50-to-1 axle ratios instead of the standard 4.11-to-1. This gives a much more economical and quiet cruising speed. The compression ratio was not altered so regular gas is used. On highway driving around 65 mph the economy is between 22 and 23 miles per gallon. (EDITOR'S NOTE: Before Bronco readers descend en masse to lynch their local Ford dealer, the reference here is to the Imperial gallon).

A Cee Bee quartz iodine driving light and a full length, full width, removable roof rack was cadmium plated and installed.

Is our modifier to the north satisfied? We doubt it, for he reports that just after writing us, he intended to install a variable ratio Saginaw power steering unit from a 1968 Cadillac, an out of the way roll bar and a swing away tire carrier for the rear.

Homer also reports that the Bronco performs superbly (we don't doubt his word one iota). It idles around 600 rpm,

pulls very strong from 20 mph in high, will exceed 80 mph in second gear and cruise effortlessly at 65-70 mph.

Problems? Yes, there was one. The front brake drums were "square," probably by at least .005-inch and Homer Rogers promptly reported this to his Ford dealer who capitulated and installed new drums all around on the warranty.

Yet, Rogers has no quarrel with the Ford people in Campbell River. He states that the engine burns no oil, starts exceedingly well and is fun to drive no matter what the road or no-road condition. (EDITOR'S NOTE: This Bronco wouldn't dare be otherwise).

Rogers has also installed four H-70 x 15 wide oval snow tires to be used when the 9:15 x 15 highway tires can't cope with mud and sand conditions often found in the backwoods of Canada. He also found that he needs the roof a little more often in his area so he removed the hood hold down for the windshield and replaced it with a Chrysler fender turn signal light modified to act as an oil

pressure indicator light.

While at times in this article we have treated Homer Rogers modified Bronco a little lightly, perhaps humorously, it is in our opinion the finest job of off-road individualization that any Bronco has yet received. His has to be a rig that any Bronco enthusiast would love to own — so much that he might even be tempted to "borrow" it without permission.

If we didn't mention it earlier, Homer Rogers is not, *just a high school teacher,* he is the Automotive Instructor for Campbell River Senior High School. And if his classes don't have a waiting list, then there must be something wrong with the boys at Campbell River.

They better get into Rogers' classes soon. After reading this article Dearborn, Michigan is liable to plan a kidnapping. Homer Rogers . . . and his ideas . . . are something that any off-road manufacturer can use — and some of them are going to start wrenches turning in the average four wheelers hand.

NEW BRONCO OVERDRIVE

Owners or prospective owners of the popular Ford "Bronco" will do themselves and their Bronco's a big favor by looking into the features of the newly developed Rancho Overdrive, designed especially for the Bronco. For our driver's test we picked up one of the first Broncos equipped with a Rancho Overdrive at Ken Roggy Ford in La Puente, California.

The surging power the Bronco 289 V-8 offers is now fully realized with the use of a Rancho Overdrive. Normal noise and vibration levels are now reduced appreciably as the engine speed is slowed 33 percent with the Rancho Overdrive engaged. Driver fatigue on most long trips can normally be attributed to these factors. We found highway cruising to be enjoyably free from noise and vibration which should reduce driver fatigue commensurately. Long grades posed no problems. We had the alternative to either return the Bronco to its normal high gear ratio by fully depressing the accelerator pedal or shifting to second-overdrive. Up the longest grades we continued without slowing, using either method.

The marked increase in the Bronco's perfor-mance and engine saving lower RPM's was decidedly apparent by the tach readings.

MPH	OVERDRIVE "IN"	OVERDRIVE "OUT"
35	1200 RPM's	3100 RPM's
65	2600 RPM's	3900 RPM's
70	2900 RPM's	LOUD

Mileage figures also reflected the advantage of the Bronco with the Rancho Overdrive. With the overdrive engaged 17.5 miles-per-gallon were obtained versus 13.7 with the overdrive disengaged. Fuel economy increased 27 percent.

Our test Bronco was not equipped with free-wheeling hubs, and the use of hubs can increase performance data as much as 10 percent.

The Bronco has long needed an overdrive unit and Rancho has delivered. Bronco owners will appreciate the immediate economy and performance the Rancho Overdrive provides plus the long range reward of extending the overhaul interval to the drive-train.

Drive a Bronco equipped with a Rancho Overdrive and we are sure you will agree. It's a "Bronco Saver".

Beating out cycles and buggies, the HMS-built Minor/Hall Motor Trend Bronco was overall winner of Baja 1000 offroad race.

"Just how tough does a car have to be to win the Baja 1000 . . . does it have to be bulletproof?"

"It's got to be an iron anvil."

Bill Stroppe started building off-road racers long before the era of the Broncos, long before the Baja 1000 and long before the absorbtion of his Long Beach, California, shop by Holman & Moody. Before all of that there were those unbelievable *Carrera Pan Americana* Lincolns, innumerable NASCAR-type Pikes Peak stockers and the African Safari Comets. Stroppe got his first Bronco in 1966, before its public release, readying it for a competion debut shortly after the official introduction. That first one, with a little six-cylinder engine, was overall winner at the Riverside Four-Wheel-Drive Grand Prix at the start of the '67 season. The prize, by the way, was a new Jeep.

In 1968, HMS Broncos won their class at the Skyline Snow Rally, the Riverside Grand Prix (again), the Mint 400, the Stardust 7-11, and the Baja 1000, where the Larry Minor/Jack Bayer stock Bronco was the first four-wheeled vehicle of any kind across the finish line. In 1969, they won that Riverside race yet another time, finished third at the Mint 400 and most recently, and spectacularly, took a class and overall win in the Baja 1000. It was Larry Minor again, this time with Rodney Hall, a Baja winner in his own right, as co-driver, in one of our *Motor Trend* Broncos. The way HMS put that machine together is representative of the extensive preparation that is a trademark of Bill Stroppe. Anybody who thinks that all that's required is a roll bar, big tires, and stiff shocks is mistaken.

Starting as a regular production vehicle, the winner-to-be was first stripped to the bare frame. Then, specially-fabricated shock absorber towers, two per wheel, were welded on. The car uses heavy-duty Gabriel racing shocks, with the fronts mounted vertically for steering clearance and the rears angled out 45° to cut piston travel (thereby conserving the the seals). The rear shocks also angle inboard to the frame at the top, helping control tire side bite. The front springs are the optional heavy-duty Bronco coils, fitted with Air Lift air bags, which are inflated to 16 psi. The air bags control bottoming and dampen spring oscillation. At the rear, the Air Lifts are fitted with coiled helper springs, giving a soft "cushy" ride even with the heavy racing fuel load. The rear springs are heavy-duty Bronco leafs, which have been re-arched. The springs are located closer to the center section than on stock Broncos, with the outrigger spring perches eliminated. This results in a quicker roll center and also increases side bite.

A heavy-duty rear axle housing, which has larger outer bearings than the standard part, is used, with a streel strap welded underneath to make it more rigid. The differential is a Detroit Locker with a 4.86:1 ratio, the same ratio as used up front. Heavy-duty Dana driveshafts, with double back-to-back U-joints, and Bronco HR axles fill out the rearend package. At the other end, Dana teflon spherical ball joints, from an F250 Ford truck front end, were used. A variable-ratio power steering box was sandwiched into the frame and all the stock steering parts modified to be compatible with it. In addition the column had to be shortened and fitted with double U-joints.

Two brake systems, one for the front and one for the rear, are actuated through a double master cylinder. Velvet-Touch metallic brake linings were fitted to the stock drums, which are drilled with small holes to release dust, sand and water. Brake action is set for 60/40 front to rear proportioning. The 10-inch wide HMS steel wheels carry modified spiders for less flange flex and mount Goodyear or Firestone Pikes Peak Special time (with inner liners).

With the chassis on wheels, the roll cage was built. The material is .125-inch wall, 1¾-inch o.d. seamless tubing, heliarced together according to SEMA (Specialty Equipment Manufacturers Association) specifications. Next came the Bronco's basic body shell, less doors and front end sheet metal. The stock body mounts were swapped for hard rubber biscuits. The dash, steering column, floor-shift tower, and battery box (under the co-driver's seat) were then fabricated. The twin 22-gallon NASCAR fuel cells, with rubber bladders, anti-slosh baffles and two H&M ball-check filler neck safety valves, were built and installed. Shock absorbing Bostrum seats, with both hydraulic and spring action, were bolted in and HMS fiberglass door and rear fender cut-outs rivetted in place.

In the cockpit, a small hydraulic jack, jack handle, first-aid kit, and parts box were securely mounted. Instrumentation

How the Bronco Builder Beats the Bronco Busters

Or, why Motor Trend's Project Bronco won the Baja 1000.

By A. B. Shuman

Most of bed is filled with dual 22-gallon fuel tanks.

Front roll cage cuts bovine damage. The Broncos are rebuilt from the frame up.

Air Lift air bag and double Gabriel racing shocks are used at each wheel. Springs are heavy-duty Bronco parts, but mounts and shock towers are Holman & Moody-Stroppe.

followed: Stewart-Warner gauges, an Auto-Meter tach and a police car speedo (for accurate distance measurements). The Purolator air cleaner element was mounted on the dash in front of the co-driver, as it is in all Holman & Moody-Stroppe-prepared Broncos, allowing it to be changed underway, with plastic and metal ducting making the connection between the carburetor and air cleaner.

For this particular car, a roll cage was built around the engine compartment before the front end sheet metal was put on. This was done to prevent any panels from being pushed into the fan in the event of collisions with stray cattle. Just the outer body panels are used, here tied to the roll cage structure.

The power steering was fitted with an oil cooler and the engine radiator was custom-built with a three-inch core, protected from clogging by a front-mounted shaker screen. The blueprinted 302 CID V8 drives a Flexi-Lite fiberglass fan and heavy-duty 55-ampere alternator. The mill uses a completely shielded ignition system, with plastic sealant applied at all points of possible dust entry on the exterior of the engine. The baffled oil pan is reinforced to prevent stone punctures and the carburetor fitted with special floats and float bowls to stand the pounding of the race. A single S-W electric fuel pump, mounted behind the driver's seat, pushes the gasoline through a Purolator filter to the engine.

A Schiefer clutch rides inside a Lakewood steel bell-housing and drives the Hurst-controlled Ford T&C four-speed trans. Other details include four Lucas quartz-iodine lights (two mounted on the roll cage), Purlux flood-beam lights, stock horns with piggy-back "diesel" horns, a rear view mirror, full Impac belts and harnesses, HMS rubber-dipped steering wheel, rubber tubing/vinyl tape covering over the roll bars, naugahyde "roof" and "doors," and two spare tire mounts at the rear of the bed. Along the way, everything is safety-wired and fitted with Marsden and Elastistop nuts. *The ignition key is safety-wired to the dash!*

The total package weighs about 3700 pounds ready to race and has a top speed of 122 mph on pavement. With the facilities at the Holman & Moody-Stroppe plant, it still takes four full weeks to prepare each car — and before each is raced again, it is completely rebuilt. Even an anvil can sometimes wear out. **/MT**

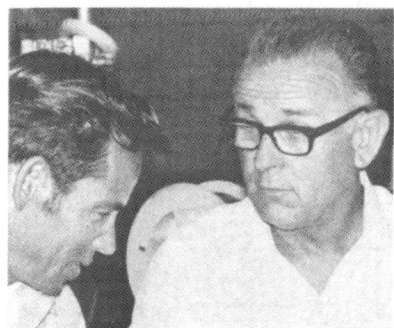

Bill Stroppe, right, maintains tight rein on the operation, personally checking on progress of each unit.

Once chassis is on wheels, roll cage can be built and basic body shell bolted on. Complete car weighs 3700 pounds and has speed of 122.

Charlie's Better Idea

A 4 SPEED FOR YOUR BRONCO

"Better Ideas From Ford" is the Ford Motor Company's catchy slogan for the consumer to identify with. However, for Charlie "Erick" Erickson, the ideas are equipment improvements and the "Ford" has become Fairway Ford of Placentia, California. It's Erickson's campaign to put Bronco on top of the 4wd hill; his method is to provide better and improved equipment for the Bronco.

A prime example of superior equipment development is his white, six-cylinder, blown Bronco with chain drive. It

In addition to the new trans, shown above, Fairway Ford's kit includes - output shaft, Hurst rubber boot, shifting linkage, transmission mounting bracket and plate, modified extension housing, fiberglass console and Hurst shifter.

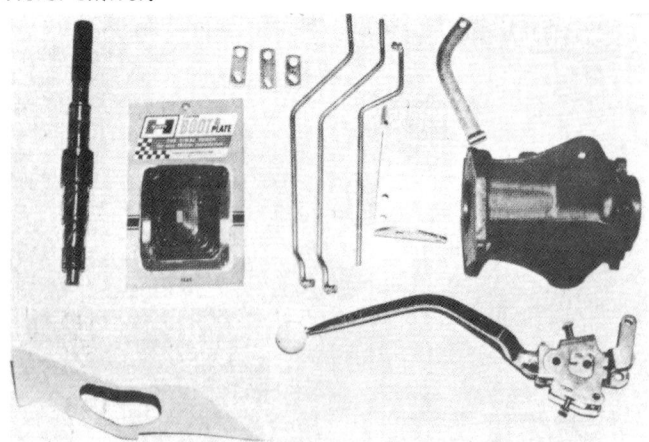

may be an over-exaggeration of the stock Bronco, but it's a a goal that was achieved through planning and development. For the owner of a Bronco, there are other vehicle improvements that can be accomplished within the trail and street confinements. A monstrous engine need not be added, nor an elaborate injection system or torque developer.

A simple improvement for the Broncos with either column shift or three-speed, which is available in two kits. With the addition of either the four-speed adapter kit or the installation of the completely new transmission and adapter kit assembled, the stock Bronco can be transformed into a gear-splitting, road-ripping machine.

For 2wd on the street, there are four gears, but once the paved highway is left behind and 4wd is locked in, the Bronco bares its teeth, digs in and lets loose for a ride unequalled, even by its name benefactor. Eight forward and two reverse gears are at the driver's disposal. The gear splitting possibilities would be tremendous, while the applications would vary with the driver and the speed in which he'd want to cover the terrain.

FOUR WHEELER's road test staff put the stock 302 cubic-inch Bronco with the four-speed gearbox to its overhill, over dale test. On the paved highway the Bronco accelerated to 35 mph in first gear with the rpm's reaching the 4,000 mark. For the remaining gears, the 4,000 rpm mark was likewise respected. The test situation wasn't to simulate competition circumstances, so the 4,000 rpm mark was used as a control setting. Quite easily the Bronco would have surpassed that mark, almost with the same ease that a Highway Patrol car would display in calling an end to the increased speeds on a speed controlled highway. With the combination of engine-gears that the FOUR WHEELER staff used, it would be an understatement to say that this Bronco would go fast enough to get the driver into trouble on any highway in the U.S.

Second gear brought the speedometer up to the 50 mph reading, while the shifting into third gear made it possible to reach 65 mph. With a watchful eye for the road hazards, the go-ahead was given and fourth gear was put to the test. A pen scribbled down a figure and the Bronco returned to the legal speed limit of 65 mph, which was a drop of almost 20 mph. The shifting was smooth and sure. In comparison with a three-speed floor shift or a column shift, the shifting of gears was as easy as turning a truck with power steering just after having the unit installed.

With the increase of speed and the rising rpm's, it might seem that there would be a noisy reminder of speed coming from the area of the floor console. Not so in this case, as the Hurst rubber boot and the fiberglass console served as a noise barrier between the passenger compartment and the underside of the vehicle. Sounds of silence were duly remembered.

Speeds and rpm's weren't registered for 4wd operation;

New 4 speed, with 8 forward and 2 reverse gears to choose from gives driver a better break in the soft stuff, as well as improved highway performance.

51

Stock 302 cubic inch Bronco used to test the new transmission paused here to pose. After complete stop, it continued on its way, oblivious to the apparent barrier.

pilot's licenses weren't provided for the road test. With the addition of the four-speed, the transmission ratios became: 2.78, 1.93, 1.36, 1.00 and 2.78 for gears one through fourth and reverse, respectively.

Parts comprising the four-speed adapter kit include a special output shaft, modified extension housing, special four-speed Hurst shifter, gasket and seal and installation instructions, all of which are used with the owner's present four-speed transmission.

For the completely new transmission and assembled adapter kit, the following parts are supplied: new four-speed transmission, modified extension housing, special four-speed Hurst shifter, gasket and seal and installation instructions.

Installation of the complete unit is simplified by its bolt-on application, Erickson pointed out. The only modification would be the filing, cutting or grinding of the edges of the transmission mount. Installation time for the adaptor kit was estimated at six hours for the practicing mechanic, while four hours time was given for the complete installation of the new transmission and adapter kit.

With the installation of the four-speed, it was recommended that a 4.11 rear axle ratio would serve the best performance interests of the vehicle.

The following chart has been drafted for the selection of buying a used four-speed transmission, and the ratios listed previously should be the same as that in the purchased transmission.

YEAR	MODEL	ENGINE		CODE MODEL NO.
1966	Mustang	289	2- or 4-barrel	HEH-BW (not H.P.)
1966	Fairlane	289	2- or 4-barrel	HEH-BV
1966	Comet	289	2- or 4-barrel	HEH-BV
1967	Falcon	289	2- or 4-barrel	RUG-D
1967	Comet	289	2- or 4-barrel	RUG-D
1967	Fairlane	289	2- or 4-barrel	RUG-D
1967	Mustang	289	2- or 4-barrel	RUG-E
1967	Cougar	289	2- or 4-barrel	RUG-E
1967	Mustang	390	4-barrel	RUG-M
1967	Cougar	390	4-barrel	RUG-M
1968	Falcon	289	2-barrel	RUG-D2
1968	Fairlane	289	2-barrel	RUG-D2
1968	Montego	289	2-barrel	RUG-D2
1968	Mustang	302	2- or 4-barrel	RUG-E2
1968	Cougar	289	2-barrel	RUG-E2
1968	Mustang	390	4-barrel	RUG-M2
1968	Cougar	390	4-barrel	RUG-M2
1969	Mustang	302, 351	2- or 4-barrel	RUG-E3
1969	Cougar	302, 351	2- or 4-barrel	RUG-E3
1969	Mustang	390	4-barrel	RUG-M3
1969	Cougar	390	4-barrel	RUG-M3

Specific questions or further information can be acquired by contacting Charlie Erickson at Fairway Ford, 1350 Yorba Linda, Placentia, California, or phone (714) 524-1200.

FOUR-WHEELERS

FORD BRONCO

The Ford Bronco is undoubtedly the best known of the 4-wheelers at the present time, due to FoMoCo's active participation in all forms of racing. The last Baja 1000 had more than a dozen Broncos entered, with six of them from the Holman-Moody, Stroppe shop. One crashed, the one driven by Parnelli Jones broke something in the transfer case, and another driven by Larry Minor and Rodney Hall won the whole ball of wax. Or "ball of sand," if you prefer. The Hall-Minor Bronco covered the 832 miles from Ensenada to La Paz in 20 hours, 48 minutes and 10 seconds, which means an overall average of about 40 mph . . . this over some of the roughest country in the world, mind you. The 2nd place Corvair buggy was 21 minutes behind, the first non-production 4-wheel-drive Jeep arrived almost 3 hours later, and the first production passenger car was over 5 hours behind that. A 2-wheel-drive Ford pickup won the utility vehicle class, driven by Ray Brock and Ak Miller, and prepared by—*surprise*—Holman-Moody, Stroppe.

The Bronco comes in two body styles only, with the open pickup considered a truck for excise tax purposes and the hardtop wagon considered a passenger vehicle. The body styling is both modern and barely distinguishable from that of the International Scout and the Chevrolet Blazer. One feature that is not too noticeable, but can be quite important, is the Bronco's wheelbase. At 92 inches, it is among the shortest in the 4-wheel-drive field, only slightly longer than the Toyota Land Cruiser's 90 inches, the British Land Rover's 88, and the Jeep CJ5's 81 inches. The Scout and the Blazer,

1. No stranger to the off-roader is Ford's Bronco, shown here in deluxe trim and factory off-road tires. Beneath good looks is a rugged frame and suspension.

2. In racing trim, Broncos have swept Baja, Ascot and other races by sheer weight of numbers, if nothing else.

3. Despite somewhat limited carrying capacity, Broncos lend themselves to just about any off-road situation.

ited-slip rear ends are also available from the factory.

Bucket seats are a $66 option, and there is a Sport Package for about $190 that includes all sorts of interior and exterior bright trim, vinyl panels, a cigarette lighter, chromed bumpers and the like. If you intend to use a Bronco for a lot of family and city use, the Sport Package is a good buy.

The optional tires offered by Ford do not cover an extremely broad range of sizes and tread patterns, but they are inexpensive. If you take the largest available without having added the GVW package, a set of five 9.15x15 4-ply-rated black sidewall B-range tires will cost less than $70. If you already have ordered the GVW package, the five will cost you a total of less than $6! Snow and mud tread patterns cost no more.

For 1970 the Bronco is basically unchanged, with minor exceptions. It now has an automatic choke, rather than a manual, and has front and rear side marker lights, replacing the reflectors. The 2-speed electric windshield wiper, introduced late in the 1969 model year, is retained. A new tire option is now offered for highway use—the G78x15 B-range fiberglass belted tire with 5-K wheels. FoMoCo claims this combination lengthens tread life, and improves traction and handling. The only transmission for the Bronco is still the column-shift, 3-speed, all-synchro manual one, with no 4-speed or automatic available, even as an option.

Dealer-installed accessories include overload air bags for the front, front power takeoff and winch, compass and tachometer, rear heater and radio speakers for the Bronco wagon, front tow hooks, 2-way radio, a trailer hitch, and even a snowplow. If you really want to go the whole route, you can always contact Holman-Moody, Stroppe in Long Beach, Calif.

The Ford Bronco is a well made and rugged 4-wheeler. From the standpoint of off-road competition, it is probably the best buy, as you are much more apt to get factory and dealer support with a Ford than with any other 4-wheel-drive vehicle on today's market.

---

by comparison, are 100 and 104 inches. This short wheelbase tends to make the vehicle nimbler and easier to handle in tight situations, but can produce a very rough and choppy ride on the pavement.

The Bronco is available with two engines — a 170-cubic-inch, 100-hp straight-6 and a 302-cubic-inch, 205-hp V-8. The V-8 is an option at about $210 extra. It should be noted, however, that these are not the only engine sizes that can legally be run in the Bronco. NORRA rules state, "Any engine that has a cylinder block of the same basic design and size as the one in the vehicle originally as standard (or factory optional) equipment may be used." The 170-cubic-inch, 100-hp inline-6 has two other variations which could be NORRA-legal: the 200-cubic-inch, 115-hp and the 250-cubic-inch, 155-hp. The optional 302-cubic-inch V-8 uses the same small block as the

351-cubic-inch, 250-hp and the 351-cubic-inch, 290-hp, so either of these would be completely legal for the production 4-wheel-drive class. The 240-cubic-inch straight-6 and the 390/428-cubic-inch Ford and Mercury V-8's are different blocks, and their use would put the Bronco in the modified or non-production class, as far as NORRA is concerned.

With its short wheelbase, the cargo space behind the front seats is understandably short, with only about 4½ feet from the seat to the tailgate. This limits its use as a live-in 4-wheeler, but there is still more than enough room to carry all the camping gear one would need for a long trip into the boonies.

For the Baja 1000 and similar off-road races, the Holman-Moody, Stroppe Broncos are equipped with roll cages, 44-gallon gas tanks, 2-way radios, full tool kits, 2 gallons of Gatorade, and specially mounted shock absorber seats with 3 inches of travel. The wheels are heavy-duty, and the tires have a special layer of plastic between the tread and the carcass to lessen the chance of punctures by cactus needles and rocks.

For heavy off-road work, the gross vehicle weight can be raised from its stock 3900 pounds to 4700 with a GVW package for $125 that includes a 3300-pound rear axle, 1280-pound rear springs, and 8.25x15 (8-ply-rated) D-range tires. Stock tires are 7.35x15 (4-ply-rated) B-range. Lim-

SPECIFICATIONS	
Wheelbase	92.0
Overall length	152.1
Width	68.8
Height	69.9
Front tread	57.4
Rear tread	57.4
Ground clearance	6.6
Box length—floor	55.2
Box length—top	46.8
Box width—floor	56.0
Box width—tailgate	56.0
Box depth	19.3
Max. gross vehicle wt.	3900*
*4700 with H-D rear axle and springs.	

3

Most 4-Wheeler for the money

Bronco:

Compare before you buy

TIGHTEST TURNING OF ALL 4-WHEELERS.
Here's an important Bronco plus right off the bat—a 33.6-ft. small turning circle. Extra-tight maneuverability to take you in a Bronco where the others have to turn back.

SHORT OVERHANG—NO HANG-UPS. Bronco has minimum overhang front and rear to let you keep going when negotiating abrupt inclines and in those places where the roads and trails give out.

MORE GROUND CLEARANCE. Bronco stands high off the ground with minimum ground clearance of nearly a foot (11.5") to clear sharp break-overs, stumps, rocks and other off-road obstacles. Bronco takes them all in stride.

SMOOTHER RIDING ON THE HIGHWAY.
For all its rugged design (and Broncos are built as tough as they come), Bronco still gives you a well-behaved ride on the highway. All this thanks to exclusive Mono-Beam front suspension, which combines the toughness of forged steel radius rods with the cushioning of resilient coil springs.

These are just a few of Bronco's strong points. A flock of options headed by a lively 302-cu. in. V-8 is another one. Whatever you're looking for in a 4-wheeler, the most for the money is now at your Ford Dealer's. Ask him for the complete story on Bronco. You'll see.

FORD BRONCO

FORD BRONCO

4 WD TEST

WE MAY BE accused of being a bit harsh in our judgments about the Ford Bronco. We'll try to give it a balanced evaluation but as the Editor has driven a Bronco for something over 60,000 miles, we are intimately acquainted with its virtues and vices and consequently inclined to be somewhat less tolerant of its weaknesses. But let's take a look.

Ford brought out the Bronco in 1965, the first of the major manufacturers to foresee the expansion that was coming in 4wd vehicles for recreational use. It seems obvious that they looked at the International Scout a long time before coming up with the Bronco but made several basic changes that gave their product a personality of its own rather than making it an imitation Scout. Ford was the first manufacturer, for instance, to offer a V-8 in a machine of this size, a rather daring thing to do at the time. But they also underestimated the number of luxuries that 4wd recreation vehicle owners would find desirable and the Bronco still comes up short in this department when the option list is examined.

The basic engine for the Bronco is an inline 6 with 170-cu-in. displacement and 105 horsepower. Frankly, this isn't enough to keep up with normal traffic but for $111 you can get the 302-cu-in. V-8 with 205 hp. And this is a good, strong, durable engine with lots of torque (300 lb-ft) and a blessed freedom from temperament.

The standard transmission is an all-synchro 3-speed manual and there are no transmission options. No 4-speed, no automatic. There are overdrives on the market, though not from Ford, that can be added to give the Bronco a longer stride in highway travel.

There are a couple unique items on the Bronco. First, instead of leaf springs under the front axle there are coil springs and leading arms. This gives better than average wheel travel at the front but also requires better than average bounce and rebound control and this means either very frequent replacement of the standard shock absorbers or replacing them with something expensive, like Konis. At the rear the suspension is the familiar live axle on leaf springs.

Also unique in the field, the Bronco comes standard with free-running front hubs. We're not altogether convinced that these are a necessity, but we freely admit that almost every 4wd recreation vehicle owner buys them anyway.

The standard suspension on the Bronco is quite soft (930 lb spring rating at the rear) which gives it a minimal payload rating but there is a heavy duty option that includes a stronger rear axle, heavier rear springs and 8-ply-rated tires that ups the GVW rating to 4700 lb.

The current Bronco comes in two body styles, pickup and wagon, and the list price includes two bucket seats in front. You can get a bench seat for the rear and, if you prefer a front bench seat (with no rear seat), you can order it and save about $70 over the price with buckets.

In size, the Bronco classifies as medium-to-small among 4wd recreation vehicles. It is built on a 92-in. wheelbase, is 152 in. long and just 68.8 in. wide. Without the rear seat there is unobstructed load space 48 by 40 by 38 inches and while this is hardly cavernous, it will accommodate a useful amount of gear. With a rear seat in the wagon model, there's practically no cargo area—especially if the spare tire is left inside. One of the options is a swingaway spare tire carrier, a practical option with or without the rear seat. The standard fuel tank holds only 12.5 gal., which makes the auxiliary tank (8.5 gal.) almost mandatory for the serious off-pavement traveler.

There's a limited amount of space under the rear sheet metal for bigger-than-standard tires and the use of anything as large as a 9.15-15 requires sheet metal to be trimmed away to avoid interference. Fiberglass fender flares at the rear are so common on Southern California Broncos that an unmodified one looks almost unfinished.

The Bronco is the only 4wd recreation vehicle for which a limited slip differential is also available at the front. We're not completely convinced that a front limited slip is a good idea because of the tendency for a locking front differential to steer itself in marginal traction conditions. On the other hand, when the going is really tough, it's the only vehicle that will really have 4-wheel drive since machines without it will lose traction on one front wheel.

Driving Impressions

Our test Bronco turned out to be a pickup version and we have to start by saying that we can't imagine why anyone would buy a pickup with such a small cargo area. It may exactly fill somebody's needs but honestly we can't imagine any application that couldn't be better filled by either the wagon version or a standard-size 4wd pickup.

The driving position is about average for 4wd recreation vehicles, not very good. The steering wheel is too close to the chest and too high for the most comfortable driving position. In front of the driver and a little to the left there's a single instrument housing and within this circle it is admirably complete.

This includes speedometer, odometer, ammeter, oil pressure, water temperature and fuel level gauges and these, wonder of wonders, are calibrated with genuine numbers rather than the commonly vague "L," "N" and "H." The transfer case—a Dana 20 2-speed—has a T-handle and a pointer clearly indicates what slot you're in. This is a good handle, one of the best in American-built 4wd vehicles, as it has a straight-through pattern and is located where the driver can reach it conveniently.

The gearshift lever is on the steering column and this has very long throws so the handle is sticking almost straight up when you're in 2nd gear. This is a good, sturdy transmission but the action is fairly slow, the powerful synchronizers taking plenty of time before letting you get from one gear to another.

The steering is slow and with big tires, it is also heavy. There is also considerable feed-back of road shock through the steering wheel though the latest model, which has ball-joint front suspension, is a little better in this respect than earlier Broncos.

In ordinary around-town and highway driving, the Bronco's ride is no better than poor-to-fair, the short wheelbase resulting in lots of fore-and-aft action and no irregularity of the road surface going unnoticed. With the optional heavy duty suspension the ride becomes very harsh when the vehicle is unladen and only improves to tolerable as the springs are partially compressed. Oh, the ride isn't all that bad, perhaps. It has to be better than the Jeep CJ-5 but somehow, with the Bronco, you

expect something better.

Off the pavement, the Bronco's short wheelbase also results in a lot of fore-and-aft pitching and the back wheels tend to come off the ground on bumps and dips. Better shock control—some Bronco owners having gone to the extent of fitting double shock absorbers in the rear—helps considerably in this respect.

The V-8 Bronco has plenty of power, the 302 engine being capable of just about anything that is asked of it. On the highway it will cruise with the fastest traffic (though with the 4.11:1 final drive ratio, the engine is whirring away at a lively pace) and still have plenty of reserve for keeping up the pace on hills.

Off the pavement, the Bronco has good traction characteristics and snorted up all four of our test hills with no complaints except a gargle in its carburetion. The maneuverability is very good, thanks to the comparatively small dimensions, but the slow steering requires a lot of fast elbow work as you twirl at the steering wheel. The turnaround capability is also better than average.

The shortcomings of the Bronco, based on the Editor's experience, are these: The wheelbase could be another foot longer (and the body lengthened an equal amount) without seriously affecting the vehicle's appeal. The steering needs to be quicker and if this means power steering, then so be it. The brakes aren't as good as they should be. An automatic transmis-

59

Ford Bronco

PRICES

Basic list, FOB Detroit:
Pickup $3467
Wagon $3570

Standard equipment: 4wd, free-running front hubs, painted bumpers, bucket seats (wagon), arm rests, floor mat.

Sport package includes bright trim, wheel covers (15-in. wheels only), cigar lighter, door trim, vinyl seat trim, grained floor mat, horn ring, headlining, rear floor mat (with rear seat option). With 16-in. wheels (no wheel covers), $190. With 15-in. wheels, $213.

Other prices for options are included in data below.

ENGINES

Standard engine . . . . inline ohv 6
Bore x stroke, in 3.50x2.94
Displacement, cu in 170
Compression ratio 8.6:1
Bhp @ rpm . . . . 100 @ 4200
Torque @ rpm, lb-ft . . . . . . 148 @ 2600
Type fuel required . . . . regular
Air cleaner type . . . . .dry

Optional 302-cu-in. V-8 . . . .$111
Bore x stroke, in 4.00x3.00
Displacement, cu in 302
Compression ratio 8.6:1
Bhp @ rpm . . . . 205 @ 4600
Torque @ rpm, lb-ft . . . . . . 300 @ 2600
Type fuel required . . . . regular
Air cleaner type . . . . .oil bath

CHASSIS & BODY

Body/frame: ladder type frame, steel body.

Brakes . . . drums, 11x2 front, 10x2.5 rear
Brake swept area, sq in 244
Power brakes . . . . .none

Steering type . . . . .worm & roller
Steering ratio 24.0:1
Turning circle, ft 31.0
Power steering . . . . .none

Wheel size, std 15x5½K
Optional wheel sizes 16x5.0
Tire size, std . . . . . ,. 4pr E78-15
Optional tires . . . . . .too numerous to list

Front axle capacity, lb 3000
Optional . . . . .none
Front spring rating, lb (at pad): 750 (6-cyl), 800 (V-8).
Optional 850 lb $3.34

Rear axle capacity 2780
Optional 3300-lb $58
Rear spring rating, lb (at pad) 930
Optional 1280-lb $6.55

Additional suspension options: HD suspension package (3300-lb rear axle, 1280-lb rear springs, 8pr 678x15 tires), $130.

ACCOMMODATION

Standard seats . . . . 2 buckets
Optional: rear bench seat $85
Headroom, in 42.0
Pedal to seatback, max 36.2
Seat to ground 31.5
Heater & defroster . . . . std
Tinted glass . . . . .not available
Air conditioning . . . . .not available

INSTRUMENTATION

Instruments: 100-mph speedometer, 99,999.9 mi odometer, ammeter, oil pressure, water temperature, fuel level.
Warning lights . . . . .none
Optional . . . . .none

DRIVE TRAIN

Transfer case . . . . 2-spd Dana 20
Transfer case ratio . . . . . .2.46 & 1.00:1
Free-running front hubs . . . . .std
Limited slip differential: front, $28; rear (when included in HD package), $49; without HD package, $40 (with 2780-lb axle), $107 (with 3300-lb axle).

Rear axle type . . . . .semi-floating hypoid
Final drive ratio: 6-cyl, 4.11:1; V-8, 3.50:1

Standard transmission . . . . . 3-spd manual
Clutch dia., in: 9.375 (6-cyl engine); 11.0 (V-8)

Transmission ratios: 6-cyl   V-8
3rd . . . . 1.00:1 . . . . 1.00:1
2nd . . . . 1.86:1 . . . . 1.75:1
1st . . . . 3.41:1 . . . . 2.99:1
Synchromesh . . . . .on all 3
Optional transmission . . . . .none

GENERAL

Curb weight, lb (test model) 3430

Maximum laden weight 3900
With HD suspension 4700
Payload rating 470
With HD suspension 1270

Wheelbase, in 92.0
Track, front/rear 57.4/57.4
Overall length 152.1
Height 70.7
Width 68.8
Overhang, front/rear 26.9/33.2

Approach angle, degrees 40
Departure angle, degrees 27
Ramp breakover angle 29

Ground clearance at differential, front 9.5
At rear differential 8.5
At oil pan 17.5
At transfer case 14.5
At fuel tank 17.0

Fuel tank capacity, U.S. gal 12.5
Optional auxiliary 8.5 gal tank (includes skid plate): $38.

MAINTENANCE

Service intervals, normal use:
Oil change, mi 6000
Filter change 12,000
Chassis lube 6000
Minor tuneup 6000
Major tuneup 12,000
Warranty, months/miles 12/12,000

OTHER OPTIONS

55-amp alternator $31
HD battery $7.72
Chrome bumpers $30
Swingaway spare tire rack $33
HD cooling (included with V-8 engine) $10
Headliner (wagon) $16
Radio & antenna $51
Skid plates (transfer case and std fuel tank): $52.
Hand throttle $3.71
Wheel covers (15-in. only) $24

PERFORMANCE DATA

Note: All performance data taken with maximum rated payload on board.

Test model: Bronco pickup with 302 V-8 engine, Sports trim, G78x15 tires, free-running front hubs, limited slip rear, radio. West Coast list price, $4229.

DRY PAVEMENT

Acceleration, time to speed, sec:
0-30 mph	4.3
0-45 mph	8.4
0-60 mph	14.5
0-70 mph	23.0

Maximum speed in gears:
High range, 4th (3700 rpm)	90
2nd (4500)	64
1st (4500)	37
Low range, 4th (3700 rpm)	37
2nd (4500)	26
1st (4500)	15

Cruising speed at 3000 rpm 74

BRAKE TESTS

Pedal pressure to achieve 1/2-g deceleration rate from 60 mph: 85.
Fade, Percentage increase in pedal pressure for 6 successive stops from 60 mph: 30.
Overall brake rating . . . . fair

OFF PAVEMENT

Hillclimbing ability:
Climb test hill no. 1 (47% grade)	yes
Climb test hill no. 2 (56% grade)	yes
Climb test hill no. 3 (63% grade)	yes
Climb test hill no. 4 (69% grade)	yes
Maneuverability	good
Turnaround capability	good

Comments . . . . choppy ride, slow steering

GENERAL

Heater rating	fair
Defroster effectiveness	fair
Wiper coverage	fair

FUEL CONSUMPTION

Normal driving, mpg	12-14
Off-pavement, test conditions, mpg	6-8
Range, normal driving, mi	150-175
Range, off-pavement	75-100

sion would make it a more satisfactory dual-purpose machine. Tinted glass and factory air conditioning would be welcome additions to the option list.

Mechanically, the Editor's Bronco has been super reliable. It has never stranded him in the back country (or anyplace else) and has never been defeated by any reasonable request on its climbing ability. The major annoyances in 60,000 miles have been one broken clutch-actuating arm (replaced under warranty without question) and, get this, three (count 'em) new constant velocity joints in the drive shafts, two rear and one front. For some reason, these CV joints don't last much longer than the warranty period and as they cost something like $100 each to replace, we consider this a serious weakness. The Editor has never run one to complete failure so he can't say how long you could travel with a bad one. We don't know what the problem was with these CV joints but Ford Motor Company assures us that all the difficulties have been solved and that Bronco owners no longer have this trouble. On the Editor's Bronco the brake linings have gone about 20,000 miles between changes and the muffler is still the one that came from the factory.

A further annoyance is the tailgate of the wagon, which has never been rattle-free for more than a few days at a time. Other than these things—plus the difficulty of keeping the front end aligned and the front wheels in balance so the highway ride isn't the motorized equivalent of a Relaxacisor—and that the brakes are poor—he has no serious complaints.

Summary in one sentence? Good . . . but not as good as it should be. WD

The Great RV Binge

Muscle Cars are out and Recreational Vehicles are in. We test three of the prime movers — the Chevrolet Blazer — Ford Bronco — AMC Jeepster — and find out why By Chuck Koch

If this is the desert and that's a Bronco, then you must be Parnelli Jones. And, if this is the desert and I'm in a Blazer, then I must be Bud Ekins. And so you shove your transfer case into four-wheel high and get it on in the Mexican 1000 style because there's a whole new bunch of heros for a whole new thing — Recreational Vehicles.

In the period since 1961, recreational vehicles have boomed a 700 percent sales increase and an annual growth rate of 31 percent. RVs are racing into the vacuum left by the demise of the muscle cars if for no other reason than it is simply no longer fun to drive in most metropolitan areas throughout the country.

There has always been the Jeep, of course, and the Land Rover and not much in between. But now, with consumer interest shifting away from the old two-overweight-cars-in-every-driveway concept, a completely novel, mushrooming market segment exists where none did before. Blazer. Bronco. Jeepster. What are these machines boiling across what's left unpaved of the American landscape? We thought you ought to know what's going on, so we got the three of them and those robust souls on the MT staff who consider themselves up to the task and took them in their element, the dust-choked, mountain-strewn wilds of southeastern California.

We climbed a 6,100-foot mountain with a

>>>

The Great RV Binge

vertical rise of 5,000 feet in only eight miles. We raced down a river wash at 60 mph hoping to avoid John Lamm who was somewhere up ahead, at a particularly vulnerable corner taking pictures. Two nights we spent at abandoned gold mines listening to Art Director Terry Bratcher sing the trucker songs and explain who "Bruce's Riders" were. But those are other stories.

To go off-roading you need certain logistical support equipment. Camping gear it's called. Sleeping bags, stoves, coolers, and gasoline cans all supplied by the good folks at Sears; and bikes, two from American Honda and one from Yamaha International. By the time we had hit a few rocks and ruts, it became apparent that if you plan to

Double opening tailgate in the Jeepster aids loading cargo; and carrying capacity is adequate.

Hills, rocks, and whatever else was encountered by the Blazer was easily conquered, as the vehicle's far superior horsepower and automatic transmission made off-road driving very simple.

Full fiberglass top on Blazer served equally to protect supplies and people from the elements. Wide track hurts car's maneuverability.

Narrow rear stance and short wheelbase increased Bronco's maneuverability in tight places. Pickup version offered no protection.

Photography: John Lamm

take bikes, you better take bumper racks on which to mount them. We put the Hondas inside the Blazer and then watched helplessly as the bikes quickly battered themselves and the vehicle every time any roughness was encountered. The Yamaha was firmly strapped in the Bronco's rear bumper and suffered no greater damage than a heavy coating of dust and a fouled plug from too much joy riding.

As for the vehicles, we ran into some problems here because the cars varied

from the all-out off-roader — Chevrolet calls theirs Blazer K5 — to the Jeepster, a casual blend of a street and dirt machine, with a price differential of $1,000, making an across-the-board comparison to the stock Ford Bronco, rather difficult. But we did discover the long and short points of each vehicle and also the excitement which is off-road driving. And that, of course, was the reason for the trip.

Perhaps best known among 4WD vehicles, for its record-setting perfor-

mances in the Baja, is Ford's Bronco. We had hoped to test the Bill Stroppe-prepared Baja Bronco but this model was unavailable, so we settled for a more or less standard pickup version and immediately decided that if you're planning to do any serious off-roading, the wagon is preferable. Not only does the hardtop allow more space to stack supplies, but also protects them against the elements and the insidious dust. In its way, the Bronco is a pioneer among

The Great RV Binge

4WD vehicles in that it introduced V8 power to the species and our test car was equipped with the 302-2v engine which had been tuned to run on premium gas, although the showroom models are designed for regular grade fuel.

Coupled to the engine is a three-speed manual transmission and the ever-present transfer case. The purpose of the transfer case is to distribute power to the wheels and allow the driver to select which drive configuration he wants to be in: two-wheel high, four-wheel high or low, depending on the type of terrain the car is traversing. While the Bronco's transfer case shift pattern was simple, a straight fore and aft movement of the lever, it took a lot of muscle power to shift. The car also had free-running front hubs, limited slip front axle and a traction-lok rear axle. Other specialized off-road items included skid plates, auxiliary gas tank, a heavy-duty cooling package, and tube-type 6.50 x 16.6 ply rated tires. In test form, the Bronco priced out at $4,125.13.

Chevrolet's Blazer, rapidly gaining in popularity among 4WD fans to the point where dealers cannot stock enough of them to meet the demand, is simply a

Bronco's 302-2v engine supplied enough power to get the car over most obstacles.

shortened version of a half-ton pickup. Of the three cars we tested, it was the largest, the most powerful and the most expensive, sporting a list of $5,560.10. Standard engine in the Blazer is the 307 V8 but ours had the 350-2v, which runs on low lead gas and produces 245 hp at 4800 rpm. It came with the full fiberglass top and when the rear seat was removed, the amount of cargo space was so phenomenal that we used the car as a catch-all for supplies which did not fit in the other vehicles. One problem with the setup, though, was lack of a proper storage location for the spare tire once the seat was out. Chevrolet

should definitely consider offering a swing-away tailgate tire carrier option, like the one you can get from Vic Hickey, to alleviate this shortcoming.

In addition to its superior power, the Blazer was also equipped with an automatic transmission, a decided advantage over the Bronco. Now, don't get us wrong. We like to shift gears as much as the next guy, but when you're in deep sand, a manual shift is about the last thing you want and it is a shame that

Ford has yet to offer an automatic in the Bronco, except in the expensive Baja version. The reason behind the automatic's superiority is in its torque converter, which more than doubles the low range torque production of the engine. This allows the driver to more precisely control the amount of power delivered to the wheels, making it possible to turn them without losing traction and digging a hole in the sand. The only way to

Above: Blazer's high clearance results from heavy front leaf springs and shock absorbers.

Above: Composed of coil springs, shocks, and a stabilizer bar, the Bronco's front suspension was good for adequate ground clearance height. Note shock absorber, which helps ease steering. Below: The Jeepster's suspension, a compromise between that of off-road and street machines, did not provide sufficient clearance to climb over the more difficult obstacles.

The Great RV Binge

approximate this process with a manual shift is to slip the clutch and this, naturally, reduces clutch life and does not guarantee full traction on starting. With the automatic it's just a matter of gently stepping on the accelerator and gradually applying pressure as you begin to move to multiply torque while the manual requires engaging the clutch, adding power, and finally hoping that those shovels you packed won't have to be used.

The Blazer was an all-out off-roader, equipped to go anywhere with skid plates, huge 10.00 x 16.5 six-ply tires, heavy-duty suspension and generator, power steering, disc brakes, auxiliary battery, a 3.73:1 axle, two hooks, and free running front hubs. It costs more than the other cars and really must be considered apart from the others.

Although the name Jeep is synonymous with four-wheel drive, the Jeepster Commando was more of a combination street/dirt car, not really suited for really rough off-roading. Its suspension

disengages the axle shaft from the hub, makes it possible to save needless wear on the front end when driving on paved roads. There is one catch; you must remember to lock or unlock the hubs when shifting in or out of four-wheel drive. They are advantageous, however, since they make adjusting brakes easier and there are those who claim that the locking hubs help slow the car when driving downhill.

The Jeepster also lacked sufficient ground clearance and the protective skid plates (which resulted in a few dents to the gas tank) but did have a full top

former. Not because it went where the others wouldn't; it didn't, but because of the ease with which it got there.

As tested, the Blazer was built for the dirt, making it somewhat obnoxious to drive on the road but pure delight in the boondocks. In addition to the powerful 350 engine and oversize tires, it was equipped with heavy-duty front and rear shock absorbers and the optional front springs with a rating of 1,750 pounds. Combine these with 5 leaf rear springs rated at 1,800 pounds each and you have a towering ground clearance of 8¾ inches. Then consider the added

Top: The Jeepster's lack of power led to its inability to climb hills. Above Left: Bucket seats in Jeepster made the car comfortable, even if legroom was not outstanding. Above Center: Bench seats made Bronco least comfortable. Above Right: Firm buckets made the Blazer best.

is too soft and ground clearance not sufficient to surmount large obstacles. On our trip, though, it did go where the Blazer and Bronco went but with more difficulty. Despite its rather calm personality, the Jeepster had a rugged OHV V6 engine with a four main bearing crankshaft. This motor is extremely light, to save front suspension wear, yet very durable and fairly powerful; displacing 225 c.i. and producing 160 hp at 4200 rpm. While the engine tended to strain traversing steep inclines, we could not fault the 13.5 mpg fuel economy, a factor to be appreciated when you're in the desert, miles from a gas station.

Like the Blazer, it was equipped with power steering and automatic transmission but lacked the free running hubs. Most serious off-road drivers will not be caught without these hubs. Their reasons vary but the basic thought is that there is no need to work the front axle machinery while traveling down a highway. The free running hubs, which consist of a dog clutch that engages or

and sufficient cargo space when the rear seat was folded down. For safety sake we had a power winch installed, at a cost of $330.62, just in case one of the cars became inextricably mired along the way. Luckily, this didn't happen but the winch did give us a facade of security. Minus the winch, the Jeepster's price came to $4,659.56.

When speaking about performance of four-wheel-drive vehicles, you must discard the normal comparisons of quarter-mile times, cornering forces, and stopping distances. These are measured on paved surfaces, something which is a second priority in off-road cars. Instead, you have to compare climbing ability, maneuverability through rocks, and the car's capacity to withstand punishment. Beyond drive trains you must consider tire size, spring rates, wheelbases, widths, and ground clearance.

Weighing these elements and after driving the three vehicles over some mighty rough country, we have to conclude that the Blazer is the real per-

protection of skid plates and there are not many obstacles capable of stopping the vehicle. Maneuverability, despite the car's size, 104-inch wheelbase and 177.5-inch overall length, was good due to the power steering and disc brakes. And punishment, the Blazer endured it all. Occasionally, when driving quickly over rough ground, we would lose our rhythm while avoiding boulders and hit one. The car would just power right over the rock, crash down, giving occupants a thorough jolt, and then continue totally unphased by the experience. In fact, the Blazer was so well adapted to its purpose that we spent most of the time in two-wheel high with an occasional stint into four-wheel high and a very short period while descending a rather precipitous trail when we shifted to four-wheel low for safety. It was a most impressive experience.

But, as great as the Blazer is, it does have its drawbacks and these concern the car's dimensions. The wheelbase

The Great RV Binge

strikes us as being on the upper limits of what you'd want for serious off-roading. While the length is nice for traveling over ruts, tending to smooth out the ride, it can get you in trouble when encountering steep rock climbs. The front wheels will make it up with no problem but the frame can get hung up since the rear wheels are so far back. On the other hand, a short wheelbase, like the Bronco's 92 inches, will simply bounce over the rocks without getting stuck.

Width is also a consideration and the Blazer had 13.8 inches on the Jeepster

and was 10.1 inches wider than the Bronco. This naturally restricts maneuverability in tight quarters, but then you could say that if the quarters are that tight you shouldn't be there in the first place. And, we sort of agree with this philosophy.

Next in performance was the Bronco, not set up as nicely as the Blazer but its power, 205 hp at 4000 rpm, was enough to pull it through without too much trouble. It was equipped with the standard suspension composed of front coil springs with a capacity of 800 pounds (rated at the pad) and longitudinally-mounted rear leafs with a pad rating of 930 pounds. Combined with the 6.50 x

16 tires, this was good for a ground clearance of 8.22 inches, enough to get over most obstacles. Because of its softer springing, as compared to the Blazer, the Bronco had a good deal of body roll, a most uncomfortable feeling while driving over rocks; yet its ride, particularly on rutted roads, was much harsher. This is due to the short wheelbase, which tends to transmit all road shocks to the passenger. If you don't let discretion be the better part of speed, the jolts can pound you to a pulp. However, this same factor made the car very maneuverable, and we like to ponder how good this machine would be with an automatic

SPECIFICATIONS FORD BRONCO

Engine	V8 ohv
Bore & stroke — ins.	4.0 x 3.0
Displacement — cu. in.	302
HP @ RPM	205 @ 4,600
Torque: lbs.-ft. @ RPM	300 @ 2,600
Compression Ratio/Fuel	8.6:1/regular
Carburetion	2 bbl
Transmission	3-spd. manual
Final Drive Ratio	3.50:1
Steering type	Worm & roller
Tire size	6.50 x 16
Brakes	Drum/Drum
Front Suspension	Coil springs, shocks, stabilizer bar
Rear Suspension	Progressive leaf springs, telescopic shocks
Body/Frame Construction	Box section
Wheelbase — ins.	92
Overall length — ins.	152.1
Width — ins.	68.8
Height — ins.	68.6
Front Track — ins.	57.4
Rear Track — ins.	57.4
Curb Weight — lbs.	3,100
Fuel Capacity — gals.	12.7
Gas Mileage range	
On road	10.1-10.9 mpg
Off road	6.7-7.1 mpg

SPECIFICATIONS CHEVROLET BLAZER

Engine	V8 ohv
Bore & stroke — ins.	4.0 x 3.48
Displacement — cu. in.	350
HP @ RPM	245 @ 4,800
Torque: lbs.-ft. @ RPM	350 @ 2,800
Compression Ratio/Fuel	8.5:1/regular
Carburetion	2 bbl
Transmission	Automatic
Final Drive Ratio	3.73:1
Steering type	Recirculating ball
Tire size	10.00 x 16.5
Brakes	Disc/Drum
Front Suspension	Longitudinally mounted leaf springs, heavy duty shocks
Rear Suspension	2-stage tapered leaf springs, heavy duty shocks
Body/Frame Construction	Perimeter
Wheelbase — ins.	104
Overall length — ins.	177.5
Width — ins.	79.0
Height — ins.	68.7
Front Track — ins.	60.4
Rear Track — ins.	60.4
Curb Weight — lbs.	3,807
Fuel Capacity — gals.	21.0
Gas Mileage range	
On road	9.1-11.0 mpg
Off road	6.1-6.6 mpg

SPECIFICATIONS JEEPSTER COMMANDO

Engine	V6 ohv
Bore & stroke — ins.	3.75 x 3.4
Displacement — cu. in.	225
HP @ RPM	160 @ 4,200
Torque: lbs.-ft. @ RPM	235 @ 2,400
Compression Ratio/Fuel	7.4:1/regular
Carburetion	2 bbl
Transmission	Automatic
Final Drive Ratio	3.31:1
Steering type	Recirculating ball
Tire size	8.55 x 15
Brakes	Drum/Drum
Front Suspension	Multi-leaf springs, telescopic shocks, stabilizer bar
Rear Suspension	Leaf springs mounted off-center, telescopic shocks
Body/Frame Construction	Box section
Wheelbase — ins.	101
Overall length — ins.	168.4
Width — ins.	65.2
Height — ins.	62.4
Front Track — ins.	50.0
Rear Track — ins.	50.0
Curb Weight — lbs.	2,966
Fuel Capacity — gals.	15.0
Gas Mileage range	
On road	13.1-13.9 mpg
Off road	9.1-9.8 mpg

FORD BRONCO

Base price	$3,466.54
Price as tested	4,125.28

Good Points
Short wheelbase
V8 engine
Ground clearance
Free running hubs
Width
Skid plates
Auxiliary fuel tank

Need Improvement
Manual steering
Manual transmission
Passenger comfort
Cargo space too limited
Bad transfer case shift movement

CHEVROLET BLAZER

Base price	$3,355.00
Price as tested	5,560.10

Good Points
Passenger comfort
Suspension
Cargo area
Tires
Ground clearance
Free running hubs
Disc brakes
Automatic transmission
Power steering
V8 engine
Skid plates

Need Improvement
Better tire storage
Body too wide
Wheelbase almost too long

JEEPSTER COMMANDO

Base price	$3,207.82
Price as tested	4,659.56

Good Points
Power steering
Power brakes
Automatic transmission
Cargo area
Passenger comfort
Narrow width
Fuel economy

Need Improvement
Insufficient ground clearance
Automatic hubs
No skid plates
Needs a little more power
Suspension too soft
Tires should be 6 ply

The Great RV Binge

transmission and power steering. Ford should offer these two items as options; they are well worth the extra money.

The Jeepster? Well, it just trundled along, going where the others went but with a great deal more effort. It was hindered by too-soft suspension, with ground rated spring capacities of 945 pounds in front and 1,185 pounds in the rear, resulting in a ground clearance of only 7.5 inches. Despite the inclusion of a front stabilizer bar, body roll was undue, and when driving in sand the car slid until the tires would dig in and throw you in the opposite direction. It was sort of a thrill but not recommended. With a medium-length wheelbase, 101 inches, and a narrow width, 65.2 inches, the Jeepster was maneuvered fairly easily; but when in rocky country more often than not the suspension would bottom out, slamming the unprotected gas tank down on some awaiting boulder. Of the three vehicles on the trip, the Jeepster was the only one to get stuck, although for a very short period. Again, insufficient ground clearance was the villain.

Adequate passenger comfort is also important to the off-roader since rough country can lead to driver fatigue and here the Blazer won out. Its bucket seats were very good, providing excellent lateral support and just enough padding to absorb blows to the rump. Legroom was sufficient and armroom adequate despite a huge steering wheel that stared you in the face. The Jeepster rates second, again on the strength of its comfortable bucket seats, but legroom was lacking and occasionally the car rocking motion would cause a leg to sharply strike the steering column. Bench seats, totally inadequate legroom and a generally awkward driving position relegate the Bronco to last place in comfort. Perhaps the wagon version improves on this situation — we would hope so — but some advancement is definitely needed in this area.

The conclusions? In our little contest the Blazer wins hands down with the Bronco a distant second. Both are decent off-road vehicles and while the Ford requires improvement in several important areas, Chevrolet seems to have the inside track on what it takes to achieve its purpose, with a smattering of style. The Jeepster needs to decide whether it wants to be a street automobile or an off-road machine. In its present, compromise configuration it is not really well suited to either.

But no matter what we have said about these three particular vehicles, one inescapable fact remains: off-road driving is fun and exciting. If we came away with any definitive statement after our three-day desert bash it was, if you want to escape the pressures of the civilization, off-roading is the way to do it. No other means we know of allows you to reach the "way back" country, free of smog and urban congestion, in the relative comfort of an automobile seat. Now we know why recreational vehicles are so popular, but we wonder how long it will last. After all, there's only so much open land left. /MT

The sure footed one - Ford Bronco

■ Most power   ■ Smoothest ride

■ Best maneuverability   ■ Best stability

The nimble 4-wheel-drive Bronco puts you on the right trail for new camping, hunting, fishing and rally thrills. And Ford's better ideas keep you ahead of the crowd on any trail or turnpike. Bronco offers the most power going with rugged Six or V-8 engines—now up to 302 cubic inches big! Underneath, Bronco has lots of ground clearance and tough components. Ford's exclusive Mono-Beam front suspension provides matchless strength and riding smoothness. Wide-track axles and steering linkage shock absorber give slope-hugging stability and the best maneuverability of all 4-wheelers—tight 33.6-ft. turning circle. For the fun way to go, roads or no, choose *the sure one* at your Ford Dealer's.

NEW POWER & STRENGTH
- New 302-cu. in. V-8 option
- Steering linkage shock absorber standard
- Improved body sealing
- New reinforced strength

FORD
BRONCO

FORD BRONCO

4WD OWNER SURVEY REPORT

FORD MOTOR CO. introduced the Bronco in 1966 and it was the first vehicle from the "Big Three" aimed directly at the 4wd recreation vehicle market. The Bronco was short, it was maneuverable, it was attractive and it was a success from the beginning. At introduction, only the 6-cylinder engine was offered, but late in 1966 Ford made a medium-sized V-8 available and there have been almost no changes in specification since.

A total of 178 Bronco owners sent in their questionnaires by the cut-off date. We were able to discard questionnaires on 1966 and 1967 models and still stay over the 100 mark which is sufficient to tabulate "typical" experience. This allowed us to base the results on 1968 and newer models, which should help to make it of maximum value to prospective Bronco customers.

We ended up with a total of 119 responses to be evaluated—22 were 1968 models, 39 were '69s, 36 were '70s and there were 22 '71 models. No vehicle with less than 5000 miles was included in the tabulation, because this would not represent "typical" experience.

First, a bit about these owners. Thirty-two percent of those included in the survey live in the Southwestern part of the U.S. (California, Nevada, Arizona), 21% are from the Midwest, 18% from the Rocky Mountain or Plains states, 10% from the Northeast and 9% from the Northern Pacific. There were also scattered responses from Bronco owners in Canada, Alaska and Hawaii but in too small numbers to be of any significance.

Seventy-five percent of the Broncos were bought new and 76% of the owners report that they are used for daily transportation as well as for recreation. The 1968s had covered an average of 44,000 miles each, the '69s 30,000, the '70s 19,000 and the '71s 9500. The highest mileage reported on any of the cars included in the survey was 94,000 on a 1968 model. This vehicle, incidentally, was the third Bronco this driver had owned and he considered its best features to be the "maneuverability, long trouble-free service and good trade-in value."

Our Bronco owners estimated that they drive about 13,000 miles a year on paved roads and about 3000 miles off. Sixty-four percent said they had an interest in competition events and of the choices given, rallies and club tours were named as those events in which they were most likely to participate.

As a group, Bronco owners do not have a very high opinion of the service they have received from their dealers. In fact, fewer Bronco dealers were rated as "good" than any other dealers in this series. Only 35% of the Bronco owners rated their dealers as "good," while 43% considered their dealers "fair" and 22% "poor" or "very poor." The most common complaint about dealer service was that service personnel had insufficient knowledge of or interest in 4wd vehicles.

The Broncos that our owners had selected for themselves showed a definite pattern of preference. Ninety-five percent had the V-8 engine, 99% had free-running hubs, 72% had limited slip at one or both ends, 91% had radios and 77% had bucket seats.

The equipment and accessories that had been added to the vehicle after it was purchased demonstrates that Bronco owners spend a considerable number of dollars on their vehicles to tailor them to their preferences. The most common additions were double shocks or heavy-duty shocks (26%), fiberglass rear fender kits (23%), and air conditioning (16%). Ten percent or more of the owners had also added a citizen band radio, a rollbar or rollcage and a winch. Between 5 and 10% had also installed a tachometer, stereo tape deck, interior lights, driving lights, helper springs, air bags, floor shifter, extra sound insulation (usually in the form of indoor-outdoor carpeting front and rear), heavy-duty bumper and compass, and made engine modifications (the most common of these was either re-jetting the 2-barrel carburetor or replacing it with one of larger capacity).

Forty percent of the owners had bought wider wheels than those that came from the factory and the two most popular rim widths were 8 and 10 inches.

There was no pattern of preference in tires being used by the Bronco owners. As an example, of the 22 1968 Broncos included in the survey, there were 18 different makes or sizes of tires! The only common characteristic seemed to be that well over half (58%) of the tires in use were larger than those originally supplied with the vehicles.

The troubles that Bronco owners have had with their vehicles makes an interesting list. At the very top, with a total of 35% reporting the same problem, was driveshaft universal joints failure. This problem had occurred as early as 600 miles on one Bronco and there was one owner who had replaced five U-joints in 52,000 miles! The worst year for U-joint failures seems to be 1969, 46% of the owners of '69s having reported this trouble. Our sample may have been too small to say this with any certainty but we can surmise that '69 was a bad year. There seems to have been an improvement with 1970 (36%) and 1971 (10%) models but because these vehicles had covered a smaller number of miles, we cannot say this with any conviction.

It was suggested from comments made by owners that U-joint troubles could be avoided by frequent lubrica-tion, several owners having reported that they had lubed their Broncos often (every 500 to 2000 miles) and had not experienced U-joint problems.

No other chronic trouble areas appeared in the survey. More than 10% of the owners reported clutch and differential replacements but there was no single weakness that could be pinpointed. The most common cause for clutch replacement seemed to result from a leaking rear main bearing seal but the incidence of failure was not large enough to allow a conclusion to be drawn. The most common failure with the differential seemed to be with the limited slip, but again the numbers are too small to be conclusive.

Several different components had given trouble to between 5 and 10% of the owners—front axle, shift linkage, starter, steering, transmission were among the culprits—but here, too, no single fault emerges.

The very small number of engine failures was extremely impressive. Less than 2% of the Broncos had had engine problems that required removal of a head and these had occurred early and been repaired under warranty. There was not a single instance of piston or rod failure reported. Time after time, owners voluntarily commented on the questionnaires, "Has never let me down," "Always gets home," and "Can't beat reliability." This adds up to an impressively favorable reaction from owners. In any make of car there seems to be the occasional "lemon," but this word was not mentioned by a single Bronco owner among those surveyed.

Even among high-mileage Broncos there was a low failure rate and this includes items that you would ordinarily expect to replace—alternator, voltage regulator, fuel pump, water pump, etc. There were so few replacements of these components that it is impossible for us to predict how long they could be expected to last.

Shock absorbers are something else. For all the Broncos in the survey, shocks were replaced after an average of 16,000 miles. Owner after owner also remarked on the need for better shock control action. It is obviously not coincidental that over a quarter of the owners had installed either heavy-duty or double shocks on their Broncos.

Other "expected" replacements on

the Bronco occurred at 12,000-15,000 miles for sparkplugs and 15,000-20,000 miles for original equipment tires. No owner reported having found a long-wearing tire and many commented, "Eats up tires," "Front tires wear fast even when properly aligned," and "Tried so-and-so brand tires without improving tire wear."

There was considerable agreement among Bronco owners about the best features of the vehicle. Maneuverability was the characteristic most often mentioned as a "best" feature (36%), with power (30%) a close second and dependability (12%) third. Also mentioned by more than 10% of the owners as a "best" feature were size, appearance and comfort. Characteristics rated as "best" by between 5 and 10% of the owners were versatility, ground clearance, the availability of limited slip for both front and rear, and the fact that the Bronco is easy to work on when service or repairs are needed.

There was also considerable agreement about the Bronco's "worst" features. First came brakes (several owners had harrowing stories to tell about panic stops from highway speed), then shift linkage, rattles (specifically rattles in the tailgate) and the choppy or bouncy ride. A significant number of owners also said the worst thing about the Bronco was the lack of automatic transmission, power steering, power brakes and air conditioning options from the factory. Also cited by over 5% of the owners as a "worst" was the fact that the rear fenders must be cut away to accept wide tires, that the steering is poor, that the ventilation leaves something to be desired and that the Bronco inclined to leak in the rain.

About the future, a total of 89% of the Bronco owners say they will be buying another 4wd vehicle. Just over a third (34%) of these have already decided that their next 4wd will also be a Bronco. This is by far the lowest "model loyalty rating" of the five vehicles in this series of surveys and we suspect that the owners' opinions about their dealers are a significant influence here.

That's what the people that own them say about the Bronco. It isn't without its faults (U-joint failure, brakes that aren't as good as they

should be), there are areas that need improvement (better shock control, larger rear fender cutouts) and the dealer service is not too highly regarded. Yet, it is apparent that the engine is super-reliable, that minor components aren't a constant source of trouble and that, overall, the Bronco has longevity of a high order.

It is also implicit from the number of owners who mentioned it that Ford could be selling more Broncos if they offered a wider variety of options.

If there was a typical reaction among our Bronco owners, it might have been this: "It isn't perfect, but it has never let me down." **4WD**

SUMMARY: FORD BRONCO

**Most Popular
Mfgr/Dealer Options**
V-8 engine
Free-running hubs
Limited slip
Bucket seats
Radio
Air conditioning
Winch

**Most Popular Accessories
Added by 10% or More of Owners**
Rear fender kit
HD or double shocks
Rollbar or rollcage
CB radio

Added by 5-10% of Owners
Tachometer
Airbags
Engine modifications
Helper springs
Interior lights
Floor shifter
Driving lights
Extra sound insulation
Bumpers
Compass

**Troubles
Reported by 5-10% of Owners**
Front axle
Starter
Shift linkage
Steering
Transmission

Reported by 10-20% of Owners
Clutch
Differential

Reported by Over 20% of Owners
U-joints

Five Best Features
Maneuverability
Power
Reliability
Size
Comfort

Five Worst Features
Brakes
Choppy ride
Shift linkage
Rattles
Lack of luxury options

Wheels/Tires
Owners using larger-than-
standard tires 58%

**How Owners Feel
About Bronco Dealers**
Rated "good" 35%
Rated "fair" 43%
Rated "poor" 22%

New or Used?
Bought new 75%
Bought used 25%

Buy Another?
Will buy another 4wd 89%
Will buy another Bronco 34%

Friendly Hostility

**It's Ford vs. Chevy. Stroppe vs. Hickey. But, driving the
Hickey Blazer and Stroppe Bronco, you soon learn that the
vehicles, like their builders, are closer than you think**

By Chuck Koch

Comparison

We met Vic Hickey and Bill Stroppe at Indian Dunes Recreational Park. Hickey: After a cursory examination of the Bronco said, "How hard was it to drop that 351 into the car, Bill?" Stroppe: Wearing the proper frown as he inspected the Blazer, allowing as how there was an abundance of chrome, "You didn't used to do that, Vic." To which Hickey replied with one of the day's few serious comments: "Christ, Bill, when the government won't let you sell power, you gotta give the people something." It went like this for the remainder of the day; two good friends taking as much pleasure in besting each other in quips as in proving the superiority of their cars.

The following weekend we decided to find out for ourselves which was the better vehicle, Stroppe's Baja Bronco or the Hickey-modified Blazer. The high desert country of eastern California gave us the obstacles and the machines provided all the fun. What the staff got out of the whole affair was a completely satisfying off-road experi-

ence in what have to be the finest four-wheel-drive vehicles sold in America.

To put it simply, the Baja Bronco and Hickey Blazer are upgraded versions of their production line counterparts. Both Hickey and Stroppe have taken careful looks at their respective vehicles, discovered areas which need improvement, and made the necessary refinements. Considered in this vein, the Bronco is more improved over its stock version than is the Blazer for the simple reason that, in showroom condition, it is the more fundamental of the two cars. In concept, the Bronco was intended to overhaul the Jeep, the Blazer is still two years away.

Stroppe begins with the basic Sportwagon model equipped with the 302-2v V8 engine and whatever else the individual purchaser might see fit to order. In our test vehicle's case, the option list, including the special red, white, and blue Baja Bronco paint treatment, ran the price to $5,432.17 before Bill did his magical tricks. When we tested the stock Bronco last June, our two primary complaints were the manual steering and transmission; both of which made the car quite difficult to drive off-road. Stroppe has ameliorated these faults by including in the Baja

package Ford's excellent 3-speed automatic transmission and a Saginaw power steering unit with a super-quick ratio of approximately 17:1. In our previous Bronco article, we had wondered how good the vehicle could be with these items and now I can say that it is like an entirely new car; much more maneuverable, far easier to urge over steep rock climbs, and generally just more pleasurable to drive.

But, Stroppe does not stop here. Realizing that the 302-2v, while possessing adequate power, is not known as Detroit's strongest offering, he has made available a 4v modification of the engine which is good for an additional 15 hp. Our test car was thusly equipped and combined with the low gearing of 4WD, the Bronco was transformed into a real performer. Other refinements center on the suspension and wheels with Stroppe improving on the basic chassis configuration by installing double shocks at all four wheels, stiff 1,280-lb. rear leaf springs, and a 3,300-lb. rear axle which act to increase the car's GVW to a hefty 4,700 lbs. In the wheel department, the standard factory treads have been replaced by Gates TX off-road tires mounted on chrome-plated 15-inch wheels, raising the Bronco's ground clearance from 8.2 inches to a towering 11.5 inches.

Safety and convenience also come in for attention on the Baja Bronco with the addition of a fuel tank skid plate (no transfer case plate is needed since the unit is located high in the chassis where only the most vicious or determined rock could find it), padded roll bar, 8-gallon auxiliary gas tank, heavy-duty cooling system, swing-away spare tire carrier, electric winch, rubber coated steering wheel, and a class II tow hitch to haul a 3,500-lb. trailer.

In a nutshell, Stroppe has retained the basic body, adding fender flares to accept the larger tires, and rugged ladder frame. He has discarded most everything else save for the slightly modified engine and stock interior components, and rebuilt the vehicle to meet his stringent off-road demands. Naturally, all this engineering does not come free; the draftsmen at Stroppe's facility perched atop Long Beach's Signal Hill must make their daily bread, too. As installed on our test Bronco, the Baja package priced out at $2,031.67; bringing the total sticker cost to $7,463.84.

Hickey, on the other hand, does not have to contend with an identical set of problems since his Blazers can be ordered from Chevrolet with power steering, automatic transmission, and a strong engine. Perhaps this is the reason behind the differing marketing concepts of the two off-road wizards. Whereas the Baja Bronco is available through any Ford dealer as an extracost option, Hickey offers only pieces sold directly to Blazer owners. The advantages of each method are readily apparent. With the Bronco, the vehicle is delivered anywhere in the U.S. finished and ready to drive while the Hickey approach allows the off-roader to choose just how serious, and expensive, he wants his hobby to become. The problems are equally obvious; if you want any part of the Stroppe package, you must buy it all and the Hickey method requires the purchaser, unless he lives close to Vic's shop in Ventura, to bolt-on the equipment himself or arrange to have it installed locally.

Because of the marketing concept, there is no absolute price on a modified Blazer; it depends on what the individual owner orders from Chevrolet and what additional parts he buys from Hickey. As ordered from the factory, our test Blazer, including the 350-2v engine, air conditioning, fiberglass top, AM/FM radio, and the CST interior option, had a sticker price of $5,534,85. Then Vic went to work.

Although the 350 V8 is a strong engine, Hickey added his dual exhaust system which helps the motor breathe better and is good for a slight power increase which makes the car even easier

〉〉〉〉

PHOTOGRAPHY BY: T. S. BRATCHER AND JOHN LAMM

Above: With a powerful V8 engine, even fording rivers were easy with the Hickey Blazer: Below: A padded 14-inch steering wheel made for fatigueless driving. Bottom: Hickey equipment includes a heavy-duty roll bar and two auxiliary fuel tanks mounted on the rear wheel wells that make total gas capacity 47 gallons.

Left: Stroppe Bronco features a padded roll bar and durable rubber floor mats. Above: Dashboard is utilitarian on the Bronco but a rubberized steering wheel does help comfort. Below: High ground clearance plus a transfer case mounted at frame rail level made the Bronco a pleasure to drive over most of the rough terrain.

Friendly Hostility

to power over obstacles than before. He corrected one of the inherent problems of the Blazer, bad ball joints, by installing a hydraulic steering stabilizer and shimmy dampener that pre-loads the ball sockets therefore controlling front end wobble and improving not only the wear on the joints but the driver fatigue factor as well. Since our test vehicle had power steering, automatic transmission, and standard power front disc brakes, Hickey concentrated on the suspension and mechanical protection devices. Double shocks were mounted at all four wheels to complement the factory-ordered high rate leaf springs while Positraction Stagger Block tires on 15-inch one-piece aluminum wheels increased ground clearance from the stock 7.3 inches to 9.5 inches. To further protect the drive train, skid plates were attached to the fuel tank and the rather low-slung transfer case and a

special engine oil and transmission cooler was added.

In the safety category, Vic added his super-trick power winch which mounts between the front frame rails and requires no bumper extension, front push bars, steering box and transfer case bolt kits that replace the stock items which have been known to shear causing extensive damage, a front axle truss assembly designed to prohibit the axle from bending and possibly breaking under strenuous off-road maneuvers, a roll bar, and quartz-iodine lamps which are a necessity if you contemplate any desert night driving.

Convenience items abound on the vehicle and include two 13-gallon auxiliary fuel tanks that bring the total gasoline capacity of the Blazer to an unbelievable 47 gallons, a swing-away spare tire carrier, tie-down rope hooks, interior dome light, a bolted-in tool box complete with block snatch and tow strap, a 14½-inch vinyl foam steering wheel, heavy-duty tow hitch, a red dashboard

light which glows when the front axle is engaged in 4WD, and an American Racing 8-track stereo tape deck.

Now, with this much equipment the Blazer is bound to cost beaucoup bread so the catalog price for the parts, $1,943.85, is not startling. Adding this to the vehicle's price before modification, we arrive at a total cash outlay of $7,478.70. While this may be only $15 more than the Bronco, don't forget that the price does not include the installation cost of the Hickey equipment. In the case of both cars, it's a lot of money, but, I think, their off-road performance is well worth it.

Comparing the Stroppe Bronco and the Hickey Blazer is at one time easy and hard; easy because they perform their intended task so superbly and hard since there is no real clear-cut victor. Driving them around on the street gave us a few notions about which would be better but, after our weekend jaunt in the boondocks the issue was even more clouded than before: when

Above: Bronco and Blazer had swing-away spare tire carriers. Top right: Going where others can't is both cars' forte. Below: If there's no road, make one.

STROPPE BAJA BRONCO

Engine	90° V8, OHV
Bore & Stroke — ins.	4.0 x 3.0
Displacement — cu. in.	302
HP @ RPM	158 @ 5000
Torque: lbs. ft. @ RPM	242 @ 2000
Compression Ratio	8.5:1
Carburetion	4 bbl.
Transmission	3-spd. auto.
Final Drive Ratio	3.50:1
Steering Type	Worm and Roller
Steering Ratio	17:1
Turning Diameter — ft.	31.0
Tire Size	9.15 x 15
Brakes	Front & Rear Drums, manual
Front Suspension	Vertically mounted double shocks, coil springs, radius rod, stabilizer bar
Rear Suspension	Vertically mounted double shocks, leaf springs
Ground Clearance — ins.	11.5
Angle of Approach	40°
Angle of Departure	27°
Body/Frame Construction	Box section
Wheelbase — ins.	92
Overall Length — ins.	152.1
Width — ins.	68.8
Height — ins.	70.7
Front Track — ins.	59.9
Rear Track — ins.	59.9
Curb Weight — lbs.	3,400
Fuel Capacity — gals. (Main)	20.2
Gas Mileage Range	
On Road	11.3-11.8
Off Road	7.1-7.7
Base Price	$3,637.85
With Factory Options	5,432.17
With Baja Package	7,463.84
Car of the Year Score	76.7

HICKEY K/5 BLAZER

Engine	90° V8, OHV
Bore & Stroke — ins.	4.0 x 3.48
Displacement — cu. in.	350
HP @ RPM	165 @ 4000
Torque: lbs. ft. @ RPM	280 @ 2400
Compression Ratio	8.5:1
Carburetion	2 bbl.
Transmission	3-spd. auto.
Final Drive Ratio	3.73:1
Steering Type	Recirculating ball
Steering Ratio	17.5:1
Turning Diameter — ft.	36.7
Tire Size	L70 x 15
Brakes	Front discs, rear drums-power assist
Front Suspension	Angular mounted double shocks, tapered leaf springs, stabilizer bar
Rear Suspension	Angular mounted double shocks, tapered leaf springs
Ground Clearance — ins.	9.5
Angle of Approach	31°
Angle of Departure	20°
Body/Frame Construction	Perimeter
Wheelbase — ins.	104
Overall Length — ins.	177.5
Width — ins.	68.7
Height — ins.	79.0
Front Track — ins.	61.6
Rear Track — ins.	61.6
Curb Weight — lbs.	3,967
Fuel Capacity — gals. (Main + 2 Aux.)	47
Gas Mileage Range	
On Road	9.3-10.8
Off Road	6.3-6.9
Base Price	$3,358.00
With Factory Options	5,534.85
With Hickey Equipment	7,478.70
Car of the Year Score	79.4

the Blazer was superior, the Bronco was a close second and vice versa. It is easier to criticize the cars since to list our praises could fill volumes.

Our primary complaint rests in the choice of tires. Both vehicles were equipped with 4-ply rated tires for reasons of road-going comfort, but once off in the desert we suffered the misery of changing flat tires on each car. Even though the street ride would be much harsher, I would opt for the more rugged 6-ply treads. The Bronco, in its Stroppe configuration, has taken care of two major areas of discontent, power steering and automatic transmission, but continues to keep manual drum brakes which require an unseemly high pedal effort to stop the vehicle. The Blazer's power discs are far superior, both on and off-road. But, when all was said and done, it turned out that the two most annoying faults of the cars were a radio in the Bronco which refused to work and the Blazer's cigarette lighter that operated only

spasmodically. And, if that's all that upsets you about a couple of trucks, it has to mean something.

In actual off-road performance, the Bronco is just a hair better although, in certain terrain you couldn't drag me out of the Blazer with a team of oxen. This is due primarily to the Ford's shorter wheelbase, tighter turning circle (31 feet), and better ground clearance. Over rolling country it was possible to drive the Bronco at incredibly fast speeds while the Blazer tended to get its rear end airborne over the humps. However, we encountered certain obstacles where the sheer power of the Chevy enabled easy passage while the short wheelbase of the Bronco had to struggle before finally gaining the upper hand.

Comfort, though, is what the Blazer excells in and the Bronco has to admit defeat in this area. I hate to think that I'm getting soft, but it was a beautiful thing to roll up the Blazer's window, switch on the air conditioning, insert a cartridge in the tape player, and do a

frenetic broadsliding dance between rocks and bushes in rhythm with the beat of Grand Funk or Leon Russell. Chevrolet and Hickey have apparently foreseen the current trend among off-roaders away from strictly utilitarian and uncomfortable vehicles towards cars that accomplish the same job with style. Perhaps Stroppe should induce Ford to follow the same tack in the Bronco; it'd be one sweet machine.

It is clearly evident, however, that Hickey and Stroppe have developed their respective vehicles almost to full potential, and that reflects well on both men. If I have to choose a winner (and The Man says I do), I would cast my vote for the Blazer. While just barely losing in off-road performance, the comfort factor makes it the better all-round vehicle. But, as far as Vic Hickey and Bill Stroppe are concerned, what we say here will not stop the good-humored quips and jibes. And frankly, that's the way it should be. We'd hate to ruin a beautiful friendship. **/MT**

MAN
VS.
BRONCO....

Spiegel takes a commanding lead early in the race. Foot power was the necessary ingredient to get through the tightest corners fast.

The outcome was often in doubt. Here Spiegel leads the Bronco into the final turn. The Bronco was often drafting Spiegel, which helped conserve fuel. Spiegel was the ultimate victor. He won going away by a tennis shoe length.

MAN WINS?!

Several months ago, Ford Division of Ford Motor Company introduced the 1973 Ford light duty trucks and the new Bronco. Now the Ford Public Relations men, being resolute as they are, laid out an obstacle course for the Bronco. The intrepid P.R. men, fearful lest a novice driver from a newspaper or elsewhere might get into the spirit of driving and get a little too spirited, made the course tight enough so no one could go fast or get in over his head.

In fact, the course was so tight and so slow, the experienced off roaders were a little bored by the pace. One dilligent four wheeler, the renowned automotive writer Marshal Spiegel (who brought you "Jeeping New York" in the April, 1972 issue of FOUR WHEELER), decided that a man on foot could get around the course faster than the vehicles. The question has been bugging mankind since the industrial revolution began: Who is faster, man or machine? To settle this vexing issue once and for all, Spiegel and a Bronco were pitted in a no-holds-barred race to the finish.

It was touch and go from the start. Our brave writer, on foot, got away fast, but the Bronco was on his heels. Both man and machine cornered furiously on the green grass of Ford's Romeo proving ground. Steadily, though, Spiegel pulled away. A couple of times the outcome was in doubt as the Bronco closed the gap. Finally, it went down to the wire: It was Spiegel by a tennis shoe! It was close, but man prevailed. And we must thank Tom Rhodes and Tom Boyle of Ford Public Relations for this outstanding photo story. ☐

4WD Earthshaker!

The Baja 500, Mint 1000, Idra and Mint 400, Mexican 1000, Riverside Grand Prix and Borrego Rough 100 are all names synonymous with the growing sport of American offroad racing. In all forms of event from the tough blast of the long distance enduros to the specialist sprints of sand dragging or just plain dune riding the all-American attitude of inventiveness and adaptability for things mechanical is evident.

All kinds of vehicles are tried, but successes have determined classes for single seat racing buggies, chopped VWs, and modified pickups with either two or four wheel drive. Perhaps the most well known of the offroaders are the traditional four wheel drive vehicles; Jeep, Jeepster, Chevy Blazer and Bronco. These big trucks are the heavy metal of the events and with all things tough perhaps have the greatest appeal.

Ford's Bronco, which has a string of major successes behind it, is one of the

beasts of the events. It starts life as a tough hard·top utility which is capable of moderate offroadability and is equally at home running to the supermarket. Ford offer the Bronco with a mass of dealer options and several engine and gearbox combinations. For all its fame and usefulness in the States the Bronco is not usually seen over here. Except one, and it is this one which we're about to describe. It belongs to Peter Stevens, and is an out and out racer fully prepared and built by the forceful Bill Stroppe and engine men Holman and Moody.

It transpires that the truck was built up in 1968—the same year that Parnelli Jones won the Baja 500 in a Bronco. Apart from the race winning car, the team built up three other race cars and two for the Press to experience the dust and the thunder. The Stevens-owned Bronco found its way over here as a 'gift' from Ford of America to Ford of Britain in return for a Mirage GT40.

Judging by the number of appearances the Bronco made it seems that the Ford people were not too interested in their newly acquired desert charger. However it was taken to a French mountain rally —The Rallye des Cimes—but didn't start probably due to the fact that the tracks it would have to ascend were too narrow to negotiate. Apart for the occasional appearance as interest value at a few autocrosses the Bronco wasn't seen until the autumn of 1971. Resurrection was for the Senior Service Hill-rally in which it failed to finish. I still remember the look of disgust on the faces of the Ford mechanics as they slaved over an exploded clutch. We were in the service area too, in other Ford-built products—a pair of thirty-year-old WWII Jeeps. Our servicing was confined to a fill of petrol and an oil check. After this demise the Bronco disappeared to the wastes of Boreham.

In the course of the following year

Peter made several attempts to purchase the Bronco from Ford, but all to no avail. Eventually he got wind of 'a big American offroad machine' in Northern Ireland of all places. Sure enough it turned out to be the wandering Bronco. A Ford tractor dealer had bought it unseen to put a crane in the back. 'Can't think what they could have used it for with those big tyres and huge engine,' he said, after Peter had bought it from him.

The Bronco took a long time returning to the UK and Peter feared for the safety of the truck every time he heard that another bomb had gone off. At last it arrived, complete with the '71 Hillrally damage. This amounted to a blown clutch which wrecked the flywheel and bellhousing as well. Replacement of these parts posed little problem as they are all Mustang/Cobra components. Nevertheless the bill came to some £70 for a racing clutch, bellhousing and steel flywheel from a 7-litre Cobra.

The engine is a big Ford 351ci V8 and is to full race specification by Holman & Moody. The unit was stripped on arrival as a precaution and was found to be in sound order. It has a solid lifter cam, and all the pistons and rods are polished and balanced. The crank and attendant clutch/flywheel assembly is balanced and lightened. A Holley 600cfm carburettor feeds the two modified heads and a pair of custom made headers take away the gases. It's not known just what the engine is producing in the way of power, but a guess of some 325bhp must be fairly accurate.

A four-speed transmission is fitted in place of the standard unit and is rated as a T10 box. The Bronco may be driven in either two or four wheel drive, the ratio selection facilitated by the big fore and aft lever next to the Hurst gearchange on the main box. Positions from the dash back are four wheel drive low, neutral, two wheel drive high and four wheel drive high. You can only be in low range if the transfer case is in fwd. All these selections may be made while the vehicle is on the move.

In standard trim the huge ladder frame chassis is substantial enough, but the Stroppe racing shop had reinforced the frame even more. Further strength is gained by building the roll cage direct to the frame rails. The already stout suspension is further modified by adding an extra shock absorber to the original, giving two per wheel. Further reinforcement is made by inserting inflatable air bags into the coil springs which can be adjusted to suit the conditions. Leaf springs are fitted to the rear of the chassis as standard and the axles are reinforced with a cross brace to prevent them fracturing. There is of course a steering damper to prevent violent shocks from tearing the steering wheel from the driver's hands.

Weight on the racing version is

drastically reduced by the removal of the hard top, doors and trim. Alternative equipment is added of course, and this must bring the weight to around 30cwt. Brakes are 11 inch drums all round fed via twin circuits and do an adequate job in slowing the truck. There were reports that after the last Mexican 1000 that Parnelli Jones's Bronco was overtaking planes which were covering the event; it's said he was doing 135mph in some places.

The auxiliary equipment is basic and necessary; the rear cargo bed is filled with the fifty gallon fuel cell which has dual fillers—one on either side. Immediately behind the two seats is a rack for a two gallon cask of Gatorade—a honey/glucose health drink—which the crew drink with a pair of tubes. At the rear, the tailgate is filled with one of the huge spare wheels fitted with a special lug wrench.

As you would expect the wheels and tyres are completely out of the ordinary. A set of 8.45x15 8-ply Gates Commandos, which have nine inches of tread is mounted on 9x15in steel rims, and as an alternative for driving in soft conditions a set of Pikes Peak Specials with 10in of tread on 10x15in rims can be fitted.

The scene in the cockpit is pretty spartan. Entry is either by climbing in from the rear deck over all the roll cage plumbing or by cocking a leg over the chicken bar and glass fibre fillet which replaces the door. There are two Bostrom sprung seats to ease the ride on the behind, and each has a full aircraft style harness with quick release hung round the frame. The co-driver's side of the cab has all the engine monitoring instruments and a foot operated horn and dipswitch. Also there is a large grab handle protruding from the side bar of the cage. Many a sweaty palm has grabbed for that in a panic. On the driver's side there are just the pedals,

a foam rubber covered wheel and the hulking Hurst shifter. Not much, but when this baby gets going it's more than enough to handle.

At the time of writing only a tarmac road test had been possible. The description of the vehicle is easy; the ride is a different horse altogether. One thing is for sure: it makes sliced bread, up-lift bras, coloured girls and oysters redundant as far as turning you on. It's an ego trip of the first degree. Other road users just don't believe that they're sitting next to a big red truck with huge tyres, their ears battered by the iron pant of a hot V8 and a couple of loonies in funny headgear grinning inanely down at them. Our apologies to the sports back Mustang driver who tried to out-stage us at a set

of lights. After all our pony could do 45mph in first gear, 70mph in second and if you work it out on revs per thousand, 95mph in third and around 120mph in top. We won.

The final account of the evening was when we we stopped at a traffic junction and heard an incredulous voice from behind say, 'What the effing hell is that?' We turned round to see a very sane looking gentleman in the car behind, which happened to be a Mercedes 280. The gentleman was actually standing on the driver's seat with his person protruding through the sun roof. Stranger things may happen in the deserts of southern California, but never did such a pair of cowboys ride such a pony down the Finchley Road one January evening. **RP**

Pic: Robert Pemberton

Do It Yourself:

BRONCO CAN AND TIRE HOLDER

Story and photos by Willie Worthy

Rear view shows two 5-gallon cans and spare. Note that there is no restriction of brake/taillights.

Bronco owners with swing-away outside tire carriers can easily rebuild them to be capable of carrying two GI cans, as well as the spare tire. My own was built from pieces of tubing I just happened to have. The idea is not original but a composite of several others I have seen on the backs of local Broncos.

Material used in construction consists of two heavy-duty gate latches, a 54-inch, a 36-inch, and a 14-inch piece of 1/8-inch wall of tubing, a 30-inch and a 36-inch piece of 1/2-inch electrical conduit, and a 1/4-inch thick, 2-inch wide, by 14-inch long piece of flat steel. The original retaining latch was used, as well as the tire holder. The can holders are from Dick Cepek, 9201 California Ave., South Gate, Calif. 90280 or J.C. Whitney Company, 1917-19 Archer Ave., Box 8410, Chicago, Ill. 60680.

Start by cutting off the curved portion of the stock carrier and throw it away. Slide the two long pieces about a foot or so into the top and bottom tubes. Adjust them so they come just to the end of the tailgate. Add the vertical piece to the end and tack weld everything together. Since tape measures always seem to lie when measuring the first time, before welding remeasure, making sure everything is parallel and equidistant.

Next, clamp the two gate bolts to the top and bottom pieces and position the latches to the fender above and below the taillights. I used some sheet metal screws in the outside holes and 1/4-inch bolts for inside holes on the brackets. Once the latches are mounted and you're sure you have the latch bolts in the proper location, weld them in place. Double check to see that everything swings and latches properly.

Location of gate latches, can holder and relocation of original latch. Note new license plate location.

Stock tire holder adapted to new unit with 3/8-inch bolt used to control excessive movement.

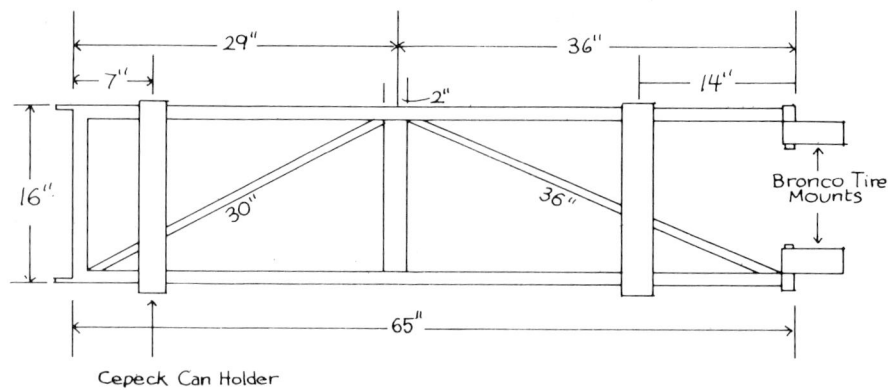

Measure from both ends to find the center and weld a piece of 2 x 1/4-inch flat stock between the top and bottom tubes. Hook the stock tire carrier over the top tube, rest it against the flat plate and weld it into place. Drill a hole for the tire hold-down bolt and square off

Continued on page 133

JIM HANSEN PHOTOS

1973 FORD BRONCO

IN THESE DAYS when the production of light trucks is running over a million-and-a-half a year and more emphasis than ever is being put on the recreation vehicle market, the Ford Bronco has to be regarded as something of an anomaly.

The Bronco is an anomaly because it is a unique vehicle in the Ford truck line. It is unique because it shares almost no components except engine and transmission with any other vehicle at Ford. With Bronco sales running under 20,000 a year, that puts it in the awkward position of not being worth changing very much. If it shared sheet metal, chassis and running gear with the pickups, then it would get the major changes along with those high-volume vehicles. But it doesn't and consequently the Bronco gets ignored a lot.

On the one hand, it's good that a vehicle can continue in production for over seven years without major change. On the other hand, this also keeps the Bronco from being as good as it

could and should be. We have no doubt at all that Ford management is aware of this conflict. Sure, they could sell more Broncos if they improved the product. But could they sell enough more to justify the investment that would be required? It's apparent that Ford doesn't think so. Not yet. So what we've got is the good old Bronco, a combination of up-to-date and out-of-date, a sparkly new 1973 model still hampered by 1965 thinking.

But that's enough philosophy. Let's look at the machine itself.

In the overall scheme of things, the Bronco is in the middle-size class of 4wd vehicles and a comparison of it with the others in its group is shown on the following page.

Under the hood the standard engine is the 200-cu-in. inline 6 and the only optional engine is the 139-horsepower 302 V-8, another example where the Bronco has come up a bit short in comparison to other 4wds. With the Ford 4x4 pickups, for example, you can get the 360

V-8, as well as the 240 and 302 engines, and Chevrolet offers the 307 and 350 V-8s in addition to the base-line 250 inline 6 in their 4wd pickups and the Blazer.

With the 1973 model Ford finally got around to offering an automatic transmission as an option for the Bronco in addition to the standard 3-speed, all-synchro, column-shift manual transmission. No 4-speed heavy duty manual transmission is available for the Bronco. The transfer case is the familiar Dana 20 with a straight-through shift pattern.

	Wheelbase	Track	Length	Width
Bronco	92.0	57.4/57.4	152.0	69.8
Blazer	106.5	65.8/62.7	184.5	79.0
Scout II	100.0	55.7/55.7	165.8	70.0
Commando	104.0	51.5/50.0	174.5	59.9
Land Cruiser	90.0	55.3/55.1	152.4	65.6

Bronco dashboard is simple and rather spartan. All instruments are contained in cluster around speedometer on left hand side.

Fully equipped Bronco includes auxiliary gas tank, swingaway spare tire carrier, plenty of chrome and fancy wheel covers.

Ranger trim option, new for '73, includes stick-on striping as well as bright-metal trim, wheel covers, spare tire rack.

The Bronco is still the only 4wd vehicle that can be ordered with a limited slip differential in the front as well as in the rear axle. Some other manufacturers will make this available on their machines if the buyer insists but all state that it is not a wise option for the average buyer because of the "steering" created by the limited slip under some conditions. PV4 concurs in this opinion and does not recommend limited slip in front except in certain rare cases.

One of the unique features of the Bronco is that coil springs are used in the front suspension instead of traditional leaf springs. A massive trailing arm is used to locate the live axle with a tube shock acting against the arm just behind the spring. At the rear there are the familiar leaf springs on a live axle and tube-type shocks are used here as well. The standard GVW (gross vehicle weight) rating is 4300 lbs and there are optional 4500 and 4900 GVW packages. Since the fully equipped Bronco weighs about 3750 lbs, we suggest that the larger of the two optional GVWs be selected unless you never plan to use your Bronco for anything more serious than a picnic.

As the Bronco has gone through its production life the option list has been simplified to a certain extent. Because so few buyers specified the bench front seat, front buckets were made part of the standard equipment. The rear bench is still an option, of course. Free-running front hubs, another high priority option, were also made standard. In addition, a hydraulic steering stabilizer is also part of the standard equipment.

In body styles there is no longer a pickup version of the Bronco, nor an open-topped utility version, the full-top station wagon being the only body style now available.

Among the luxury touches offered with the latest Bronco is the top-of-the-line Ranger trim package which includes full carpeting, bright metal trim, vinyl covered seats with fabric inserts, molded vinyl door trim, swingaway rear tire carrier complete with cover and full wheel covers. The stick-on striping is also part of the Ranger package.

Also new for '73 is a power steering option, which we consider a good thing since it reduces the steering ratio, making it easier to get those quick changes in direction that are often needed off the pavement. The brakes remain as before, small drums at each corner, and no power brake option

1973 FORD BRONCO

PRICES

Basic list, FOB Detroit: $2037

Standard equipment: 200-cu.-in. 6-cyl engine, 3-spd manual transmission, bucket seats, free-running front hubs, E78-15 tires

ENGINES

Standard	200-cu.-in. inline 6
Bore x stroke, in.	3.68 x 3.13
Displacement, cu. in.	200
Compression ratio	8.3:1
Net horsepower @ rpm	89 @ 3800
Net torque @ rpm, lb-ft	156 @ 2200
Type fuel required	regular

Optional 302 V-8	$124
Bore x stroke, in.	4.00 x 3.00
Displacement, cu. in.	302
Compression ratio	8.0:1
Net horsepower @ rpm	137 @ 3800
Net torque @ rpm, lb-ft	222 @ 2600
Type fuel required	regular

DRIVE TRAIN

Standard transmission . . . . . 3-spd manual
Clutch dia., in. 11.0
Transmission ratios:
   3rd 1.00:1 (6-cyl), 1.00:1 (V-8)
   2nd 1.86:1 (6-cyl), 1.75:1 (V-8)
   1st 3.41:1 (6-cyl), 2.99:1 (V-8)

Optional 3-spd automatic (V-8 only) $236

Transmission ratios: 3rd 1.00:1
2nd 1.46:1
1st 2.46:1

Rear axle type . . . . . .semi-floating hypoid
Final drive ratio: 4.11 (6-cyl), 3.50:1 (V-8)
Optional final drive ratios: 4.57 (6-cyl), 4.11 (V-8)
Overdrive . . . . none
Limited slip differential (rear) $39

Transfer case . . . . 2-spd Dana 20
Transfer case ratios: . . . . . .2.46 & 1.00:1

CHASSIS & BODY

Body/frame: ladder type frame with separate steel body.

Brakes (std): drums, 11 x 2 front, 10 x 2½ rear
Brake swept area, sq in. 244
Swept area/ton (max load) 98
Power brakes . . . . none

Steering type (std) . . . . . . worm & roller
Steering ratio 24:1
Power steering $131
Power steering ratio 17:1
Turning circle, ft 31.0

Wheel size (std) . . . . 15 x 5.5
Optional wheel sizes: . . . . none
Tire size (std) E78-15 (4PR)
Optional tire sizes: . . . . . . up to L78-15

SUSPENSION

Front suspension: trailing arms & coil springs on live axle, tube shocks
Front axle capacity, lb 3000
   Optional .none

Rear suspension: live axle on leaf springs, tube shocks
Rear axle capacity, lb 2780
   Optional 3300

Additional suspension options: heavy duty springs

ACCOMMODATION

Standard seats . . . . front buckets
   Optional . . . . rear bench
Headroom, in 43
Pedal to seatback, max 36.5
Steering wheel to seat back, max 15
Seat to ground 33.5
Floor to ground 22
Heater & defroster . . . . std
Tinted glass . . . . na
Air conditioning . . . . na

Unobstructed load space (length x width x height), in.
   With seats in place . . . . . . .13 x 39 x 38
   Rear folded or removed . . .49 x 39 x 38

INSTRUMENTATION

Instruments: 100-mph speedometer, 99,999.9-mi odometer, fuel level, temp, ammeter, oil pressure
Warning lights: high beam, turn signals
Optional . . . . none

MAINTENANCE

Service intervals, normal use, miles:
   Oil change 6000
   Filter change 6000
Warranty, months/miles 12/12,000

GENERAL

Curb weight, lb (test model) 3750

GVW (max. laden weight), lb 4300
   Optional GVWs 4500, 4900

Wheelbase, in 92.0
Track, front/rear 57.4/57.4
Overall length 152.1
Overall height 71.1
Overall width 68.8
Overhang, front/rear 26.9/33.2

Approach angle, degrees 40
Departure angle 27

Ground clearances   (test model):
   Oil pan 16.8
   Transfer case 14.7
   Fuel tank 18.0
   Exhaust system (lowest point) 21.0

Fuel tank capacity, U.S. gal 12.2
Auxiliary 7.5-gal $38

OTHER OPTIONS

Sport trim $197
Ranger trim $405
Chrome bumpers $32
Swingaway spare carrier $32
Auxiliary 7.5-gal. fuel tank $38
AM radio $59
Rear seat $104
Skid plates, transfer case & fuel tank .$51
Hand throttle $4.38

TEST MODEL

302 V-8 engine, automatic transmission, power steering, Ranger trim, AM radio, L78-15 Firestone Deluxe Champion tires.
West coast list price $5406

ACCELERATION

Time to speed, sec:
   0-30 mph 5.1
   0-45 mph 8.9
   0-60 mph 14.9
   0-70 mph 20.9
   Standing start ¼-mile, sec 19.5
   Speed at end, mph 68

CORNERING

Speed on 100-ft radius, mph 31.0
Lateral acceleration, g 0.64

SPEED IN GEARS

High range, 3rd(3800 rpm) 90
   2nd (3800 rpm) 62
   1st (3800 rpm) 37

Low range, 3rd (3800 rpm) 35
   2nd (3800 rpm) 24
   1st (3800 rpm) 15

BRAKE TESTS

Pedal pressure required for ½-g deceleration rate from 60 mph, lb 80
Stopping distance from 60 mph, ft . . .238
Fade: Percent increase in pedal pressure for 6 stops from 60 mph 37
Overall brake rating . . . . fair

INTERIOR NOISE

Idle in neutral, dBA 55
Maximum during acceleration 78
At steady 70-mph cruising speed 79

OFF PAVEMENT

Hillclimbing ability . . . . .very good
Maneuverability . . . . .excellent
Turnaround capability . . . . . . .excellent
Handling . . . . .good
Ride . . . . fair

GENERAL

Heater rating . . . . .good
Defroster effectiveness . . . . fair
Wiper coverage . . . . .poor

FUEL CONSUMPTION

Normal driving, mpg 10-12
Off pavement 7-8
Range, normal driving, miles 190-220
Range, off pavement 135-150

is available. Also missing from the option list is factory air conditioning though many dealers will arrange for that accessory to be installed locally.

TESTS & IMPRESSIONS

Our test Bronco was a top-of-the-line model with the 302 V-8, automatic transmission, power steering, the new Ranger trim package and was fitted with L78-15 Firestone Deluxe Champion tires with street treads. The all-up list price on the west coast is $5140.

Compared to the plain-jane appearance of the early Broncos, this latest model is a pretty flashy machine. The Ranger trim option is comprehensive and the full carpeting covers not only the rear wheel arches but the inside of the tailgate as well.

The bucket seats are comfortable and while these are not deeply contoured they do a good job of offering lateral support in ordinary driving. The steering wheel is a bit close to the chest to suit us and also a bit higher than we find comfortable. The instruments are all housed in one round frame and there is a complete set of gauges, not idiot lights.

The 302 V-8 effectively occupies most of the space under the hood. Smog control extras complicate access on left side.

This is also part of the standard equipment, not optional as on the Blazer.

The 302 V-8 engine is an old favorite of ours. It's been in the Ford family for many years now, is thoroughly de-bugged and as dependable a piece of iron as you'll find under any hood. Thanks to the latest smog equipment there are some drivability problems during the warm-up period but after that it churns along in good fashion.

The power steering is an improvement over the non-assisted variety, primarily because it allows the steering ratio to be reduced from 24:1 to about 18:1 and this makes a real difference in maneuverability. Another benefit from the power steering is that it reduces the steering feedback present in the manual steering Bronco and the wheel no longer acts like it wants to tear off your thumbs when you're inching through

rough terrain. The overall steering, with or without power, is still far from ideal and this probably results from a combination of steering geometry, high center of gravity and weight transfer. This manifests itself in a non-linear effect where the steering behaves predictably up to a point but then just a little more effort at the steering wheel causes the vehicle to turn more sharply than you would expect. Tire squirm may also have something to do with this and the effect can be minimized by running the tires at comparatively high inflation pressures.

The new automatic transmission works very well and is a vast improvement over the 3-speed manual with which all Broncos have been equipped up till now. In off-pavement driving we found it most effective to leave the automatic in "D2" most of the time since it offers some hold-back on deceleration yet also has the torque at the tip of your toe when it is needed.

What doesn't work well and is still in serious need of improvement is the brake system. These are extremely heavy in operation, requiring a horrendous 80-lbs of pressure to achieve a half-g deceleration rate. Even worse, if you jump on the brakes for a panic stop you'll be sideways faster than you can wind the steering wheel.

The down-the-highway behavior of the Bronco is pretty good and the directional stability excellent, assuming there are no stiff sidewinds. The ride isn't as good as it would be with another foot or so of wheelbase, the fore-and-aft pitching over small irregularities being a characteristic that Bronco drivers have to learn to live with.

The driving position is very good in the Bronco because you sit up high and have a good view down over a comparatively short hood. It is far better in this respect than the Blazer, for instance. Taller drivers may find they are sitting a bit too high, however, as the plastic shroud covering the windshield wiper mechanism does tend to interfere with the view.

Off the pavement the Bronco is what we would call an honest machine. The ride in our test vehicle was rather harsh, especially on rebound, since ours had the 4900-lb GVW suspension but this could be greatly improved by better shock absorbers. There isn't a lot of front wheel travel and many Bronco owners have found double shocks to be worth the investment for off-pavement stability.

The transfer case on our test Bronco wasn't easy to operate but previous experience with Broncos indicates that this will loosen up with use. There's a handy indicator needle to tell you what range you're in, a feature that other manufacturers would do well to consider.

Our Bronco had the 7.5-gal. auxiliary fuel tank, giving a total fuel capacity of 19.7 gallons, a respectable quantity for the traveler. The switchover system, which includes a handle under the righthand side of the driver's seat and a flip switch on the dash, worked quickly and well as long as we could remember which way the handle was pointed for which tank.

There was a lot of slack in the drive train of our test model, which we hope isn't typical of the '73 version, but other than that we found nothing except a few rattles and squeaks to complain about.

Overall, we like the Bronco. It's a good size, it's an excellent off-road performer, the new power steering improves what was already good in maneuverability, the automatic transmission makes it easier to drive and we also like the fact that it has been around long enough to become one of the standards for comparison among 4-wheel-drive vehicles. But we do have two serious reservations: be careful until you get used to the steering and avoid situations where you need a lot of brakes. ●

1974 FORD BRONCO

THE 1974 FORD BRONCO RANGER IS A DELIGHT TO BEHOLD

THOS. L. BRYANT PHOTOS

FORD BRONCOS HAVE the distinct advantage of looking like a good off-pavement performer. They are not too long nor too wide and they certainly have a rugged appearance. Evidently the Ford Motor Company has similar feelings because they have done little or nothing to change the basic styling of the Bronco since its introduction in 1965. There have been some trim changes and some engineering improvements, but the '74 Bronco looks very much like its 9-year-old brother.

Most manufacturers of 4wd machines in the U.S. build their specialized off-pavement runners from components that are shared with higher production volume pickups and other trucks. Ford does very little of this with the Bronco, except, of course, for the drivetrain components. In 1973 Ford introduced automatic transmission and power steering into the optional equipment lineup along with a new Ranger trim package which includes full carpeting,

PV4 TEST

bright metal trim, vinyl covered seats with fabric inserts, swingaway rear tire carrier and full wheel covers. This is a very good looking package and our '74 test model was so equipped.

The Ford Bronco has several unique features which are not offered in other 4wds. You can order limited-slip in the front axle from the factory and the front suspension is made up of coil springs with a massive trailing arm instead of the traditional leaf springs. Bronco rear suspension does use the leaf spring on a live axle with tube shocks common to other 4wd machines. The standard Gross Vehicle Weight Rating (GVWR) is 4300 pounds but you can opt for two larger GVWs: 4500 and 4900 pounds.

The powerplant in the standard Bronco is a 200-cu-in. inline 6-cylinder with a rated net horsepower of 89. The optional V-8 is the 302-cu-in. which develops 137 horsepower. The 302 is the only engine available in California this year due to emission controls.

The dashboard panel of the Bronco is clean and uncluttered. The quality of the finish is unusually good and full carpeting keeps noise down.

The Bronco has changed little since its introduction in 1965. It's still a good 4wd.

The swingaway spare tire carrier at the rear is included in the Ranger package which costs $405. It's a nice addition.

We like the Ford Bronco and feel it has a well deserved reputation as a nimble and good handling off-road vehicle.

As with just about everybody else, the standard transmission is a 3-speed manual and the only alternative is the 3-speed automatic. The 6-cylinder engine model includes a 4.11:1 final drive ratio, while with the V-8 you get 3.50:1. There are two additional final drive ratios: 4.57:1 (6-cyl) and 4.11:1 (V-8). There is no overdrive offered.

Among the optional extras you can order are the previously mentioned power steering and Ranger trim package, auxiliary fuel tank, AM radio, rear seat, skid plates and a hand throttle. There are no power brakes available, so the Bronco still runs along with the relatively small drum brakes at all four corners. Nor can you obtain factory installed air conditioning, although many local dealers will arrange to have it put in for you after delivery.

The Bronco sits on a 92-in. wheelbase which is shorter than most of the competitors except the Toyota Land Cruiser and the Jeep CJ-5. The overall length is 152 inches which makes it just about as short as anything around. It's a good size for off-pavement maneuvering and getting into and out of tight places.

TEST & IMPRESSIONS

We picked up the Bronco Ranger at the Bill Stroppe & Associates facility in Long Beach, Calif. and drove off into the rush hour freeway traffic of Los Angeles one evening. We were very impressed with the trim and the overall appearance of the Ranger model and were delighted to show it off to the rest of the populace who were inching along the traffic-choked freeways. As with any new vehicle it took some getting used to at first, but we soon had the hang of it and were able to maneuver through the pack with relative ease.

Our test model was equipped with the 302 V-8, automatic transmission, the free-running front hubs which are offered as standard equipment by Ford, which is a nice touch, the Ranger trim package, optional rear seat and the auxiliary fuel tank in addition to an AM radio. The Stroppe people had added a roll bar which is a good idea in any off-pavement vehicle.

Our earliest impressions of driving the Bronco on the highway were that it felt rather tippy and that you should exercise a lot of caution in making lane changes at high speeds. After a couple hours, however, we soon got used to the handling and were more at home with the short wheelbase. We never did get accustomed to the steering, however, and were often surprised that beginning a turn resulted in the need to back off a bit on the cranking of the wheel.

The ride in the Bronco was surprisingly good for such a short wheelbase. We had expected rather a large amount of choppiness, but we were pleasantly surprised to discover that the suspension works quite well to avoid this characteristic. Off the pavement, the Bronco rides as well as any vehicle we have driven in some time, with good handling and quick response to driver inputs. At our off-pavement test facility at Saddleback Park in Tustin, Calif. we were able to motor along

1974 FORD BRONCO

PRICES

Basic list, FOB Detroit $3715
Standard equipment: 200-cu.-in. 6-cyl engine, 3-spd manual transmission, bucket seats, free-running front hubs, E78 x 15B tires, 2-spd electric washers/wipers, painted bumpers

ENGINES

Standard . . . . 200-cu.-in. inline 6
Bore x stroke, in. . . . . 3.68 x 3.13
Compression ratio 8.3:1
Net horsepower @ rpm . . . . . . 89 @ 3800
Net torque @ rpm, lb-ft . . . . . 156 @ 2200
Type fuel required . . . . 91 octane

Optional 302-cu.-in. V-8 . . . . $124
Bore x stroke, in. . . . . 4.00 x 3.00
Compression ratio 8.0:1
Net horsepower @ rpm . . . . . 137 @ 3800
Net torque @ rpm, lb-ft . . . . . 222 @ 2600
Type fuel required . . . . 91 octane

DRIVE TRAIN

Standard transmission . . . . 3-spd manual
Clutch dia., in. . 9.375 (6-cyl), 11.0 (V-8)
Transmission ratios:
  3rd 1.00:1 (6-cyl) 1.00:1 (V-8)
  2nd 1.86:1 (6-cyl) 1.75:1 (V-8)
  1st 3.41:1 (6-cyl) 2.99:1 (V-8)
Synchromesh . . . . all forward gears
Optional 3-spd automatic $236
Transmission ratios: 3rd 1.00:1
  2nd 1.46:1
  1st 2.46:1
Rear axle type . . . . semi-floating hypoid
Final drive ratios: 4.09 front/4.11 rear or 4.55 front/4.57 rear (6-cyl); 3.54 front/3.50 rear or 4.09 front/4.11 rear (V-8)
Overdrive . . . . none
Free-running front hubs . . . . std
Limited slip differential: $39 (2780 axle); $55 (3300 axle)
Transfer case 2-spd
Transfer case ratios . . . 2.46:1 & 1.00:1

CHASSIS & BODY

Body/frame: ladder-type frame with separate steel body

BRAKES

Brakes (std) 11 x 2 in. drums front, 10 x 2.5-in. drums rear (11 x 1.75-in. drums w/3300-lb axle)
Brake swept area, sq in. 295 (278)
  Swept area/ton (max load) . 120 (113)
Power brakes . . . . none
Steering type (std) . . . . . worm & roller
Steering ratio 24:1
Power steering $131
Power steering ratio 17:1
Turning circle, ft 31.0
Wheel size (std) . . . . 15 x 5.5K
Optional wheel sizes . . . . none
Tire size (std) . . . . E78 x 15B
Optional tire sizes: G78 x 15B, G78 x 15D, L78 x 15B, 7.00 x 15C

SUSPENSION

Front suspension: trailing arms & coil springs on live axle with tube shocks
Front axle capacity, lb 3000
  Optional . . . . none
Rear suspension: leaf springs on live axle with tube shocks
Rear axle capacity, lb 2780
  Optional 3300
Additional suspension options: HD front and rear springs, $11

ACCOMMODATION

Standard seats . . . . front buckets
Optional seats . . . . rear bench
Headroom, in. 37
Pedal to seatback, max. 41
Steering wheel to seatback, max. . . 15.5
Seat to ground 36.5
Floor to ground 23
Heater & defroster . . . . std
Tinted glass . . . . none
Air conditioning . . . . none
Unobstructed load space (length x width x height) in.
  With seats in place . . . . . 13 x 39 x 38
  Rear folded or removed . . 49 x 39 x 38
Tailgate (width x height) . . . . . 58 x 21.5

INSTRUMENTATION

Instruments: 0-100-mph speedometer, 99,999.9-mi. odometer, fuel gauge, water temp, ammeter, oil pressure
Warning lights: hazard warning, brake system warning
Optional . . . . none

MAINTENANCE

Service intervals, normal use, miles:
  Oil change 6000
  Filter change 12,000
  Chassis lube 6000
  Minor tuneup 12,000
  Major tuneup 24,000
Warranty, months/miles 12/12,000

GENERAL

Curb weight, lb (test model) 3945
GVW (max. laden weight) 4500
  Optional GVWs 4300, 4450, 4900
Wheelbase, in. 92.0
Track, front/rear 57.4/57.4
Overall length 152.1
Overall height 71.1
Overall width 68.8
Overhang, front/rear 27.5/33
Approach angle, degrees 35
Departure angle 33
Ground clearances (test model):
  Front axle 8.5
  Rear axle 8.5
  Oil pan 17.8
  Transfer case 14.5
  Fuel tank . . . . 18.5 (17.0 aux)
  Exhaust system (lowest point) . . 12.0
Fuel tank capacity (U.S. gal) 12.2
Auxiliary tank 7.5 gal. $38

OTHER OPTIONS

Ranger pkg $405
Sport pkg $197
Chrome bumpers, front & rear $32
AM radio $59
Skidplates $51
Swing-a-way tire carrier $32
Convenience group $22
Rear seat $104
Hand throttle $5
4500 pound GVW pkg $48
4900 pound GVW pkg $104

PERFORMANCE DATA

TEST MODEL

Ranger option, 302-cu.-in. V-8, automatic transmission, power steering, AM radio, L78 x 15B w/w tires, auxiliary gas tank, wheel covers, chrome bumpers, skidplates, roll bar, limited slip differential
West Coast list price $5412

ACCELERATION

Time to speed, sec:
  0-30 mph 4.8
  0-45 mph 8.4
  0-60 mph 13.8
  0-70 mph 20.2
  Standing start, 1/4-mile, sec 19.4
  Speed at end, mph 69

SPEED IN GEARS

High range, 3rd (4000 rpm) 79
2nd (4000 rpm) 55
1st (4000 rpm) 33
Low range, 3rd (4000 rpm) 33
2nd (4000 rpm) 23
1st (4000 rpm) 13

BRAKE TESTS

Pedal pressure required for 1/2-g deceleration rate from 60 mph, lb 75
Stopping distance from 60 mph, ft . 211
Fade: Percent increase in pedal pressure for 6 stops from 60 mph 113
Overall brake rating . . . . fair

INTERIOR NOISE

Idle in neutral, dBA 55
Maximum during acceleration 81
At steady 70-mph cruising speed . . . 75

OFF PAVEMENT

Hillclimbing ability . . . . excellent
Maneuverability . . . . very good
Turnaround capability . . . . . . excellent
Handling . . . . very good
Ride . . . . good/very good

GENERAL

Heater rating . . . . excellent
Defroster effectiveness . . . . . . very good
Wiper coverage . . . . good

FUEL CONSUMPTION

Normal driving, mpg 11.4
Off pavement 8.6
Range, normal driving, miles 140
Range, off pavement 105

The 302-cu-in. V-8 is the only optional engine. The standard powerplant is the 200-cu-in. 6-cylinder. The 302 has lively performance and good economy.

The Bronco is quite comfortable off the pavement with good handling.

The Ranger trim package incorporates many nice features into the Bronco. The tailgate is easily soiled off road.

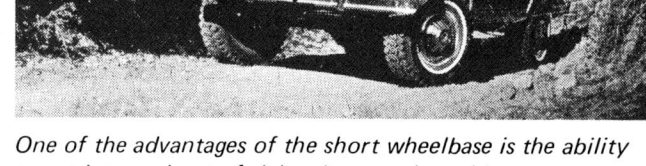

One of the advantages of the short wheelbase is the ability to get into and out of tight places such as this.

at a moderate rate of speed with little discomfort from the bumps and whoop-de-doos.

Our hillclimbing tests were exceptional. The Bronco Ranger went right up our Hill No. 2, a 63 percent grade, in 2-wheel drive. We believe this is the first time we have ever performed this feat except in rear-engined vehicles. We were also able to easily climb even our steepest hills in 4-wheel drive low range, going up and over with aplomb. The rating for the Bronco was excellent in these regards. All in all, our entire time off the pavement in the Bronco was fun and it is a sure-footed vehicle in nearly all types of terrain.

At the Orange County International Raceway we were impressed foremost with the quietness of the Bronco, as it registered less on our noise meter than nearly every other 4wd vehicle tested in recent months. The full carpeting of the Ranger trim package certainly added to this. In acceleration, the Bronco showed a lot of spirit, hustling from 0-60 mph in 13.8 seconds and covering the measured quarter-mile run in 19.4 seconds at a speed of 69 mph at the finish. The 302 V-8 is among the smallest of the V-8s offered these days, but it still has lots of performance.

The brakes of the Bronco are not as good as they should or could be. Ford still clings to relatively small drum brakes at all

four corners, so we used up 211 feet of pavement in making our panic stop from 60 mph. Also, because of their limited size, the brakes faded quite badly and the pedal pressure required for six ½-g stops from 60 mph increased more than 100 per cent. The brakes we rate only as fair and it seems overdue for Ford to put disc brakes into the Bronco.

In the area of comfort, we found the Bronco to be very good. It is not so high that the shorter driver will have to climb to get aboard and yet there is ample ground clearance for most situations. The bucket seats, which are standard equipment, are very comfortable and even spending all day driving around does not get tiresome. The controls are clearly labeled and are within easy reach. The transfer case shift lever was quite stiff but we were probably the first persons to ever put it to use and it did begin to loosen up by the time we were finished with out testing.

By and large we think the Ford Bronco is an outstanding 4-wheel-drive vehicle. It handles very well and has the ability to go just about anywhere with its abbreviated size and good approach and departure angles. It also has the advantage of looking like a good off-pavement machine. The most serious drawback is the braking ability. Overall, we have to give it very good ratings as the kind of 4wd we would be proud to own. ●

PERFORMANCE
with a price tag!

CHEVY BLAZER
V
FORD BRONCO

IF anyone asked us why we chose the Bronco and Blazer as our first ever four-wheel-drive comparison, we'd have to be honest and say "because they've created more interest and conversation amongst off-roaders than any single item since the first Sunraysia Desert Rally."

Let's face it, we didn't select them because they're easy-to-get, cheap, or widely available. In fact, from what we've heard (despite denials by at least one of the importers) there won't be any more imported for some time to come. It seems our ever-tightening ADRs make all but Holdens, Falcons and Valiants illegal on Australian road.

But let's dispense with the hum-drum and sort out a little of the nitty-gritty. Both vehicles sell in the same price range — the Chevy Blazer varying between $11,500 and $12,500 depending on where you buy it and who does the left/right conversion, and the Ford Bronco sells at $11,500 inclusive of the conversion.

Both are equipped with V8 engines. In the Blazer's case its the low compression 350 CID Chevrolet unit all hung up with anti-smog and emission control devices (although there are less of these fitted if your Chev was purchased in Alabama, and not

California), and in the case of the Bronco it's the Cleveland 302 CID powerplant, suitabley toned-down with emission controls, an inefficient exhaust system and a small-throat two-barrell carburettor. Both also have power steering and four-wheel-drive, but here the similarities end.

The Chevrolet Blazer is big, brutish, powerful, good-looking and extremely well equipped with creative comforts. The Bronco (and here I know I'm asking for trouble) on the other hand is not much more than a short, small, stubby, ugly (though lovable) pre-war Jeep with a V8 stuffed under the bonnet and a horn paint job.

The Bronco dash is a flat metal sheet, housing a speedo and a few switches; the seats are too small, too flat and too thin; and the back seat is nothing more than a "jump seat" for a couple of kids or a third adult should an emergency present itself. The whole vehicle presents an image of total utilitarianism. That may well be a good point — but for $11,500?

On the other hand, the interior of the Blazer positively exudes "luxury" and comfort, although no-one can convince me either vehicle is really worth the capital outlay demanded to own one in Australia. The dash in the

Blazer is fully padded and full instrumentation is housed in a "wrap-around" cockpit right in front of the driver. On the Cheyenne package Blazers imported to Australia air-conditioning and radio are standard. The front bucket seats are big and comfortable, providing plenty of cushioning, support and holding power even in the roughest off-road situations. The seats are separated by a "parcel bin" big enough to house a small refrigerator, and the steering column has a tilt adjustment to suit even the most unusually-shaped driver. In the rear of the wagon, the back seat provides comfortable accommodation for two, and would probably not be uncomfortable even for three or four people at a pinch.

Our test unit was privately-owned and one of the first Blazers to arrive in Australia. It came equipped with factory-standard options such as the 16.5 x 9.00 wheels and 16.5 x 10.00 tyres, and a rubber encased roll bar just behind the front seats. The Blazer is carpeted throughout — something which is of doubtful value to an off-roader and of course has the full-time four-wheel-drive.

The Bronco however is a "no nonsense" bit of gear. The interior is functional, although again the interior is carpeted. The seating is color-coded to the exterior paintwork, and all sheet-metal inside the cab is a straight continuationof the exterior paint job. However it is lacking in easy-to-read instrumentation, something which is most important in a proper off-road situation.

Both vehicles have three-speed column selector automatic gearboxes and in the case of the Bronco the four-wheel-drive/high/low range selection is a separate operation. It's sometimes a difficult one also, with the changes from low to high range and from four-wheel-drive to two-wheel-drive being very stiff and hard to find. Normally I'd put this down to the newness of the car — but I've since noticed that several American magazines picked this same point when the first of the 1973 models were released last year.

On the Chev the operation is simplified somewhat by the constant four wheel-drive system. Selection of high/low range is an easy crash type change using the floor-mounted Hurst shifter and can be carried out at almost any speed. Lo-loc and hi-loc (the extra

positions, on the şelector quadrant) allow the driver to lock the limited slip diffs to allow all four wheels to turn at exactly the same speed in really tough going.

Once off the road and in four-wheel-drive however, the Bronco begins to shape up very well. In both cases the automatic gearbox shows its value immediately you hit hard going. Gear changes are faultless, ensuring the vehicles are kept moving without loosing revs or momentum normally lost with a gear change. The Bronco also has a tremendous weight advantage over the Blazer which checks in at a staggering 44cwt and obviously with little improvement would outperform the Blazer with very little trouble. However a "modified Bronco" test will come later.

. Speaking of modifications though, it's interesting to note some of the changes made to the Blazer — and the effects they've had. First up the Blazer returned a hungry 8mpg, a good indication that something had to go. The first things to go were some of the anti-pollution fittings not required in Australia. The standard carburettor and manifold were also replaced — and a 725 Holley carbie and a Torquer manifold fitted. This lifted fuel consumption to 12mpg. The latest change has been the fitting of a 2in. Phillips twin exhaust system, which has increased consumption to around 15mpg. The changes have also had staggering effects on performance.

John Warren has promised a rework of the Bronco (four-barrel carbie, hi-riser manifold, twin straight-throughs etc.) so it will be interesting to compare notes again in a future issue.

The Blazer's constant four-wheel-drive eliminates another small but significant "creature problem"...that of lunging in and out of the cab to lock the free-wheeling front hubs (as on the Bronco) for four-wheel-driving.

Both vehicles perform well off the road, although the standard road-rubber on the Bronco precluded us from any serious four-wheel-driving. But the potential is there and we plan to explore it fully at a later date. However our comparison drives at least emphasised the need for proper rubber, even in the easiest of off-road situations. The Blazer on the other hand made good use of its ten inch wide feet and clawed its way up sand dunes, through swamp water and mud, over rocks and up clay gullies...all without a falter.

Visibility from both the Blazer and the Bronco rates an all-round good on the flat in most situations. However the width and height of the Blazer can become awesome in many off-road situations. In fact the wide, flat bonnet

THE Bronco interior is just the opposite. The flat metal dash is painted the same color as the rest of the bodywork. There's no padding, no ornamentation . . . just two plain round instrument panels. One is the speedo, the other houses the ancilliary gauges. The seats are too flat and lack proper lateral support.

can cut off visibility completely as you approach the crest of an uphill run, making it impossible for the driver to see over the ridge until you're almost on the way down. By that time it's too late — and believe me it can frighten hell out of you!

The sensible driver of course knows this and will stop and ease over the edge. In situations like this the big 350-cube engine and automatic transmission really show their worth. You can stop and move off again without digging in, stalling or rolling backwards.

The visibility problem of course doesn't affect the Bronco which is much more compact and nowhere near as bulky as the Blazer.

On the highway both the Bronco and the Blazer were hard to separate in the ride categories. Both were relatively smooth and certainly free of the fore and aft chop which is so characteristic of four-wheel-drives. Comfortwise the Blazer edges slightly ahead — mainly because of its more luxurious interior trim. Sound levels in the Bronco again are higher, and again this fact is attributable purely to the fact that it is virtually an unlined shell.

In the handling department the Blazer is a long way ahead, but to those who are familiar with full time

THE interior of the Chevrolet Blazer reeks of opulence with its deep carpets, air-conditioning, radio, wrap-around dash console with full instrumentation, and leather finish padding. The huge "bits bin" between the two front bucket seats is almost big enough to house a small refrigerator.

SPECIFICATIONS — CHEVROLET BLAZER v FORD BRONCO

	Chevrolet	Ford
Make:	Chevrolet	Ford
Model:	Blazer Cheyenne two-door wagon.	Bronco Ranger, two-door wagon.
Supplier:	Arthur Greig, North East Crescent, Lillipilli NSW	Peter Warren Ford P/L, Hume Highway, Liverpool, NSW.
Price:	$12,500 (incl. right-hand drive conversion).	$11,500 (incl. right-hand drive conversion.)

ENGINE

Cylinders:	V8	V8
Displacement:	350CID	302CID
Bore x Stroke:	4.00in x 3.50in	4.00in x 3.00in
Compression ratio:	8.5 to 1	9.4 to 1
Maximum power:	160bhp @ 3800rpm	230bhp @ 5000rpm
Maximum torque:	250lb.ft @ 2400rpm	300lb.ft @ 2600rpm
Carburettor:	four-barrel	two-barrel
Fuel pump:	mechanical	mechanical

TRANSMISSION

Type:	Three-speed turbo-hydramatic, column selector. Constant four-wheel-drive. Floor-mounted Muncie range selector. Lockable differentials.	Three-speed auto, column selector, console mounted two/four-wheel-drive selector and transfer case lever. Constant-mesh, two-speed transfer case.

SUSPENSION

Front:	Hypoid drive axle with tapered leaf spring.	Mono-beam with coils and radius rods, free-wheeling hubs.
Rear:	Semi-floating axles with progressive multi-leaf springs.	Semi-floating axle with progressive multi-leaf springs.
Shock Absorbers:	Double-acting hydraulic.	Double-acting hydraulic.

STEERING

System:	Recirculating ball with variable ratios, power assisted.	Ross worm and roller with linkage shock absorber and power assistance.

BRAKES

	Power-assisted, dual-circuit, hydraulic discs front, drums rear. Self-adjusting.	Power-assisted, dual-circuit, hydraulic. Drums all round. Self adjusting.

DIMENSIONS

Wheelbase:	106.5in.	92.0in.
Overall length:	184.5in.	152.2in.
Overall width:	79.5in.	69.1in.
Overall height:	71.5in.	70.6in.
Front track:	65.76in.	57.4in.
Rear track:	71.25in.	57.4in.
Front overhang:	33.5in.	26.9in.
Rear overhang:	44.5in.	33.2in.
Ground clearance:	7.0in. (min)	6.4in. (min)

WHEELS AND TYRES

	Pressed steel disc 10.00 x 16.50 wheels with Uniroyal off road dual-purpose tyres.	Pressed steel disc, 5.5K rims with E78 x 15 Conventional cross-plys.

CAPACITIES

Fuel tank:	Not available	12.2 gal.
Transmission:	16 pints	Not available
Transfer case:	6.75 pints	Not available
Engine:	9.5 pints (incl. filter)	8 pint (incl. filter)
Cooling system:	27 pints	Not available

ELECTRICAL

Alternator:		55 amp
Battery:	12 volt, 66 plate 70 amp/hr	12 volt, 66 plate 70 amp/hr
Headlights:	Twin, 7.25in diameter	Twin, 7.25in diameter

four-wheel-drive (Jensen, Range Rover and several very advanced prototype Formula One racers) this will come as no surprise. Cornering, even at high speed is flat and comfortable with absolutely no hint of body roll or front-end kneel. The Blazer in fact handles like a sports car. The Bronco however is a little prone to kneeling in corners with a shade of understeer which becomes quite piggish and heavy to handle (even with power steering) when approaching the apex of a corner at a rapid rate of knots. On the standard wheels and tyres the Bronco also feels a little top-heavy, although never really unstable.

The power steering on both vehicles is very easy to get used to, with the variable ratios balancing out the extremes at either end of the lock-to-lock swing. Turning circles put the Bronco ahead with its shorter wheelbase on 33.6ft (maximum clearance, bumper to bumper) with the bulkier Chev coming in at 40.3ft.

By comparison with some of our more common sedans, the turning circles, even on the Chev, are not to be laughed at. The Bronco of course is even well inside the turning circles of some of the smaller sedans available on the Australian market.

Manouvreability in the bush is good on both vehicles, again a point which is attributable to the power steering. The Yanks have been the first to realise and admit that you don't really need hairy arms and giant biceps to be an off-roader.

Both steering systems are light, fast and responsive even in heavy sand or mud, and with the variable ratios there is no fear of over-correction in emergency situation. The value shows up even more so when crawling over tricky terrain — a situation which normally demands the strength of a Sumo wrestler to control, or hold the steering steady.

The automatic transmissions can of course be locked in first or second, and do afford excellent low-speed crawling capabilities. However the automatic doesn't give as much braking effect when used as an engine brake on steep downhill runs. In this situation the manual version would probably shape up a lot more successfully.

Both vehicles have definate potential and until such time as we are able to spend a week or so with each, both properly set up for off-roading (the Chev already qualifies in this category) and really put them through their paces off road, there's little more to be said.

But keep heart, we'll get them sooner or later and see how they really stack up against the more conventional and cheaper models available.

FORD SUSPENSION IMPROVEMENTS

BY THOS. L. BRYANT

BEEFING UP YOUR FORD FOR BETTER OFF-PAVEMENT PERFORMANCE

DICK LANDFIELD OF Fairway Ford in Placentia, Calif. called us one day to invite us to a demonstration of a new suspension system for the Ford Bronco and 4wd pickups. The demonstration was to be held in the Anza-Borrego Desert the following Sunday and so Jim Hansen, PV4 Advertising Director, and I decided to truck on down and see what it was all about.

We arrived at the test site to find a variety of vehicles and people, including some of the executives of the Bilstein Shock Absorber company from San Diego and the home plant in Germany. Dick introduced us to everyone and then took us over to explain what the new suspension device consisted of and how it worked. After that, he turned us loose, first in a Bronco and then in a pickup, to do all the driving around the desert terrain that we wanted. To say that we were pleased would be an understatement. The suspension felt a lot stronger and more effective and we decided that a more detailed analysis was in order.

A couple of weeks later we made arrangement with Landfield to loan us the Bronco with the modified suspension and we also contacted the Ford public relations office in Los Angeles and requested a stock Bronco for comparison. In a convoy of vehicles early the following Friday, the PV4 staff set out for the desert again with plans for

The stock Bronco we used for our tests had a tendency to nosedive during hard stops as you can see. The Fairway kit solved this problem.

92

We set up a 2-mile loop in the desert to test the Fairway suspension kit against a stock Bronco. This is the modified vehicle at speed.

In the sand wash we found the modified Bronco was better.

The Fairway Ford suspension kit for Broncos and 4x4 pickups consists of a new stiffer front coil spring and Bilstein shocks front and rear.

conducting a test to attempt to make some objective comparisons between the stock suspension and the Fairway Ford modification.

The Fairway kit consists of new front coil springs and four specially designed Bilstein shock absorbers. It is a simple bolt-on unit that replaces the stock pieces and fits the stock mounting brackets, so there is no need for welding or cutting to make the switch. The kit comes complete for less than $120, which we think is quite reasonable for the resulting improvement.

We arrived at our selected location and mapped out a course of two miles

of bumps, grades, whoop-de-doos, sand washes, holes and small cliffs. The plan was for three drivers to make one lap in each of the two vehicles. All of the laps would be timed with stopwatches in order to have some hard-fact input. The basic evaluation, of course, would have to be subjective, based on the feel of the vehicles during the laps and the reactions of the various drivers. If we had had the time, the ideal would have been to continue circling the course until one or the other of the Broncos broke something in the suspension area. However, we did not have the time for that and we did not want to break anything

on vehicles that didn't belong to us. In between each lap, the vehicles would be rested for five minutes in order for the shocks to cool somewhat for the next driver so that he would not be making a judgment about shocks which had been overworked by someone else.

We had a lot of fun making the test and we learned a good deal as well. The modified suspension was definitely superior. We found that there was a difference in the average of the three runs in each vehicle of 18 seconds. The modified Bronco was running the loop in slightly under four minutes while the stock Bronco was taking over four minutes. We also discovered that the stock Bronco was not stock. Someone along the way before the vehicle was turned over to us had substituted a set of heavy-duty Gabriel shock absorbers for the factory ones. Otherwise, we are certain the difference would have been even greater.

Although we felt the time differential was significant in a course that short, it doesn't really sound that impressive. The seat of the pants feel, however, is more resounding. The "stock" Bronco was bottoming the front end about six times per lap while the Fairway Ford Bronco was bottoming once. It was apparent to us that the major difference, the important difference, was not the speed at which you could drive. Rather, it was the knowl-

The Quadrashock system provides a bolt-on unit for running double shock absorbers on the front of Fords with Twin I-beam suspension. It really made a difference on the E-200 van which got the treatment for this photograph.

edge that you could drive the modified suspension all day long in those conditions and still not do any damage to the front suspension or axle or other components. It worked quite well. The principal job of the shock absorber is to dampen rebound and that was exactly what the Fairway unit was doing and it was doing it superbly. In addition, the beefier coil spring was reducing the pitching effect of the whoop-de-doos and other sharp jolts.

We left the scene with a feeling of having discovered a real improvement for Ford 4wd owners, one that will give them better off-pavement capability and comfort without sacrificing on-pavement ride and handling. If you want more information or want to talk to Landfield, who has an extensive history in off-road racing and knows what is needed, you can write to Fairway Ford 4x4 Center, 1350 Yorba Linda Blvd., Placentia, Calif. 92670.

QUADRASHOCK

While we are on the subject of suspension, we would also like to tell you about another improvement that we have tried and found worthwhile. Quadrashock is a device which is available for Ford trucks with Twin I-beam front suspension. It is designed to give a firmer and more stable ride and can be installed on both vans and 2-wheel-drive pickups.

Basically, the unit is a bolt-on mount for running double shock absorbers in front. There is no need for welding or other modification of the vehicle. What it does is replace the original spring

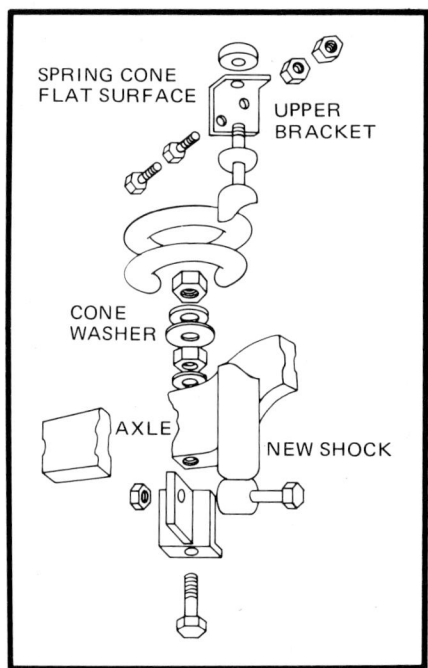

The diagram included with the kit provides an easy guide.

brackets with new ones that have fittings for placing another shock in front of the coil in addition to the stock one behind. The additional shock can be of any make, according to Charles Carvajal, developer of Quadrashock, as long as it is equivalent to the Motorcraft (Ford) No. AB102.

INSTALLATION

The first step in the installation, which was performed in our case on the Advertising Director's Ford E-200 Econoline van, is to jack up the truck by the frame and remove the spring retainer nut inside the coil. After placing a stand under the axle, the jack is let down to take the tension off the original shock so that it can be disconnected at the bottom and then the truck is jacked up once again.

The next step is to remove all the nuts and bolts holding the spring and the bracket to the axle. Then, 3/8-in. holes are drilled in the upper bracket and it is mounted to a flat surface. The bottom bracket is slipped onto the bottom spring bolt and the whole thing is reassembled. The bottom bracket should be toed-out against the axle toward the tire so that the new shock can be mounted on the tire side. The new shock is bolted in and the original one reconnected. The final step, according to Carvajal, is to have the front end realigned with ¼-degree minimum to ½-degree maximum positive camber and 1/16-in. toe in.

IMPRESSIONS

As we drove away from Charlie's shop in Lemon Grove, a suburb of San Diego, it was immediately apparent that we had found a good thing. The van responded to bumps and irregularities so much better and without the wallowing we had learned to live with. The kit sells for $37.95 to $48.95 depending on the model of vehicle and it seems to make a world of difference. If you want more information, you can contact Quadrashock Systems, Inc., P.O. Box 13446, San Diego, Calif. 92113. ●

FORD BRONCO

Not really one of Ford's better ideas, the bucking Bronc has some catching up to do.

BACKGROUND/Jeep's CJ-5 and International's Scout faced their first taste of competition in the marketplace in '65 when Ford introduced its Bronco. The Scout, already in production for 5 years, had enjoyed increasing sales with each year and the time seemed right for Ford to get a piece of the action. International's recipe had proven successful, so, to minimize any risks, Ford patterned its new truck after the Scout. The plan worked and the public responded... Bronco sales began to grow.

Initially, the Bronco looked very promising, but as with any new product there were some major shortcomings; somewhat mysteriously, however, Ford chose to ignore them and the Bronco improved little in 7 years. For '73, Bronco finally received what it had lacked for so long—power steering, a more powerful 6, and an automatic transmission; but, for many, the changes came too late. Jeep and Scout had gotten better with age—and as interest in four-wheeling grew, other trucks were introduced. Bronco owners, potential or actual, began turning to the Blazer, Jimmy, Scout, Dodge and Jeep. Bronco is now the vehicle it should have been in '66 and, hopefully, the improvements will continue.

Like the Scout, the Bronco falls into the short-wheelbase category shared by Jeep's CJ-5 and the Toyota Land Cruiser. Until '73 there were two Broncos, a 2-door wagon and a very short-bed pickup. Due to lack of cargo space, pickup sales dropped, and for '73 only the wagon returned; with it came a new wagon called the Ranger. Merely a trim package, the Ranger is a standard Bronco with body striping, swing-away spare tire carrier (until then, sold only by aftermarket dealers), plated bumpers, interior carpeting front and rear, high-backed bucket seats and a vinyl spare tire cover.

Until 1975, Bronco engine selection amounted to just two choices—one 6-cylinder and one V-8. For '66 the 6 displaced 170 cu ins.; later in the year, a 200-hp 289 was offered as an option. The 289 continued at 200 hp until 1968 when it was replaced with a 205-hp 302. The 170-cu.-in. 6 survived as the standard engine until '73 when a new and stronger 200-cu.-in. 6 took its place. An all-synchro 3-speed manual transmission was the only transmission you could get until '73, when an automatic was made optional. Heavy-duty suspension became standard late in '66 and has changed little since. For '75, only the 302 remains.

GENERAL/Like the Jeep and Scout, the Bronco was designed as a utility vehicle. For 7 years, passenger car frills like power steering and automatic transmission had not been included because the Bronco was intended to be rugged—not necessarily comfortable. It was built for abuse—off-road transportation for the rancher, the farmer and the hunter. For those people, it served the purpose well; but as the years passed, off-roading became more of a pastime—a recreation—rather than a means of getting from the cattle in the south 40 to the sheep on the hills. People who couldn't afford the price of a Blazer bought Broncos instead; for them, the truck was a sports/utility wagon, even though it was designed for pure utility. During the week, it took the kids to school, shared car-pool duties or carried the groceries; on weekends, it was out in the boonies going where a lot of Blazers couldn't. Off-pavement, the Bronco really shines—but as a commuter, it gets pretty tiring (literally). Apparently, an increasing number of owners were using them for more than utility, however, and eventually the complaints came rolling in. The standard steering made parking difficult and long rides *felt* longer; for city driving, that clutch had to go. For some reason, Ford ignored these complaints until '73, when power steering, automatic transmission and an even more powerful 6 were made available. For the commuter, 1973 brought the extra comforts of the Ranger package. At last, the Bronco was becoming versatile. Its appeal had spread from a '72 sales figure of under 20,000 units to a '73 figure of 22,245.

Other than some minor grille changes and trim alterations, the Bronco had not changed in appearance since 1966—and 1974 and '75 were no exceptions. The Bronco Sport package, an optional trim model, was added to the '74 line to fill a slot between the standard model and the Ranger. Like the Ranger, it has chrome bumpers rather than painted ones, bright grille moldings, headlining, and door trim panels—but no swingaway spare tire. For '75 the 6-cylinder was dropped and the 302 became the standard engine. For the first time, front disc brakes (non-power) were offered as an option—and because the Bronco is rated below 6000 lbs. gross vehicle weight (GVW), it comes equipped with a catalytic converter for '75.

At 4300 lbs, the standard GVW for the '75 Bronco remains unchanged from '74; that rating applies only to the 2-passenger model. If the optional rear seat is ordered (standard on the Ranger), the GVW increases to 4500 lbs. Bigger tires and stiffer rear springs raise it even further to 4600 lbs. If the Traction-Lok rear differential is ordered, then the GVW reaches its maximum of 4900 lbs.

CHASSIS/The Bronco uses a ladder-type frame and a separate steel body. The majority of four-wheel-drive vehicles use leaf springs front and rear, but Bronco has continued with coils in front and leafs in the rear. This permits greater wheel travel—but that requires better-than-average bounce control, which in turn means rapid wear on standard shocks. Bronco shock selection varies according to which GVW package is ordered.

For '75, Ford offers four different suspension packages, all referred to by GVW. The standard Bronco is a 2-passenger wagon with a GVW of 4300 lbs.; with that package you get standard springs, shocks and tires. The front springs are rated at the ground at 1075, the rear leaf springs are progressive with a ground rating of 1240, and the tires are E78X15B—the "B" signifying 4-ply. A rear seat is optional, and with it come heavier shocks to handle the additional passenger weight. Consequently, this elevates the 4300-lb. package to the optional 4500-lb. class; with it, maximum payload increases from 755 lbs. (4300) to 915. The next package is the 4600-lb. GVW and it includes: stiffer rear springs (1475), an increase in the rear gross axle weight rating (GAWR) from 2480 lbs. to 2900 lbs., heavy-duty shocks, and an increase in tire size from E78X15B to G78X15B. The larger tires and springs raise the payload from 915 to 1030 lbs. The largest package has a 4900-lb. GVW and differs from the 4600-lb. option in minimum rear GAWR, shocks and rear axle. The GAWR is 40 lbs. greater, the shocks are extra heavy-duty and the heavy-duty rear end in-

FORD BRONCO

cludes a Traction-Lok (limited-slip) differential, which gives it a capacity rating of 3300 lbs.—compared to the 2900-lb. axle of the 4600 package. The result is a payload increase from 1030 lbs. to 1315 lbs., which is only 150 lbs. less than Jeep's larger Cherokee Chief.

Optional tires are available on all four packages in sizes as large as G78X15D (8-ply) and L78X15B (4-ply). Standard steering is a worm and roller (non-power) with a ratio of 24:1 and a turning circle of 31 ft. It includes a linkage-type shock absorber. This was the only steering available until '73, when power became optional. For years, a major objection to the Bronco was its inadequate brakes. Non-power drum brakes are okay for street use, but most Bronco owners spend a lot of time off-pavement. Hard and frequent braking and puddle jumping makes those standard brakes fade faster than a blush on a burlesque queen—but it wasn't until '75 that Ford decided to listen. For '75, Bronco can be ordered with front disc brakes, and even though they're non-power, they're a great improvement on or off road. They resist fade from frequent use and water retention is minimal.

DRIVELINE/Due to the Bronco's infrequent changes, driveline discussion is strictly yawn city. You could probably say it all in one breath while drinking water at the same time—but for you, we'll take three and hold the water. As mentioned earlier, the Bronco was introduced as a '66 model with only one engine, a 170-cu.-in. 6. Later in the year, a 200-hp 289 V-8 was made optional. (The Bronco was the first 4X4 entry to offer a V-8.) The 6 produced 105 hp at 4400 rpm and 158 lbs.-ft. of torque at 2400 rpm. Its compression was 9.1:1, lifters were noisy

mechanicals and it breathed through a 1-bbl. carburetor. For '68, compression dropped to 8.7:1, resulting in a 5-hp drop and a reduction in torque to 156 lbs.-ft. at 2200 rpm. This situation continued until '72, when another drop in compression (8.3:1) brought a reduction in horsepower to 97; torque also dropped noticeably to 137 lbs.-ft. at 2600 rpm. For '72 the 6 was rejected by California's Air Resources Board as being too dirty. The old 170 was already choking from restrictive smog devices and adding one more would have cut power even further. The engine was obviously past due for a replacement. For '73 a new legal-everywhere 200-cu.-in. 6 took its place. Seven main bearings gave extra support to the crankshaft and made this engine stronger than the 170. Hydraulic lifters replaced the solids for quiet, maintenance-free operation. A 302 V-8—new for '68—remained the popular (optional) engine. For '75 there is no 6 and the only power choice is the 2-bbl. 302 V-8.

An all-synchro 3-speed was the only transmission until '73, when the optional Cruise-O-Matic was introduced. A 4-speed is not offered. The transfer case is a 2-speed Dana 20 with a 4-position floor-mounted selector. From the top, the positions are low 4X4, neutral, high 2-wheel drive and high 4X4. Lockable front hubs are standard and, as with any part-time system, the vehicle is in two-wheel drive when the hubs are unlocked. An option shared by few competitors is a limited-slip front differential. Getting stuck is less likely because both front wheels share traction duties, but when traction is marginal—light sand, mud or shallow snow—power is shifted from one wheel to the other; in reaction, the front end pulls with it.

BODY/The Bronco body is all-steel and it's available in only one style—a

2-door wagon. It's nothing fancy, just a very basic vehicle; for a few dollars more, though—$237 to be exact—you can buy a touch of "fancy" in the form of the Sport Bronco. It includes chrome bumpers rather than painted ones, a hard-board headliner, floor mats, door trim panels, touches of chrome, wheel covers and fender emblems. If you desire something fancier still, then you can get the Ranger for $431. It includes all of the above plus a swing-away rear spare tire with vinyl cover, a rear bench seat, carpeting, and hood and body stripes. A rear seat is required in the Ranger and optional in all but the 4300-lb.-GVW package.

The standard interior includes front buckets with retractable seat belts, door-mounted armrests, padded dash, windshield washers, sun visors, floor mats, heater and defroster. Speaking of heaters, Ford provides the long-johns crowd with a different type of heater—one for the engine block. It comes in a package called the Northland Special, which also includes Traction-Lok rear axle, 70-amp/hr. battery and 55-amp alternator.

TEST VEHICLE/When it came time to test a '75 Bronco, we contacted the proper people for a loaner; however, their 4X4's had apparently all been consigned. If it hadn't been for Bill Stroppe, these pages would have been empty. As many of you know, Stroppe is no stranger to Fords or off-road racing. He's the man who built the Mexican Road Race Lincolns in the early '50's and, currently, his shop is filled with Ford trucks being readied for upcoming off-road events. As the white-knuckled co-driver for Parnelli Jones, Bill's experience in off-roading has produced some consistent winners.

Our test car was Bill's personal Bronco, and although it was only a few months old the odometer showed 19,000 hard miles. It had pre-run the Baja 500 a couple of times but it was, nevertheless, ready for more. On customer request, Stroppe prepares the Baja Bronco for dealership sale. This package usually consists of dual shocks, padded roll bar, padded steering wheel and, for the rear, flared fenderwells. The test vehicle had the Baja options, but everything else was stock Ranger—with automatic transmission, power steering, front disc brakes and 302 V-8. The rear axle was the standard 3.50:1 ratio without Traction-Lok. The front axle was the 3.54 Dana. It had the standard Ranger (4500-lb. GVW) suspension, but the back seat had been removed.

OBSERVATIONS/En route to our off-road testing grounds, we fell by Cruse and Co.'s dyno facilities in Van Nuys, Calif. The Bronco was driven onto the dyno rollers and, within minutes, it looked more like a patient ready for surgery than a piece of machinery. A

BOX SCORE

Each of the following factors was rated on a scale of 1 to 10, as: Poor, 1 to 2. Fair, 3 to 4. Good, 5 to 7. Excellent, 8 to 10. An 8-point award, for example, was given if the category warranted better than a GOOD rating, but not the highest of EXCELLENT. Each book staff member compiled his own Box Score, then averages were drawn accordingly. Here's how the Ford Bronco stacked up.

On-pavement handling/performance	5
Off-pavement handling/performance	8
Maneuverability	8
Stability	7
Acceleration	7.5
Gearing	7.5
Braking	7.5
Hillclimbing ability	7.5
Prolonged travel comfort	6
City travel comfort	7
Interior access (front seat)	7
Rear seat access (if applicable)	N/A
Load space access	6
Engine access	8
Engine splash shielding	7.5
Instrument/controls layout and access	6.5
Visibility	7.5

sensor was placed in the tailpipe to determine the amounts of CO and HC being emitted. The Sun engine analyzer resembled an electrocardiograph as its wires were extended to the engine to monitor vital life signs.

ON-PAVEMENT/Motoring down the highway in a Bronco is reasonably comfortable; however, at certain speeds, the ride gets choppy as the front end pitches up and down. But with a wheelbase of only 92 ins., that's to be expected (although it's not nearly as rough as the ride of the 84-in. CJ-5). The shorter the wheelbase, the more agile and maneuverable the car—and off-road, the shorter CJ will go places the Bronco can't; but on the highway, the CJ owner pays for that with a greater sacrifice in comfort. The Bronco's power steering is responsive, and even with L78 tires parking is effortless. The center of gravity is lower in the Bronco than the CJ; as a result, the Bronco feels more stable when negotiating a curve, and tipping over is less likely.

OFF-PAVEMENT/After entering the Park, we shifted into four-wheel low, dismounted and locked the hubs. We started off with a series of whoop-de-do's (closely spaced ruts), and then began looking for a saddle horn to hold on to . . . that Bronco was really bucking. But that's normal for the short wheelbase. If the ruts had been farther apart, we could have jumped from peak to peak. The stream was next: The water was about 6 ins. deep and the Bronco entered at 25 mph; it exited without a sputter or a trace of brake fade. The Bronco got a running start in Drive and with a steady throttle climbed the 40° hill. The peak levels sharply and a longer-wheelbase truck might have gotten high-centered—but the Bronco crested it without any problem.

TRAILER AND RV USE/Ford doesn't recommend towing trailers of more than 2000 lbs.; furthermore, they don't even offer any trailering options. For trailers up to 2000 lbs., the Bronco should be equipped with the 4500-lb.-GVW package, the V-8, a 3.50:1 rear axle, larger radiator, power steering, front disc brakes, G78X15 tires and a frame-mounted hitch.

SUMMATION/As a utility vehicle, the Bronco does a good job. For those wanting a weekly commuter car/weekend booniemobile combination, a '73 or newer model is the one to buy. The Bronco is more comfortable than the CJ-5, it's got more cargo space, and the transfer case selector is easier to operate than any other floor-mounted unit. Power disc brakes should be offered as an option, as well as a 4-speed for more economical highway operation—and, hopefully, the catalytic converter will be dropped from the Bronco before the brush fires begin. 🐎

FORD BRONCO—GENERAL

Curb weight (lbs.)	3800
Payload (lbs.)	650
Track (ins.) front/rear	57.5/57.5
Overall length (ins.)	113.3
Overall height (ins.)	71
Overall width (ins.)	69
Overhang (ins.) front/rear	27/33
Ground clearance (ins.):	
Mid-wheelbase	13
At lowest differential	7.5
At lowest chassis point/component	13/muffler
Approach angle (degrees)	40
Departure angle (degrees)	26
Floor height (ins.) front door	21
Floor height (ins.) tailgate	28
Tailgate width (ins.)	58
Tailgate height (ins.)	21.5
Cargo length (ins.) w/rear seat	N/A
Cargo length (ins.) w/o rear seat	54
Cargo width (ins.) extreme	55
Cargo width (ins.) between wheelwells	39.5
Cargo height (ins.) (N/A pickups)	43.5
Steering (turns lock-to-lock)	N/A

ENGINES

	Displacement (cu. ins.)	Bore (ins.)	Stroke (ins.)	Compression ratio	Net hp @ rpm	Net torque @ rpm
Standard	302 V-8 (2-bbl.)	4.002	3.000	8.0:1	125 @ 3600	218 @ 2200

DRIVETRAIN COMBINATIONS

Engine	Transmission	Transfer case	Axle ratios
302 V-8	3-speed manual **Automatic**	**Conventional**	3.50/**3.54**/ 4.09/4.11

CHASSIS

		GVW's (lbs.)		
Model	Wheelbase (ins.)	Stand.	Opt.	Turning circle (ft.)
Ford Bronco	92	4300	4500 4600 4900	31

Brakes		Tire sizes		Steering		Fuel capacity (gals.)	
Stand.	Opt.	Stand.	Opt.	Stand.	Opt.	Stand.	Opt.
Drum	**Disc/drum**	E78X15B to	**78X15B**	Conventional	**Power**	12.2	7.5 (aux.)

BASE PRICE
(FOB factory. Manufacturer's suggested retail.)

Model	Price
Ford Bronco	$5347.30

TEST VEHICLE PERFORMANCE

Fuel consumption (mpg)—on-pavement	11.4
Fuel consumption (mpg)—off-pavement	4.2
On-pavement acceleration: 0-30 mph (secs.)	5
On-pavement acceleration: 0-55 mph (secs.)	13
Rear wheel horsepower @ 2500 rpm	70
Rear wheel horsepower @ 3000 rpm	84
Rear wheel horsepower @ 3500 rpm	90

Emissions at idle: **100** HC parts per millio.

● Certain equipment, option combinations may not be available in some ....

Sport Bronco with optional radio, rear seat, and special order solid exterior paint treatment (in addition to front winch and bumper)

FORD BRONCOS HAVE ALL THE RIGHT ANGLES

Rugged Ford Broncos combine all the right angles for off-road agility with V-8 performance and your choice of power and dress-up options. A spirited 302-cu. in. V-8 is standard, and features Solid State Ignition system for "breakerless" electrical reliability. Both SelectShift Cruise-O-Matic and power steering are optional. SelectShift Cruise-O-Matic gives you a choice of fully automatic or manual shifting for driving ease in traffic with full off-road control. Ford's integral type power steering provides quick steering response and easy handling in some of the roughest terrain.

Bronco's interior is uncluttered, functional, roomy and practical. Sporty front bucket seats with foam padding in seat cushion and back are standard. A two-passenger rear seat is available. Standard seats are upholstered with attractive, long-wearing vinyl. The convenient transmission shift lever is in the familiar steering-column location.

Bronco interior with optional Ranger Package, Cruise-O-Matic and radio

Sport Bronco interior

Bronco's tight body and suspended foot pedals help seal out noise, dust and road splash. Fresh air heater/defroster, lockable glove compartment, dome light, padded instrument panel, two-speed electric windshield wipers, sun visors, vinyl-coated rubber floor mat and painted channel-type steel bumpers (front and rear) are all standard.

AND OPTIONS FOR DRIVING EASE, COMFORT!

POWER

Sport Bronco features, in addition to or in place of standard, include: Vinyl door trim panels with bright moldings • Hardboard headliner with bright retainers • Vinyl parchment simulated carpet front floor mat with bright retainers (matching rear mat with optional rear seat) • Cigar lighter • Steering wheel with woodtone horn pad • Bright-metal windshield and window frames • Bright grille frame molding and tailgate release handle • Bright headlight, side marker light and rear reflector bezels • Argent painted grille • Bright bumpers • Bright front bumper guards • Bright-metal wheel covers.

Ranger Package features, in addition to or in place of Sport Bronco, include: Color-keyed, full carpeting (including tailgate and wheelhousings) • Color-keyed vinyl door trim panels with burl woodtone accent • Color-keyed vinyl trim with insulation on rear quarter panels • Cloth and vinyl seat trim in ginger, blue or green • Color-keyed instrument panel paint • Hood and lower bodyside tape stripes, white stripe with orange accent • Swing-away spare tire carrier • Spare tire cover, white vinyl with orange accent and Bronco insignia • Coat hook.

FORD BRONCO

It's 12 years young and getting better with age.

BACKGROUND/Except for foreign imports, Jeep had the four-wheel-drive market pretty much to itself until 1961, when International introduced the Scout. The Scout, although underpowered even by contemporary standards, enjoyed sales growth for its first 5 years. Armed with this information and not wanting to butt heads with the "old man" of the off-road field, Ford minimized risks by patterning its new truck after the Scout. The plan worked. The public responded and Bronco sales figures began to grow.

About the same time Bronco was introduced, off-road racing began taking its first tentative steps out of infancy toward the adulthood of full-blown professionalism that it enjoys today. Initially the Bronco looked very promising as a family four-wheeler. By its size, shape, wheelbase and width, however, the Bronco lent itself immediately to racing, which it has dominated up until the recent introduction of the Jeep CJ-7.

Such off-road racing greats as Parnelli Jones, Larry Minor, Rodney Hall and Bill Rush signed up to drive Broncos for Bill Stroppe in the early days, and they almost literally drove everyone else off the racecourses. Broncos even saw competition on the slopes of Mt. Fuji in a Japanese off-road event. Continual victories in off-road racing proved Bronco's durability, and sales of the vehicle were sustained at a comfortable level.

The profit margin, however, was not great enough to warrant Ford engineers spending a great deal of money on new product development. Many minor engineering changes and a one-step-in-front-of-the-sheriff approach to the smog control problem kept Bronco engineers busy for many years. Although rumors of a new, larger Bronco waiting to appear on the horizon have been bandied about since before 1970, they should be taken with a large grain of salt. Ford personnel continue to deny any knowledge of such a vehicle. We'll just have to wait and see. The rumors do say the new vehicle will be comparable in size to the Blazer/Ramcharger class.

The model year 1977 marks the 12th year of production for the Ford Bronco with virtually no sheetmetal changes and very few major under-the-skin engineering changes. The 1966 debut of

Ford's new idea saw the Bronco powered by a 170-cu.-in. inline 6-cyl. engine, which was quickly supplemented with a 289-cu.-in. V-8 option for the '67 model year. The Bronco's 3-speed manual transmission was the first all-synchro trans to be offered in a 4X4 and one of the strongest 3-speeds ever made. It is still the standard transmission, with a C-4 Cruise-O-Matic 3-speed automatic as an option.

For the first 3 years of production, Broncos were covered with an excellent warranty (5 years or 50,000 miles, whichever came first). However, after a few years, some weak links in the Bronco chain began to show, and the guarantee period was drastically reduced to the present 12 months or 12,000 miles. One of the more glaring defects in the Bronco's initial design was vacuum-powered windshield wipers—not very helpful during a blizzard. These were changed to electric wipers for '69. (It has been said, under one's breath of course, that the Bronco was designed so quickly that somehow no one remembered to include electrics in the approved design.)

Another engineering change in '69 was the upgrading of the front differential; Ford changed from a Dana 30 to a Dana 44, increasing ring gear size from 7½ ins. to 9 ins. In 1969, really a banner year for the Bronco, it also received a different V-8 engine option—a 205-hp, 302-cu.-in., updated version of the 289. Why the 351W was not also included in the option list is a question that has long been asked among four-wheeler enthusiasts.

Bouncing merrily along, the Bronco remained untouched in its engineering until 1973, when it was again marked heavily by the engineering pencil. It was awarded the C-4 automatic option, a larger 6-cyl. (200-cu.-in.) engine as the standard powerplant and power steering as an option. The 6-cyl. was dropped in 1975, and the 302 is the only engine currently available in the '77 Bronco.

GENERAL/Like the Jeep and Scout, the Bronco was designed as a utility vehicle—a bobtail. Broncos were built for families that liked to have fun off-road, but needed more room than the basic CJ-5 afforded—room for both cargo and kids. It was also built to take abuse, abuse that a working off-roader

must take to get the work done for the rancher, the farmer and the hunter. For those people, the Bronco served its purpose well.

For 7 years, however, passenger-car frills like power steering and automatic transmission were not included, because the Bronco was intended to be rugged—not necessarily comfortable. People who couldn't afford the price or size of a Blazer bought Broncos instead; for them the truck was a sports/utility wagon, even though it was designed for pure utility. During the week it took the kids to school, shared car-pool duties or carried the groceries. On weekends it was out in the boonies, going where a lot of Blazers couldn't. Off-pavement, the Bronco really shone (with the proper tires). But as a commuter, it became literally pretty tiring to operate.

Apparently an increasing number of owners were using Broncos for more than utility purposes, and eventually the complaints came rolling in. Standard steering made parking difficult, and long rides *felt* longer. In city traffic, an automatic was definitely needed. These complaints were finally heeded in 1973, and the Bronco became a much more versatile vehicle.

As mentioned, for 1975 the 6-cyl. engine was dropped and the 302 became the standard engine. Front disc brakes (non-power) were first offered in 1976 as an option; for '77 they are standard, with a power-assist unit as an option. Because the Bronco is rated below 6000 lbs. gross vehicle weight (GVW), it comes equipped with a catalytic converter. The converter and unleaded fuel were introduced to the Bronco in '75.

At 4400 lbs., the standard GVW for the '77 Bronco has been upgraded from 1975's 4300 lbs. That minimum rating still only applies to the 2-passenger model. If the optional rear seat is ordered (required in the Ranger package), the GVW increases to 4600 lbs. If the Traction-Lok rear differential is ordered (as in the test vehicle we drove), then the GVW reaches its maximum of 4900 lbs.

CHASSIS/The Bronco uses a ladder-type frame and a separate steel body. The majority of four-wheel-drive vehicles use leaf springs front and rear, but Bronco has continued with coils in

FORD BRONCO

front and leaves in the rear. This permits greater wheel travel, but that in turn requires better-than-average bounce control, which means rapid wear on standard shocks. For this reason, most serious off-roaders purchase aftermarket double shock assemblies for the front axle, increasing the life of the shocks and improving handling at the same time. Bronco factory shock selection varies according to which GVW package is ordered.

For '77, Ford offers three different suspension packages, all referred to by GVW. The standard Bronco is a 2-passenger wagon with a GVW of 4400 lbs.; with that package you get standard springs, shocks and tires. There are two variations of front springs available on the Bronco, both coils. Standard coils have a capacity at the ground of 1140 lbs. each; the optional rate is 1190 lbs. per coil. The rear leaf springs are progressive, with a ground rating of 1240 lbs., and the tires are E78X15B—the "B" signifying a 4-ply rating.

A rear seat is optional, and with it come heavier shocks to handle the additional passenger weight. Consequently, this option elevates the 4400-lb. package to the 4600-lb. class. It also increases maximum payload from 540 lbs. to 740 lbs.

The largest GVW package has a 4900-lb. GVWR and differs from the 4600-lb. option in minimum rear GAWR shocks and rear axle. The GAWR is 180 lbs. greater, the shocks are extra heavy-duty, and the heavy-duty rear end includes a Traction-Lok (limited-slip) differential, which gives it a capacity rating of 2840 lbs., compared to the 2460-lb. axle of the 4600-lb. package. The result is a payload

increase from 740 lbs. to 1040 lbs.

Standard steering is a worm and roller (non-power) with a ratio of 24:1; it includes a linkage-type shock absorber. This was the only steering available until '73, when a power steering unit became an option.

For years a major objection to the Bronco was its inadequate brakes. Non-power drum brakes are okay for street use, but most Bronco owners spend a great deal of time off-pavement. Hard, frequent braking and puddle jumping make drum brakes fade faster than a blush on a burlesque queen, but it wasn't until '75 that Ford decided to act. For '75, Bronco could be ordered with front disc brakes. Even though they were non-power, they were still a great improvement, on- or off-road. They resisted fade from frequent use and water retention was minimal. These non-power discs are now standard, with power discs optional.

DRIVELINE/Only the Bronco powertrain option list is shorter than its list of engineering changes over the years. One engine (302 V-8), two transmissions (3-speed manual or Cruise-O-Matic), one transfer case (Dana 20) and one gear ratio (3.50:1) are available. About the only choices you have when ordering a new '77 Bronco are color and what operations you wish assisted with power: steering, braking or shifting. Lockable front hubs are no longer standard but are optional. Also, front "posi" is no longer available. For years, Bronco was the only four-wheel-drive vehicle with this option.

BODY/The Bronco body is all-steel and available in only one style—a 2-door wagon. It's nothing fancy, just a very basic vehicle. For a few dollars more, though, you can buy a touch of fancy in the form of the Sport Bronco. It includes chrome bumpers rather than painted ones, a hard board head-

liner, floor mats, door trim panels, touches of chrome, wheel covers and fender emblems. If you desire something fancier still, you can get the Ranger. It includes all of the above plus a swing-away rear spare tire with vinyl cover, carpeting, and hood and body stripes. Included in both trim packages is the front passenger bucket seat and sun visor. A rear seat (bench type) is required in the Ranger and optional in all but the 4400-lb.-GVW package.

The standard interior includes one front bucket with retractable seat belts, door-mounted armrests, padded dash, windshield washers, a sun visor, floor mats, heater (a damn good one!) and defroster. Speaking of heaters, Ford provides the long-johns crowd with a different type of heater—one for the engine block. It comes in a package called the Northland Special, which also includes a Traction-Lok rear axle, 70-amp-hr battery, 60-amp alternator and 50/50 antifreeze mix.

TEST VEHICLE/When it again became time to test a Bronco, we contacted the proper people for a loaner, and we were again sent to Bill Stroppe and Son. This time, though, it was a factory car and not Bill's personal off-road rig. It was a bright red Ranger with an auto trans and heavy-duty suspension. A Traction-Lok rear end provided the go-power and power disc brakes provided the slow-power. With all the extras, this little Dearborn jewel listed at $7206.50. The option list alone nearly broke two grand.

In looking over the rig, we really didn't expect too much from it off-road because of the street tread on the G78X15D tires. But the Bronco fooled us—it turned out to be the best climber of the eight vehicles tested for this issue. It boggles the mind to consider what it might have done with decent off-road rubber. Forward visibility rivals that of the CJ, except for the wiper motor bulkhead. This overhead bulge forces the driver to crouch over the steering wheel during off-pavement maneuvers in order to see up hillsides or check overhanging branches.

Another off-road fault is the smog system, although 4000 miles on the odometer without a tune-up could also be the culprit. Hitting a bump hard caused a dashpot effect, in which raw fuel choked off power momentarily. This could get a little hairy during steep hillclimbs. Definitely attributable to smog controls is the increase in rpm at idle whenever the engine heats up. A vacuum-controlled device on the carb increases engine rpm in order to burn expanded fuel. A Ford engineer indicated that this could be controlled quite simply by rerouting the vacuum tube to a petcock attached to the dashboard. The amount of vacuum

---

BOX SCORE

Each of the following factors was rated on a scale of 1 to 10, as: Poor, 1 to 2. Fair, 3 to 4. Good, 5 to 7. Excellent, 8 to 10. An 8-point award, for example, was given if the category warranted better than a GOOD rating, but not the highest of EXCELLENT. Each book staff member compiled his own Box Score; then averages were drawn accordingly. Here's how the Ford Bronco stacked up:

On-pavement handling/performance	6.6
Off-pavement handling/performance	7
Maneuverability	9.2
Stability	7.3
Acceleration	6
Gearing	6.3
Braking	6.3
Hillclimbing ability	8.5
Prolonged travel comfort	7
City travel comfort	7.2
Interior access (front seat)	7
Rear seat access (if applicable)	6.3
Load space access	7.3
Engine access	7.3
Engine splash shielding	7.5
Instrument/controls layout and access	7.3
Visibility	8.3

could then be controlled from inside the cab. This little rpm-increasing device can be extremely dangerous off-road, especially when you're trying to descend a hill.

One test driver, long associated with Broncos, voiced his dissatisfaction with the new transfer case shift lever. He preferred the earlier T-handle, which he said made shifting much easier. Speedometer error was negligible on the Bronco; the speedo read 28 at 30 mph and was dead-on at 55 mph. With Ford's new engineering features on the 302 V-8, including Dura-Spark, the gas mileage figures should have been better, but the sooty exhaust pipe indicated that raw gas was being blown away needlessly. A tune-up would undoubtedly provide a possible 40-50% increase in mileage.

OBSERVATIONS/While not the most popular vehicle among the staff (the CJ-7 and Terra pickup vied for this somewhat dubious honor), the Bronco was in the top three. A direct competitor in the marketplace with Jeep's CJ-7 (if Ford does decide to cancel the Bronco, Jeep will reap the rewards), the Bronco is fun to drive both on and off the road. Adding dual shocks up front and maybe a stabilizer bar in the rear would give it cat-like stability. A judicious choice of gearing and tires would improve both hillclimbing and acceleration.

ON-PAVEMENT/Motoring down the highway in a Bronco is reasonably comfortable; however, at certain speeds the ride gets choppy because the front end pitches up and down. But with a wheelbase of only 92 ins., that's to be expected. At that, it's not nearly as rough as the ride of an 84-in. Jeep CJ-5.

OFF-PAVEMENT/The Bronco was among the top three (all Fords) in water shielding, both for engine and interior. Repeated water dunkings and stream crossings failed to make the engine sputter, the brakes fade or the driver damp.

TRAILER AND RV USE/Ford doesn't recommend towing trailers of more than 2000 lbs. Furthermore, they don't even offer any trailering options. For trailers up to 2000 lbs., the Bronco should be equipped with the 4600-lb. GVW package, larger radiator, power steering, G78X15 tires and a frame-mounted hitch.

SUMMATION/As a utility vehicle, the Bronco does a good job. For those wanting a weekday commuter car/weekend booniemobile combination, a '73 or newer model is the one to buy. The Bronco is more comfortable than its direct competition and it's got more cargo space as well.

FORD BRONCO—GENERAL

Curb weight (lbs.)	3860
Payload (lbs.)	1040
Track (ins.) front/rear	58.5/57.5
Overall length (ins.)	161
Overall height (ins.)	73
Overall width (ins.)	74.25
Overhang (ins.) front/rear	28.5/33.25
Ground clearance (ins.):	
Mid-wheelbase	15.5
At lowest differential	7.25
At lowest chassis point/component	12/exhaust
Approach angle (degrees)	43
Departure angle (degrees)	37
Floor height (ins.) front door	22.5
Floor height (ins.) tailgate	29.5
Tailgate width (ins.)	55
Tailgate height (ins.)	37.5
Cargo length (ins.) w/rear seat	13
Cargo length (ins.) w/o rear seat	53
Cargo width (ins.) extreme	54
Cargo width (ins.) between wheelwells	39
Cargo height (ins.—N/A pickups)	41.5
Steering (turns lock-to-lock)	4.25

ENGINES

	Displacement (cu. ins.)	Bore (ins.)	Stroke (ins.)	Compression ratio	Net hp @ rpm	Net torque @ rpm
Standard	302 V-8 (2-bbl.)	4.002	3.000	8.4:1	133 @ 3600	236 @ 1800

DRIVETRAIN COMBINATIONS

Engine	Transmission	Transfer case	Axle ratios
302 V-8	3-speed manual Automatic	Conventional	3.50 / 3.54

CHASSIS

		GVW's (lbs.)		
Model	Wheelbase (ins.)	Stand.	Opt.	Turning circle (ft.)
Ford Bronco	92	4400	4600 4900	33 R; 34.1 L

Brakes		Tire sizes		Steering		Fuel capacity (gals.)	
Stand.	Opt.	Stand.	Opt.	Stand.	Opt.	Stand.	Opt.
Drum	Disc/drum	E78X15B to	G78X15D	Conventional	Power	14	7.5 (aux.)

BASE PRICE
(FOB factory. Manufacturer's suggested retail.)

Model	Price
Bronco	$5260.05

TEST VEHICLE PERFORMANCE

Fuel consumption (mpg)—on-pavement	9.81
Fuel consumption (mpg)—off-pavement	5.04
On-pavement acceleration: 0-30 mph (secs.)	4.93
On-pavement acceleration: 0-55 mph (secs.)	11.8
Rear wheel horsepower @ 2000 rpm	56
Rear wheel horsepower @ 2500 rpm	76
Rear wheel horsepower @ 3000 rpm	90

Emissions at idle: **600** HC parts per million; **4.5%** carbon monoxide.

● Certain equipment, option combinations may not be available in some areas. See your dealer.

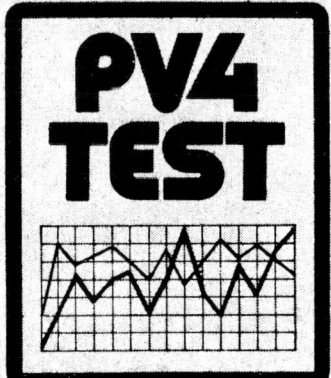

INT'L SCOUT VS. FORD BRONCO

ONE IS EXCELLENT ON THE PAVEMENT, THE OTHER IS EXCELLENT OFF THE PAVEMENT

SCOUT VS. BRONCO. That sort of has a nice ring about it and when we decided to do this comparison of the two popular mid-size 4-wheel-drive utility vehicles we felt that it would be worthwhile to make a long-distance trip in them to really learn what they are like. In addition, we wanted to get in some snow time and the nearest white stuff we could find was in the mountains of Utah near Salt Lake City. Well, we reasoned, that's only 750 miles away and the round trip would enable us to become thoroughly familiar and conversant with the two vehicles.

The Scout from International and the Bronco from Ford are two of the older 4wd utility vehicles around. The Scout seems to have been with us since year one and the Bronco made its appearance in 1966, both predating the Blazer, Ramcharger, Cherokee and others. Over the years both vehicles have built up a substantial following among off-pavement enthusiasts and a good argument can be

heard on either side any time 4wd folks get together.

These two vehicles are essentially similar in size although the redesign of the Scout in 1973 with the concomitant change in designation to Scout II has put this vehicle in a sort of in-between state. . .larger than the Bronco but smaller than the Cherokee, Blazer and Ramcharger.

The Bronco has a wheelbase of 92 inches and an overall length of 152.1 inches while the Scout II stands on a 100-in. wheelbase with a total length of 165.8 inches. Conversely, the Scout II is less tall than the Bronco—66.2 versus 70.6 inches. It could be argued that the size difference between the two puts the Scout more in the class with the bigger 4wds, but we are resisting that train of thought due to tradition and the fact that we still feel they are close enough to be valid competitors. Also, anyone who has done much off-pavement driving in all of these vehicles as we have will realize that the difference in size between the Scout→

Both Bronco and Scout are fitted with 3-speed manuals as standard equipment, but Scout offers 4-speed optional gearbox while the Bronco has only a 3-speed automatic optionally available.

Bronco has drum brakes all around, trailing arm and coil spring suspension in the front and longitudinal leaf springs in the rear. Ford offers limited-slip differentials for both front and rear drive units. Free-running front hubs are standard.

and the Bronco does not *feel* as great as the difference between the Scout and the Blazer, for example. Size differentials seem to take on a geometric rate of growth at a certain point and become accentuated.

A quick rundown of the vehicles shows that the Scout II comes with a 4-cylinder engine as standard equipment and this is new for 1975. Actually, it's a return to the past when the old Scouts always came with a 4-cylinder powerplant and was done in recognition of the interest in fuel saving. The base engine for the Ford Bronco is the 302-cu-in. V-8 and, in fact, this is now the only engine for the Bronco. The emission situation has caused the loss of the 6-cylinder Ford engines for Bronco application due to its low volume output in comparison with the remainder of the Ford truck line. Both the Scout and the Bronco have a 3-speed manual transmission as standard equipment but the Scout offers a choice of a 4-speed manual or 3-speed automatic for extra money while the Ford only has a 3-speed automatic on the option list.

Other dissimilarities worth mentioning are the Scout's choice of manual or automatic front hubs, both costing extra while the Bronco has free-running front hubs as standard equipment, but not automatic. Ford is the only manufacturer of 4wds which offers limited-slip differentials for the front as well as the rear. The Scout has front disc brakes as standard equipment and the Bronco has drums all the way around with no provision for the discs. In terms of suspension, the Scout utilizes the more common leaf springs on a live axle both front and rear while the Ford has trailing arms and coil springs on the front with the leaf spring arrangement at the back.

In terms of money, the basic list price for the Scout is $4712, FOB Fort Wayne, Ind. while the Bronco has a base price of $4973 at Detroit. However, it should be pointed out that the Bronco price does include the V-8 engine and the front hubs along with the 2-speed Dana 20 transfer case instead of the single-speed as in the Scout's base price.

We were quite lucky to get our hands on two of the first

Side-by-side placement of Bronco and Scout II emphasizes longer wheelbase of the International vehicle. And this photo emphasizes Scout II's longitudinal front springs in contrast to the Bronco's coil spring setup.

Scout II interior has the look of a family station wagon rather than the look of a rough country utility vehicle.

Column shift, stark panel, floor-mounted transfer case shift lever, lend a spartan look to the Ford Bronco.

'75 models of each vehicle with the Bronco coming to us through the courtesy of Dick Landfield at Fairway Ford in Placentia, Calif. Early on a Wednesday morning we began the long drive to the Utah snow, planning on being back in southern California by Friday night. We got our first glimpse of snow on the peaks of Utah late that afternoon and after spending the night in Salt Lake, we bundled our California bodies up and proceeded to take the Scout and the Bronco into that magical white ground.

We were delighted to find that both of the vehicles performed in an admirable style throughout the day but, of course, we were never in any powder deeper than about seven inches. On the other hand, it was such a sunny day the snow was melting and that gave it a nice slippery quality which allowed us to obtain a good feel for the tractive power of both vehicles.

The trip totalled just about 1600 miles and was primarily highway driving. We did some 75 or 80 miles off the pavement in Utah at the upper elevations and threw in a short off-pavement drive in the desert area near Zion National Park to get a few more photos.

Let's take a look now at the measurable differences we found in our normal tests of the two 4wds and then get into the impressions we received druing our driving of them.

Acceleration measurements at Orange County International Raceway showed that the Bronco was somewhat better than the Scout, getting to 60 mph in almost two seconds less time. The difference in the quarter-mile run, however, was much less with the Bronco beating the Scout by only .4 seconds. Both

INT'L SCOUT

PRICES

Basic list, FOB Ft. Wayne, Ind.
Scout II Traveltop 4wd $4712

Standard Equipment: 196-cu-in. inline 4-cyl engine, 3-spd manual transmission, single-speed transfer case, full instrumentation, front bench seat, heater/defroster, 2-spd electric wiper/washers, backup lights, painted front bumper, power front disc brakes, H78 x 15B tires, electronic ignition

ENGINES

Standard ...... 196-cu-in. inline 4-cyl
Bore x stroke, in. ...... 4.125 x 3.656
Compression ratio 8.02:1
Net horsepower @ rpm ..... 92 @ 3600
Net torque @ rpm, lb-ft .... 164 @ 2000
Type fuel required .. leaded or unleaded

Optional 304-cu-in. V-8 .... $99
Bore x stroke, in. ...... 3.875 x 3.218
Compression ratio 8.19:1
Net horsepower @ rpm ..... 141 @ 4000
Net torque @ rpm, lb-ft .... 243 @ 2400
Type fuel required .. leaded or unleaded

Optional 345-cu-in. V-8 .... $135
Bore x stroke, in. ...... 3.875 x 3.656
Compression ratio 8.05:1
Net horsepower @ rpm .... 158 @ 3600
Net torque @ rpm, lb-ft .... 288 @ 2000
Type fuel required .. leaded or unleaded

DRIVE TRAIN

Standard transmission: .... 3-spd manual
Clutch dia., in. .... 10.5 & 11.0
Transmission ratios: 3rd 1.00:1
2nd 1.85:1
1st 2.80:1
Synchromesh ...... all forward gears

Optional 4-spd manual $125
Transmission ratios: 4th 1.00:1
3rd 1.41:1
2nd 2.41:1
1st 4.02:1
Synchromesh ...... 2nd, 3rd & 4th gear

Optional 3-spd automatic $269
Transmission ratios: 3rd 1.00:1
2nd 1.45:1
1st 2.45:1

Rear axle type .... semi-floating hypoid
Final drive ratios: 3.07:1, 3.54:1, 4.09:1
Overdrive .... none

Free-running front hubs:
manual $82
automatic $120
Limited slip differential $68
Transfer case .... single & 2-spd
Transfer case ratios .. 1.00:1 & 2.03:1

CHASSIS & BODY

Body/frame: ladder-type frame with separate steel body

Brakes (std): front, 11.75-in. dia. disc; rear, 11 x 2.5-in. drums
Brake swept area, sq in. 417
Swept area/ton (max load) 134
Power brakes .... std

Steering type (std) ...... worm & roller
Steering ratio 24.1
Power steering $159
Power steering ratio 17.5:1
Turning circle, ft 34

Wheel size (std) .... 15 x 6.0JK
Optional wheel sizes: ...... 15 x 7.0JJ
Tire size (std) .... H78 x 15LRB
Optional tire sizes: HR78 x 15 steel belted radials

SUSPENSION

Front suspension: semi-elliptic leaf springs on live axle with tube shocks
Front axle capacity, lb 3200
Optional .... none
Rear suspension: semi-elliptic leaf springs on live axle with tube shocks
Rear axle capacity, lb 3500
Optional .... none
Additional suspension options: HD front springs and shocks, $10; HD rear springs, $18

ACCOMMODATION

Standard seats ... full width front bench
Optional seats: 1/3-2/3 split back front bench, $40; folding full width rear bench, $136; front buckets, $121
Headroom in. 36.0
Accelerator pedal to seatback, max . 46.0
Steering wheel to seatback, max ... 18.7
Seat to ground 31.5
Floor to ground 17.5

Unobstructed load space (length x width x height) in.
With seats in place ..... 40 x 41 x 41.2
Rear folded or removed 66.5 x 41 x 41.2
Tailgate (width x height) ...... 53 x 22

INSTRUMENTATION

Instruments: speedometer, odometer, fuel gauge, oil pressure, water temp, ammeter
Warning lights: hazard warning, brake system warning, front axle engaged signal light
Optional: .... none

GENERAL

Curb weight, lb (test model) 4400
GVWR (test model) 6200
Optional GVWRs .... none

Wheelbase, in. 100.0
Track, front/rear 57.1/57.1
Overall length 165.8
Overall height 66.2

Overall width 70.0
Overhang, front/rear 23.0/43.0

Approach angle, degrees 42
Departure angle 21

Ground clearances (test model):
Front axle 8.2
Rear axle 8.2
Oil pan 13.7
Transfer case 11.9
Fuel tank 13.3
Exhaust system (lowest point) .. 11.3
Fuel tank capacity (U.S. gal) 19
Auxiliary tank .... none

PERFORMANCE DATA

TEST MODEL

Scout II Traveltop, 304-cu-in. V-8, automatic transmission, 2-spd transfer case, rear stepbumper, free-running front hubs, HD front springs & shocks, HD rear springs, power steering, dual exhausts, trailer wiring, AM radio, 2-tone paint, modulated fan, fuel tank skid plate, evaporative emission control, bucket seats, custom interior, deluxe exterior trim, luggage rack, folding rear seat, air conditioning, storage box console, 3.54:1 limited slip rear axle, H78 x 15B tires
West Coast list price $7570

ACCELERATION

Time to speed, sec:
0-30 mph 5.0
0-45 mph 9.2
0-60 mph 15.3
Standing start, ¼-mile, sec 19.6
Speed at end, mph 68

SPEED IN GEARS

High range,
3rd (4000 rpm) 90
2nd (4000 rpm) 63
1st (4000 rpm) 38

Low range,
3rd (4000 rpm) 44
2nd (4000 rpm) 31
1st (4000 rpm) 19
Engine rpm @ 55 mph 2500

BRAKE TESTS

Pedal pressure required for ½-g deceleration rate from 60 mph, lb 38
Stopping distance from 60 mph, ft . 158
Fade: Percent increase in pedal pressure for 6 stops from 60 mph 52
Overall brake rating .... excellent

INTERIOR NOISE

Idle in neutral, dBA 63
Maximum during acceleration 79
At steady 60 mph cruising speed ... 78

OFF PAVEMENT

Hillclimbing ability .... excellent
Maneuverability .... very good
Turnaround capability ...... very good
Handling .... very good
Ride .... excellent

ON PAVEMENT

Handling .... very good
Ride .... very good
Driver visibility .... good
Driver comfort .... very good
Engine response .... good

FUEL CONSUMPTION

Normal driving, mpg 14.4
Off pavement 10.8
Range, normal driving, miles 273
Range, off pavement 205

FORD BRONCO

PRICES

Basic list, FOB Detroit
Bronco U-100 . . . . $4973

Standard Equipment: 302-cu-in. V-8, 3-spd manual transmission, 2-spd transfer case, bucket seats, free-running front hubs, heater/defroster, 2-spd electric wiper/washers, painted bumpers, backup lights, E78 x 15B tires, full instrumentation, electronic ignition

ENGINES

Standard 302-cu-in. V-8
Bore x stroke, in. . . . . .4.00 x 3.00
Compression ratio 8.0:1
Net horsepower @ rpm . . . . 125 @ 3600*
Net torque @ rpm, lb-ft. . . . 218 @ 2200*
Type fuel required . . . . .unleaded only
*For Calif. hp rating is 121 @ 3400 and torque is 216 @ 1600
Optional . . . . none

DRIVE TRAIN

Standard transmission: . . . . 3-spd manual
Clutch dia., in. 11.0
Transmission ratios: 3rd 1.00:1
　　2nd 1.75:1
　　1st 2.99:1
Synchromesh . . . . .all forward gears
Optional . . . . 3-spd automatic $246

Transmission ratios: 3rd 1.00:1
　　2nd 1.46:1
　　1st 2.46:1

Rear axle type . . . . . semi-floating hypoid
Final drive ratios: 3.54:1 front/3.50:1 rear; 4.09:1 front/4.11:1 rear
Overdrive . . . . none
Free-running front hubs . . . . std

Limited slip differential . . . . $106 (front), $56 (2900 lb. axle); $63 (3300 lb. axle)

Transfer case . . . . .Dana 2-spd
Transfer case ratios: . . . 2.46 & 1.00:1

CHASSIS & BODY

Body/frame: ladder-type frame with separate steel body
Brakes (std): front, 11 x 2-in. drum; rear, 10 x 2.5-in. drum (11 x 1.75-in. w/3300-lb. axle)
Brake swept area, sq in. 295 (258)
　Swept area/ton (max load) . . .120 (105)
Power brakes . . . . .none
Steering type (std) . . . . . .worm & roller
Steering ratio 24:1
Power steering $173
Power steering ratio 17:1
Turning circle, ft. 31

Wheel size (std) . . . . .15 x 5.5K
Optional wheel sizes: . . . . .none
Tire size (std) . . . . E78 x 15B
Optional tire sizes: G78 x 15B, G78 x 15D, L78 x 15B, 7.00 x 15C

SUSPENSION

Front suspension: trailing arms and coil springs on live axle with tube shocks
Front axle capacity, lb. 3000
　Optional . . . . .none
Rear suspension: leaf springs on live axle with tube shocks
Rear axle capacity, lb. 2900
　Optional 3300
Additional suspension options: HD front and rear springs, $14

ACCOMMODATION

Standard seats . . . . front buckets
Optional seats . . . . rear bench $107
Headroom in. 38.6
Accelerator pedal to seatback, max. . . 43.7
Steering wheel to seatback, max. . . . 14.8
Seat to ground 33.5
Floor to ground 22.0

Unobstructed load space (length x width x height) in.
　With seats in place . . . . . . .13 x 39 x 38
　Rear folded or removed . .49 x 39 x 38
Tailgate (width x height) . . . . . 58 x 21.5

INSTRUMENTATION

Instruments: speedometer, odometer, fuel gauge, ammeter, oil pressure, water temp
Warning lights: hazard warning, brake system warning
Optional: . . . . .none

GENERAL

Curb weight, lb. (test model) 3660
GVWR (test model) 4500
　Optional GVWRs 4300, 4450, 4900
Wheelbase, in. 92.0
Track, front/rear 57.4/57.4
Overall length 152.1
Overall height 70.6
Overall width 69.1
Overhang, front/rear 26.0/33
Approach angle, degrees 38
Departure angle 29
Ground clearances (test model):
　Front axle 8.2
　Rear axle 8.3
　Oil pan 17.0
　Transfer case 14.3
　Fuel tank 15.5
　Exhaust system (lowest point) . . .12.9
Fuel tank capacity (U.S. gal) 12.1
Auxiliary 7.5-gal. tank $40

PERFORMANCE DATA

TEST MODEL

Bronco U-100, 302-cu-in. V-8, automatic transmission, rear bench seat, remote control side mirror, reduced sound level exhaust, 55-amp alternator, extra cooling radiator, hardboard headliner, 70-amp battery, auxiliary fuel tank, chrome bumpers, 3.50:1 limited slip rear axle, L78 x 15B tires, Calif. emissions certificate.
West Coast list price $6122

ACCELERATION

Time to speed, sec:
　0-30 mph 4.5
　0-45 mph 8.1
　0-60 mph 13.6
Standing start, 1/4-mile, sec 19.2
　Speed at end, mph 69

SPEED IN GEARS

High range
　3rd (4000 rpm) 90
　2nd (4000 rpm) 64
　1st (4000 rpm) 39
Low range
　3rd (4000 rpm) 36
　2nd (4000 rpm) 26
　1st (4000 rpm) 16
Engine rpm @ 55 mph 2500

BRAKE TESTS

Pedal pressure required for ½-g deceleration rate from 60 mph, lb 83
Stopping distance from 60 mph, ft . 206
Fade: Percent increase in pedal pressure for 6 stops from 60 mph 102
Overall brake rating . . . . fair

INTERIOR NOISE

Idle in neutral, dBA 54
Maximum during acceleration 82
At steady 60 mph cruising speed 80

OFF PAVEMENT

Hillclimbing ability . . . . .excellent
Maneuverability . . . . .excellent
Turnaround capability . . . . . . .excellent
Handling . . . . .very good
Ride . . . . .good

ON PAVEMENT

Handling . . . . .good
Ride . . . . .good
Driver visibility . . . . .very good
Driver comfort . . . . .good
Engine response . . . . .good

FUEL CONSUMPTION

Normal driving, mpg 14.0
Off pavement 10.5
Range, normal driving, miles 170
Range, off pavement 128

Scout II's spare tire stowage permits easy cargo loading, and ready access when tire change becomes necessary.

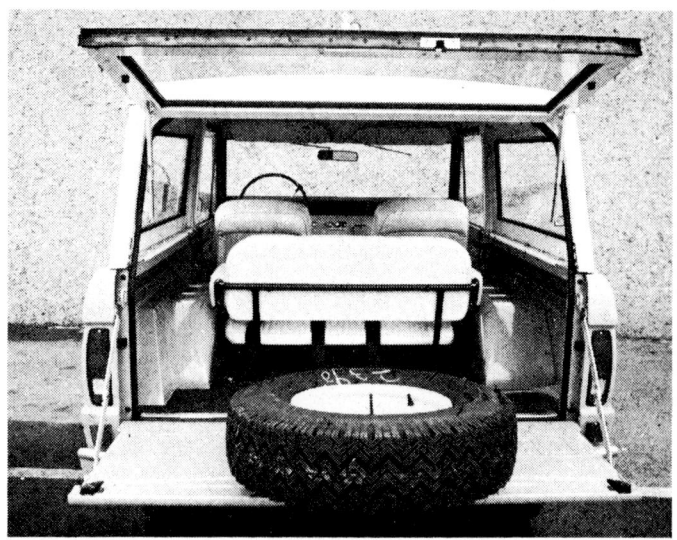

Bronco's tailgate mounting interferes with loading and takes up space that could be used for carrying cargo.

vehicles were equipped with limited-slip differentials and the axle ratios were as close as possible: 3.50 in the Ford and 3.54 in the International. Also, we had asked for and received the Scout with the 304-cu-in. V-8 so that it would be as close as possible to the Bronco's 302. We should point out that the Scout had almost all the extra equipment available from the factory while the Bronco was pretty much a plain-jane which could easily account for the Bronco's slightly quicker performance. The weight of the Scout's air conditioning and power steering, plus all the interior refinements, could easily make the difference. On the other hand, the Bronco was outfitted with all of the necessary emission control equipment including a catalytic converter while the Scout had a Gross Vehicle Weight Rating (GVWR) of 6200 lbs so it did not have as much smog-prohibiting machinery.

The largest difference between the Scout and the Bronco in our tests was in the braking ability where the Scout performed excellently while the Bronco achieved a rating of fair. This should be no great surprise to anyone as we have long contended that Broncos may have the worst brakes on an average of anything we have driven since our last outing in the Editor's late '41 Ford pickup. To give you some numbers for comparison, the Scout braked from 60 mph to zero in a very short 158 feet while the Bronco rolled up more than 200 feet in accomplishing the same test.

Getting down to the crunch, we like the Scout better than the Bronco in most cases. Obviously, our experience with the two vehicles was primarily on the road for all-day cruising. We also did a lot of around-town driving in both and found the Scout was a more pleasant vehicle to drive. Off the pavement, we have a draw with the Editor preferring the Bronco and the Technical Editor preferring the Scout.

Looking down a list of features, the Scout was bound to be the winner of the highway portion of the trip by reason of its high-backed bucket seats; its ample carpeting and paneling, which offer good noise insulation; plus its air conditioning and other comfort features. When you spend 16-18 hours driving, it's impossible not to prefer the more comfortable of the two. Also, of course, the longer wheelbase of the Scout gave it a better ride and the lower noise level helps in keeping fatigue down.

In terms of fuel economy, both the Scout and the Bronco gave a fairly decent account of themselves. The figures on the data panels accompanying this report show very little differ-

ence: 14.4 mpg for the Scout and 14.0 for the Bronco. Those figures are taken with our special fuel metering equipment and include driving out to the freeway through town and then cruising at a steady 55 mph. On the trip to Utah we found there were more variances between the two vehicles. Generally, the Scout was getting about 1.5 mpg better than the Bronco on the highway but we were driving at fairly rapid speeds and this undoubtedly accounts for the disparity.

Off the pavement, the ride is somewhat smoother in the Scout but the handling of the Bronco is superior. It gives you the feeling that you can go just about anywhere, any time and not be too concerned about whether you will fit between the trees, canyon walls or along side another vehicle on a narrow trail. The visibility from within the Bronco is second only to a CJ-5 without a top, although we do object to the windshield wiper position (at the top of the windshield) which forces the tallest drivers to slump a bit in the seat in order to see out. The ride of the Bronco is not as good as that of the Scout in the rougher areas but it is not punishing at all and is worth putting up with for the maneuverability and agility.

So, we come down to the same old dilemma. Which vehicle is best for you depends on your personal driving. From our offices here in southern California and keeping in mind that we are on the fringe of the Los Angeles megalopolis, we would probably choose the Scout. We do a lot of freeway driving into the city for entertainment so that our ratio of on-pavement versus off-pavement driving is probably about 80/20, which is still more than the average for off-pavement trips. Under those conditions we would want the highway capability of the Scout and be willing to sacrifice a little in terms of off-pavement characteristics. Also, this is qualified by the fact that we are making this choice in terms of this being our only vehicle. Obviously, if you own more than one vehicle, your choice may be altered.

The Bronco is an outstanding off-pavement vehicle. It does everything asked of it, within reason, and seems pleased to deliver miles of going even in the roughest of conditions. On the pavement, as a town car, it suffers only by comparison with the Scout. It is not bad. . . .in fact, it is good. . .but it is not *as good* as the Scout.

We like both of these 4-wheel drives. We would not hesitate to own either one of them. But, we like the Scout just a little bit better considering we have to exist in a world of paved roads and highways.
●

PV4 TEST

Ford's veteran four-wheeler is terrain tough, street soft...

FORD'S 1976 **BRONCO** suffers a pleasant schizophrenia. It's a purist's machine in some eyes. It has the slimness, shortness of wheelbase, sharp departure angle and nimbleness to put it in the same class with overtly hard-core machines such as the CJ-series Jeeps and Toyota Land Cruiser. But 11 years of refinement and softening of style have also positioned the Bronco as an almost cute Shooting Break for affluents who dread Losing It on a cowpie in front of the local gun club.

The Bronco is too good to be cast solely as a suburban snowplow. But it wasn't always that way.

As Dick Landfield, an off-road enthusiast who poses as a successful, mild-mannered Ford dealer, said, "The first Bronco was a disaster. It had a 6-cylinder engine, 3-speed manual transmission, poor brakes, no power and no options to improve it. It leaked, rattled and had a Dana 30 axle that split gears faster than you could replace them. Handling? You could never figure out where it was going to go!"

The intervening years have been kind to Bronco. Detroit doesn't often stick to one body style that long. So the little quirks have been quietly removed. The rattles and leaks have largely disappeared. And the Bronco can now be

purchased with a strong 302-cu-in. V-8, automatic transmission, power disc brakes and steering, excellent sound and road shock isolation, and trim items that add finish to what is basically a no-nonsense, functional sort of vehicle. Yes, Virginia, closet off-roaders may pass this vehicle through country club gates.

Who will be happy with the Bronco? That depends on both lifestyle and family size. The Bronco owner is more than likely

the person who would buy a 2 + 2 sports car, rather than a bigger one. Another motivation is serious contemplation of more than just an occasional drive up a dirt road. The Bronco is one of the few 4wd vehicles narrow enough to make it through a run like the Wentworth Jeep Trail without aid of a derrick or unduly clobbered body metal.

Enthusiasts who like to use their 4wds as tents will prefer a larger type of vehicle such as Blazer or Ramcharger. Space between the Bronco's wheelwells, with rear bench seat removed, is tight for a camping couple, and the tailgate would have to be dropped open for stretch room. The rear bench seat is strictly a short ride affair for two small children or two very friendly adults, in contrast to the two front buckets which wear well in a 500-mile day.

Baggage space behind the rear seat is minimal. So the Bronco is best seen as a handy 2 + 2 in town, and a two-seater with plenty of camping gear space for trips into the country. The back seat may be removed or replaced in about 3 minutes, requiring only a socket wrench on the four securing bolts.

The driving part is the best aspect of the Bronco. Highway handling is quick, as would be expected from a 92-in. wheelbase. But resistance to wind wander is

BRONCO

excellent in gusts to 24 mph, which were encountered in a 1000-mile run over the highways and choppy interior trails of the upper half of Baja California, Mexico. The quick steering works to good benefit on the trail. The driver is further aided by a steep over-the-hood sight line in picking the right way over bad ground. For 1976, the power steering ratio was quickened from 5.3 turns lock-to-lock to only 3.8 turns.

The tendency of the older Broncos to self-steer over bumps is gone. This annoying characteristic, which accounted for much of the unpredictability of the Bronco's front end, was eliminated by redesign of the front track bar. The prior arrangement caused the front axle assembly to move laterally 1 to 2 in. under compression, leaving the driver to guess when the vehicle would oversteer or understeer. While the front end still hunts mildly at high speeds, the effect is driver-induced by the quicker steering rather than Bronco-induced. In fast curve entries, the suspension now sets positively and the vehicle locks into a predictable oversteer.

On sandy dirt roads, the back end tends to have a mind of its own in 2wd only. The 4wd setting, made manually with a floor lever (2wd, 4wd-high, 4wd-low) and externally operated locking front hubs, offers the best high-speed handling. Turn entry is prettily accomplished with a quick, short release of the throttle accompanied by a pitch of the wheel, followed by throttle application as the Bronco drifts sideways. Full throttle cornering in 4wd yields neutral to mild understeer, depending on the depth of the dirt.

The Ford coil spring 4wd front end, available on Bronco, and F-100 and F-150 half-ton pickups, is unique among American 4wd sport machines. It minimizes the jarring sensations normally associated with conventional semi-elliptical leaf springs found on other U.S.-made 4wd vehicles, especially over rough ground. The standard shock units, being little different than any other manufacturer's, go away in half an hour of rough going. Because the front spring rate is kept moderate on the showroom machine, in deference to the Snowplow Set, the Bronco hobby-horses, albeit with marvelous travel length. Ford is offering a heavy-duty shock option which may help some. But, for those who really want to get the purist potential that is in the Bronco, a savvy dealer like Landfield can provide a moderately priced heavy-duty spring and matching shock absorber kit. The increased spring rate requires increased rebound damping, so Landfield prescribes either a gas-type unit such as the Bilstein or the new Mickey Thompson unit with three choices of rebound and compression damping.

Bronco interior, with Ranger trim package, is smooth and functional looking. Swing-away tire/wheel mount permits easy access to cargo area which, with rear seat removed, offers adequate accommodation for weekend off-roading.

PRICES

Basic list, FOB Detroit
Bronco U-100 V-8 .... $5078

Standard Equipment: 302-cu-in. V-8 engine, 3-spd manual transmission, Dana 20 2-spd transfer case, power front disc brakes, painted front and rear bumpers, free-running front hubs, front bucket seats, 2-spd electric wiper/washers, heater/defroster, E78 x 15B tires

GENERAL

Curb weight, lb (test model)	3650
GVWR (test model)	4600
Optional GVWRs	4400, 4900
Wheelbase, in.	92.0
Track, front/rear	57.4/57.4
Overall length	152.1
Overall height	70.8
Overall width	69.1
Overhang, front/rear	26.9/33.2
Approach angle, degrees	40.3
Departure angle, degrees	26.6

Ground clearances (test model):

Front axle	8.1
Rear axle	8.2
Oil pan	17.0
Transfer case	14.3
Fuel tank	15.4
Exhaust system (lowest point)	12.7

Fuel tank capacity (U.S. gal.)	12.2
Auxiliary .... 7.5-gal. tank,	$50

ACCOMMODATION

Standard seats	front bucket seats
Optional seats .... rear bench seat,	$122
Headroom, in.	38.7
Accelerator pedal to seatback, max	43.5
Steering wheel to seatback, max	14.9
Seat to ground	33.6
Floor to ground	22.0

Unobstructed load space (length x width x height)
With seats in place	13.2 x 40.0 x 38.0
Rear folded or removed ..	55.0 x 40.0 x 38.0
Tailgate (width x height)	56.0 x 19.3

INSTRUMENTATION

Instruments: speedometer, odometer, fuel gauge, ammeter, oil pressure, water temp
Warning lights: hazard warning, brake system warning
Optional .... none

ENGINES

Standard	302-cu-in. V-8
Bore x stroke, in.	4.00 x 3.00
Compression ratio	8.0:1
Net horsepower @ rpm	121 @ 3600*
Net torque @ rpm, lb-ft	217 @ 1800*
Type fuel required	unleaded

*Horsepower and torque ratings not available for Calif.

Optional	none

DRIVETRAIN

Standard transmission	3-spd manual
Clutch dia., in.	11.0
Transmission ratios: 3rd	1.00:1
2nd	1.75:1
1st	2.99:1
Synchromesh	all forward gears

Optional 3-spd automatic	$300
Transmission ratios: 3rd	1.00:1
2nd	1.46:1
1st	2.46:1

Rear axle type	semi-floating hypoid
Final drive ratios: front, 3.54:1; rear 3.50:1/front 4.09:1; rear 4.11:1*	
Overdrive	none

Free-running front hubs	std
Limited slip differential	$72
Transfer case	Dana 20 2-spd
Transfer case ratios	2.34:1 and 1.00:1

*4.09/4.11 ratio not available in Calif.

CHASSIS & BODY

Body/frame: ladder-type frame with separate steel body	
Brakes (std): front, 11.54-in. dia disc; rear, 11.03 x 2.25-in. drum	
Brake swept area, sq in.	375
Swept area/ton (max load)	153
Power brakes	std

Steering type (std)	worm and roller
Steering ratio	24:1
Power steering	$179
Power steering ratio	17.5:1
Turning circle, ft	31.0

Wheel size (std)	15 x 5.5K
Optional wheel size	none
Tire size (std)	E78 x 15B
Optional tire sizes: G78 x 15B, G78 x 15D, L78 x 15B, 7.00 x 15D	

SUSPENSION

Front suspension: trailing arms and coil springs on live axle with tube shocks	
Front axle capacity, lb	3000
Optional	none
Rear suspension: semi-elliptic leaf springs on live axle with tube shocks	
Rear axle capacity, lb	2900
Optional	none

Additional suspension options: HD front and rear shocks, $19; HD front springs, $4; HD rear springs, $10

With 302 V-8, automatic and 2-speed transfer case, Bronco shows both crawling capability and reasonable road performance.

The aftermarket items that would eliminate most of the objections in the Bronco would be the spring and shock improvements mentioned, plus a commonly available anti-skid device to prevent rear wheel lockup during panic stops. The stock brakes have been improved for 1976 with larger rear hubs and new power front disc units, and they do provide good stopping power, fade resistance and controllability. But front-to-rear brake proportioning on a short wheelbase 4wd is difficult, and conspires to cause rear lockup, even though the Bronco was fitted with a set of Western Tracker spoke wheels and oversize Armstrong dual purpose tires.

The 302 V-8, coupled with the Ford 3-speed automatic transmission, performs smoothly on no-lead gasoline with no surging or pinging. Measured acceleration performance is about the same as that of the 1974 and 1975 models.

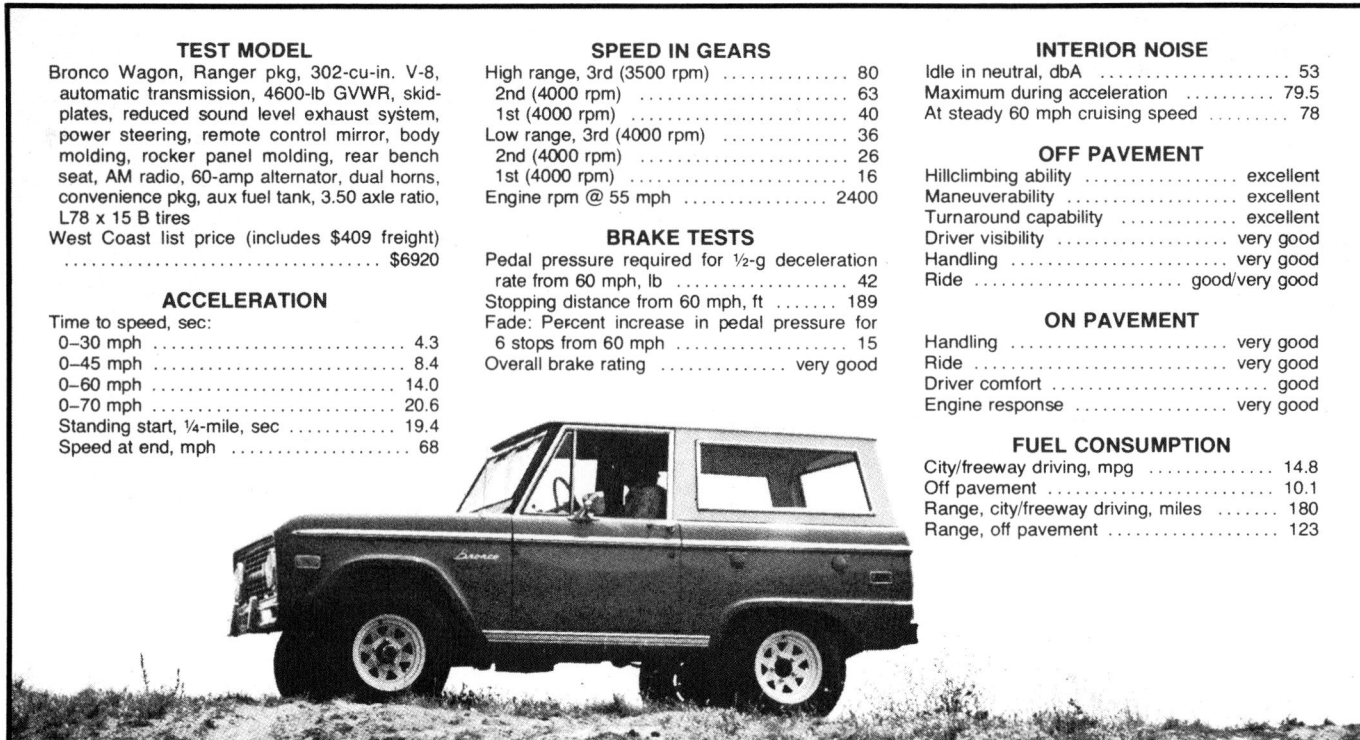

TEST MODEL

Bronco Wagon, Ranger pkg, 302-cu.-in. V-8, automatic transmission, 4600-lb GVWR, skidplates, reduced sound level exhaust system, power steering, remote control mirror, body molding, rocker panel molding, rear bench seat, AM radio, 60-amp alternator, dual horns, convenience pkg, aux fuel tank, 3.50 axle ratio, L78 x 15 B tires

West Coast list price (includes $409 freight)
.... $6920

ACCELERATION

Time to speed, sec:
0–30 mph	4.3
0–45 mph	8.4
0–60 mph	14.0
0–70 mph	20.6
Standing start, ¼-mile, sec	19.4
Speed at end, mph	68

SPEED IN GEARS

High range, 3rd (3500 rpm)	80
2nd (4000 rpm)	63
1st (4000 rpm)	40
Low range, 3rd (4000 rpm)	36
2nd (4000 rpm)	26
1st (4000 rpm)	16
Engine rpm @ 55 mph	2400

BRAKE TESTS

Pedal pressure required for ½-g deceleration rate from 60 mph, lb 42
Stopping distance from 60 mph, ft 189
Fade: Percent increase in pedal pressure for 6 stops from 60 mph 15
Overall brake rating .... very good

INTERIOR NOISE

Idle in neutral, dbA	53
Maximum during acceleration	79.5
At steady 60 mph cruising speed	78

OFF PAVEMENT

Hillclimbing ability	excellent
Maneuverability	excellent
Turnaround capability	excellent
Driver visibility	very good
Handling	very good
Ride	good/very good

ON PAVEMENT

Handling	very good
Ride	very good
Driver comfort	good
Engine response	very good

FUEL CONSUMPTION

City/freeway driving, mpg	14.8
Off pavement	10.1
Range, city/freeway driving, miles	180
Range, off pavement	123

BRONCO

While the 302 V-8 is about the biggest engine that can be stuffed into a smallish, hose-infested engine compartment, aftermarket transmission modifications can help bring this compact engine to its full potential. The Dana 2-speed transfer case for actuating 4wd is somewhat stiff and reluctant to move from one mode to the other without piddling back and forth to loosen up mating surfaces, even after 8000 miles appeared on the odometer.

Most buyers would be wise to order the optional auxiliary fuel tank as the main tank holds only 12.2 gal. The auxiliary offers only 7.5 additional gallons, but the total offers reasonable range, as the combination city-highway figure of 14.8 mpg is quite good. Having spent 50 bucks for the extra fuel tank, an owner can save $77.70 by not ordering the AM-only radio. It's okay for an AM radio, but is easily met or beaten in price by many AM/FM/Stereo units available elsewhere. Omission of the rear bench seat will save another $122.40.

The total Bronco package is really a fun thing to drive. It's a genuine form of American sports car, light in feel, easy to wheel around town or on the trail, but with V-8 reliability and substantial feel. Now, just when Bronco is getting its act together, it seems on the verge of extinction. Ford is eyeballing the big sales in the Blazer/Ramcharger category and wondering whether it ought to get in on the action. Bronco has sold steadily through the years and long since paid for its tooling. It could keep on selling profitability, even though it is geared to a smaller fol-

lowing than that of the wide-body 4wds. Resale is excellent, and a clean 1968 Bronco sells for only a few hundred dollars less now than when it sold new.

Hopefully, the Bronco will persist. It's one of the finest American vehicles made. If you agree, you ought to let the folks in Dearborn know how you feel. ●

FORD BRONCO

IT'S 12 YEARS YOUNG AND GETTING BETTER WITH AGE

Except for foreign imports, Jeep had the four-wheel-drive market pretty much to itself until 1961, when International introduced the Scout. The Scout, although underpowered even by contemporary standards, enjoyed sales growth for its first five years. Armed with this information, and not wanting to butt heads with the "old man" of the off-road field, Ford minimized risks by patterning its new truck after the Scout. The plan worked.

About the same time Bronco was introduced, off-road racing began taking its first tentative steps out of infancy toward the adulthood of full-blown professionalism that it enjoys today. Initially the Bronco looked very promising as a family four-wheeler. By its size, shape, wheelbase and width, however, the Bronco lent itself immediately to racing, which it dominated up until the recent introduction of the Jeep CJ-7.

Although rumors of a new, larger Bronco waiting to appear on the horizon have been bandied about since before 1970, they should be taken with a large grain of salt. Ford personnel continue to deny any knowledge of such a vehicle. We'll just have to wait and see.

The model year 1977 marks the 12th year of production for the Ford Bronco, with virtually no sheetmetal

TEST

changes and very few major under-the-skin engineering changes. The 1966 debut of Ford's new idea saw the Bronco powered by a 170-cubic-inch inline 6-cylinder engine, which was quickly supplemented with a 289-cubic-inch V8 option for the '67 model year. The Bronco's 3-speed manual transmission was the first all-synchro trans to be offered in

a 4x4 and one of the strongest 3-speeds ever made. It is still the standard transmission, with a C-4 Cruise-O-Matic 3-speed automatic as an option.

For the first three years of production, Broncos were covered with an excellent warranty (five years or 50,000 miles, whichever came first). However, after a few years some weak links in the Bronco chain began to show, and the guarantee period was drastically reduced to the present 12 months or 12,000 miles. One of the more glaring defects in the Bronco's initial design was vacuum-powered windshield wipers—not very helpful during a blizzard. These were changed to electric wipers for '69.

Another engineering change in '69 was the upgrading of the front differential; Ford changed from a Dana 30 to a Dana 44, increasing ring gear size from 7½ inches to 9 inches. In 1969, really a banner year for the Bronco, it also received a different

A pleasant surprise awaited us when we set off up some steep hills with the street-tired Bronco. Partly because of the light weight of the car, it climbed as well, or better, than most of the other vehicles that had flotation rubber already mounted.

PHOTOGRAPHY: ERIC RICKMAN

V8 engine option—a 205-hp, 302-cubic-inch, updated version of the 289. Why the 351W was not also included in the option list is a question that has long been asked among four-wheeler enthusiasts.

Bouncing merrily along, the Bronco remained untouched in its engineering until 1973, when it was again marked heavily by the engineering pencil. It was awarded the C-4 automatic option, a larger 6-cylinder (200-cubic-inch) engine as the standard powerplant and power steering as an option. The 6-cylinder was dropped in 1975, and the 302 is the only engine currently available in the '77 Bronco.

Like the Jeep and Scout, the Bronco was designed as a utility vehicle—a bobtail. Broncos were built for families that liked to have fun off-road, but needed more room than the basic CJ-5 afforded—room for both cargo and kids. They were also built to take abuse—abuse that a working off-roader must take to get the work done for the rancher, the farmer and the hunter. For those people, the Bronco served its purpose well.

For seven years, however, passenger-car frills like power steering and automatic transmission were not included, because the Bronco was intended to be rugged—not necessarily comfortable. People who couldn't afford the price or size of a Blazer bought Broncos instead; for them the truck was a sports/utility wagon, even though it was designed for pure utility.

TEST

Apparently an increasing number of owners were using Broncos for more than utility purposes, and eventually the complaints came rolling in. Standard steering made parking difficult, and long rides felt longer. In city traffic, an automatic was definitely needed. These complaints were finally heeded in 1973, and the Bronco became a more versatile vehicle.

As mentioned, for 1975 the 6-cylinder engine was dropped and the 302 became the standard engine. Front disc brakes (non-power) were first offered in 1976 as an option; for '77 they are standard, with a power-assist unit as an option. Because the Bronco is rated below 6000 pounds gross vehicle weight (GVW), it comes equipped with a catalytic converter.

The converter and unleaded fuel were introduced to the Bronco in '75.

At 4400 pounds, the standard GVW for the '77 Bronco has been upgraded from 1975's 4300 pounds. That minimum rating still applies only to the two-passenger model. If the optional rear seat is ordered (required in the Ranger package), the GVW increases to 4600 pounds. If the Traction-Lok rear differential is ordered (as in the test vehicle we drove), then the GVW reaches its maximum of 4900 pounds.

The Bronco uses a ladder-type frame and a separate steel body. The majority of four-wheel-drive vehicles use leaf springs front and rear, but Bronco has continued with coils in front and leaves in the rear. This permits greater wheel travel, but that, in turn, requires better-than-average bounce control, which means rapid wear on standard shocks. This is the reason why most serious off-roaders

purchase aftermarket double shock assemblies for the front axle, increasing the life of the shocks and improving handling at the same time. Bronco factory shock selection varies according to which GVW package is ordered.

For '77, Ford offers three different suspension packages, all referred to by GVW. The standard Bronco is a two-passenger wagon with a GVW of 4400 pounds; with that package you get standard springs, shocks and tires. There are two variations of front springs available on the Bronco, both coils. Standard coils have a capacity at the ground of 1140 pounds each; the optional rate is 1190 pounds per coil. The rear leaf springs are progressive, with a ground rating of 1240 pounds, and the tires are E78x15B—the "B" signifying a 4-ply rating.

A rear seat is optional, and with it come heavier shocks to handle the

We missed the old T handle for controlling the four-wheel-drive selection lever. Like the various Jeep models, the dash is more that of a utility vehicle.

This year the lockable front hubs were taken off the standard list and placed in the option category. High flotation rubber is a must for serious off-road driving.

Visually the Bronco has changed very little during the 12 years it has been produced. However, the powertrain has undergone many changes, until today the base powerplant is a 302-c.i.d. engine with a 3-speed manual trans.

The Bronco has one of the better air-cleaner arrangements. Dust has a rough time getting into the engine. The standard 302-c.i.d. engine is quite adequate, but it would be nice if, in the future, Ford decided to offer the 351 as an option.

additional passenger weight. Consequently, this option elevates the 4400-pound package to the 4600-pound class. It also increases maximum payload from 540 pounds to 740 pounds.

The largest GVW package has a 4900-pound GVWR and differs from the 4600-pound option in minimum rear GAWR shocks and rear axle. The GAWR is 180 pounds greater, the shocks are extra heavy-duty, and the heavy-duty rear end includes a Traction-Lok (limited-slip) differential, which gives it a capacity rating of 2840 pounds, compared to the 2460-pound axle of the 4600-pound package. The result is a payload increase from 740 pounds to 1040 pounds.

Standard steering is a worm and roller (non-power) with a ratio of 24:1; it includes a linkage-type shock absorber. This was the only steering available until '73, when a power steering unit became an option.

For years a major objection to the Bronco was its inadequate brakes. Non-power drum brakes are okay for street use, but most Bronco owners spend a great deal of time off-pavement. Hard, frequent braking and puddle jumping make drum brakes fade faster than a blush on a burlesque queen; but it wasn't until '75 that Ford decided to act. For '75, Bronco could be ordered with front disc brakes. Even though they were non-power, they were still a great improvement, on- or off-road. They resisted fade from frequent use and water retention was minimal. These non-power discs are now standard, with power discs optional.

Only the Bronco powertrain option list is shorter than its list of engineering changes over the years. One engine (302 V8), two transmissions (3-speed manual or Cruise-O-Matic), one transfer case (Dana 20) and one gear ratio (3.50:1) are available.

About the only choices you have when ordering a new '77 Bronco are color and what operations you wish assisted with power: steering, braking or shifting. Lockable front hubs are no longer standard but are optional. Also, front "posi" is no longer available. For years, Bronco was the only 4x4 vehicle with this option.

The Bronco body is all-steel and available in only one style—a two-door wagon. It's nothing fancy, just a very basic vehicle. For a few dollars more, though, you can buy a touch of fancy in the form of the Sport Bronco. This model includes chrome bumpers rather than painted ones, a hardboard headliner, floor mats, door trim panels, touches of chrome, wheel covers and fender emblems. If you desire something fancier still, you can get the Ranger. It includes all of the above plus a swing-away rear spare tire with vinyl cover, carpeting, and hood and body stripes.

Included in both trim packages is the front passenger bucket seat and sun visor. A rear seat (bench type) is required in the Ranger and is optional in all but the 4400-pound package.

The standard interior includes one front bucket with retractable seat belts, door-mounted armrests, padded dash, windshield washers, a sun visor, floor mats, heater and defroster. Speaking of heaters, Ford provides the long-johns crowd with a different type of heater—one for the engine block. It comes in a package called the Northland Special, which also includes a Traction-Lok rear axle, 70-amp-hour battery, 60-amp alternator and a 50/50 antifreeze mix.

Our test Bronco was a bright red Ranger with an auto trans and heavy-duty suspension. A Traction-Lok rear end provided the go-power, and power disc brakes provided the slow-power. With all the extras, this little Dearborn jewel listed at $7206.50. The option list alone nearly broke two grand.

TEST

In looking over the rig, we really didn't expect too much from it off-road because of the street tread on the G78x15D tires. But the Bronco fooled us—it turned out to be the best climber of the vehicles tested for this issue. It boggles the mind to consider what it might have done with decent off-road rubber. Forward visibility rivals that of the CJ, except for the wiper motor bulkhead. This overhead bulge forces the driver to crouch over the steering wheel during off-pavement maneuvers in order to see up hillsides or check overhanging branches.

Another off-road fault is the smog system, although 4000 miles on the odometer without a tune-up could also be the culprit. Hitting a bump hard caused a dashpot effect, in which raw fuel choked off power momentarily. This could get a little hairy during steep hillclimbs. Definitely attributable to smog controls is the in-

CONTINUED ON PAGE 133

HOT ROD 4-WHEEL & OFF-ROAD ROAD TEST SPECIFICATIONS
Ford Bronco

Base List Price $5260
Options .... Cruise-O-Matic, 3-speed, Ranger package, locking hubs, radio
Price As Tested $7206

ENGINE:

Type V8
Displacement .... 302 cubic inches
Bore & Stroke .... 4.00x3.00 inches
Compression Ratio 8.4:1
Net Power .... 133 hp @ 3600 rpm
Net Torque .... 236 ft/lbs @ 1800 rpm
Carburetion .... Motorcraft 2V
Recommended Fuel .... Regular
Emissions Control .... California

DRIVETRAIN:

Transmission .... Cruise-O-Matic
Transfer Case .... Dana 20
Reduction Ratio 2.34:1
Gear Ratios ... Third: 1.00:1; Second: 1.46:1; First: 2.46:1; Reverse: 2.18:1; Final Drive Ratio: 3.54:1

CHASSIS:

Body/Frame .... All-steel body with separate frame
Suspension .... Front: Coil springs; Rear: Leaf springs
Steering ...... 4.25 turns lock to lock; turning circle 34.1 ft
Brake System .... Front: Disc; Rear: Drum
Wheels 15x5.5K
Tires G78x15D
Gross Vehicle Weight Rating .... 4900 lbs

DIMENSIONS:

Wheelbase .... 92 inches
Ground Clearance At Lowest Point .... 7.25 inches
Track .... 58.5 inches front; 57.5 inches rear
Length .... 161 inches
Width .... 69.1 inches
Height .... 73 inches
Overhang .... 28.5 inches front; 33.25 inches rear
Fuel Capacity .... 14 gallons
Cargo Area .... Length: 53 inches; Width: 54 inches; Height: 41.5 inches
Curb Weight .... 3860 lbs

FUEL ECONOMY:

Mileage On 114-Mile Test Loop .... 14.6 mpg

OVERALL COMMENTS: (On a scale of 1-10, 5 is average.)

Exterior Finish Quality 7
Interior Finish Quality 8
Handling 8
Brakes 9
Driver Comfort 7
Dashboard Readability/Accessibility 8
Acceleration In Traffic 8

Rear access is easy because of the unique hinging method of the seat. The seats offer good lateral support during evasive maneuvers. Door-panel trim is part of the Ranger package.

One of the best ways to describe the Bronco is to say it's a "fun" vehicle. The addition of power steering and brakes means that women will enjoy driving it too.

1976 BRONCO

New front disc brakes and a beefed up suspension

Story and photos by Bill Sanders

FOUR WHEELER ROAD TEST

Ford has finally made some of the long awaited improvements to the Bronco that enthusiasts have been clamoring for: front disc brakes, and a modified front suspension to eliminate bottoming off road. These long sought after changes have made a dramatic improvement in the '76 Bronco.

POWERTRAIN AND PERFORMANCE

To cut down on production costs and keep the ultimate price to the consumer as low as possible, only one engine is now available in the Bronco, the 302-cu. in. V-8. That is your only engine selection; there are no options. Of course, there are special emission applications for California, but everywhere else it is the same. The 302 is rated at 121 horsepower at 3600 RPM, with torque listed at 217 at 1800 RPM. The latter is pretty good considering the small V-8 and all the emission controls that are tacked on for 1976.

There is a transmission option. Standard tranny is a 3-speed manual. Our test truck had the optional 3-speed automatic. Although it costs an extra $300, we would recommend the automatic with the Bronco for most types of driving. Three hundred bucks is a cheap price to pay for the added convenience.

As with most of the smaller 4x4s, the Bronco still uses manual four wheel drive instead of full-time. Ford uses a constant-mesh, Dana 20 2-speed transfer case in the Bronco.

There are still options, of sorts, when it comes to axle ratios for the Bronco. Standard ratio is 3.50:1, with an optional 4.11:1. However, again, if you live in California, you are not allowed to buy the 4.11 optional ratio. It takes too much trouble and costs too much to get emission approval for extra axle ratios in the Golden State. Entire series of tests have to be run over many thousands of miles, so evidently the number of 4.11 gears that would be sold don't justify the expense. For all you die-hard, rugged, mountain goat four wheelers who like extra low gearing, all we can say is: sorry about that!

Anyway. Equipped with the 302 V-8, automatic tranny, Dana 20 2-speed transfer case, and 3.50:1 axle ratio, our Bronco test truck was ready to go. Performance was peppy and acceleration good, considering the latest emission controls. Our test truck had a GVW package totaling 4600 lbs., well below the 6000 lb. rating limit for catalytic converters. So, our test rig had the pesky converter mounted underneath. Actually, the converter on the Bronco doesn't seem as noticeable as, say, on

Looks are deceptive; new Bronco has beefier front suspension and front disc brakes. Both auxiliary and stock gas tank fillers are on left side for easier filling. Norseman tires fit well under Bronco without modifications.

Clean dash area has all controls within easy reach for driver. Bronco lets you sit up high for good over-hood visibility.

FORD BRONCO

PRICES AND OPTIONS

Base price $5078.05
Ranger package 633.90
Skid plates 112.00
Low sound exhaust 24.30
Automatic transmission 300.00
Power steering 179.00
Left remote control mirror 18.20
Body and tailgate moldings 41.80
Rocker panel moldings 33.60
Rear bench seat 122.40
AM radio 77.70
60 amp alternator 38.10
Free running hubs 90.20
Dual electric horns 10.30
Auxiliary fuel tank w/skid plate 49.70

SPECIFICATIONS

Engine .90° OHV
Bore & Stroke (ins.) . . . . 4.00 x 3.00
Displacement (cu. in.) 302
HP @ RPM . . . . .121 @ 3600
Torque: lbs.-ft. @ RPM . . . . . .217 @ 1800
Compression Ratio/Fuel . . 8.0:1/Unleaded
Carburetion . . . . .2-bbl.
Transmission . . . . Automatic
Transfer Case . . . . .Dana 20 2-spd.
Final Drive Ratio (axle ratio) 3.50:1
Steering type . . . . .Power/Integral

Steering Ratio . . . . N.A.
Turning diameter (ft.) . . . . N.A.
Tire Size 9.50x15
Brakes . . . . Disc Front/Drum Rear
Front Suspension . . .Coil Spring/Mono Beam
Rear Suspension . . . . Leaf Spring
Wheelbase (ins.) 92.0
Overall length (ins.) 152.1
Width (ins.) 69.1
Height (ins.) 70.8

Front tread width (ins.) 57.4
Rear tread width (ins.) 57.4
Fuel tank capacity (gals.) 12.2
Auxiliary fuel tank capacity (gals.) 7.5
Engine oil capacity (qts.) 5.0
Ground clearance,
   front & rear differential (ins.) . . 8.6 Front
                                         8.1 Rear
Approach angle . . . . 44.1°
Departure angle . . . . 29.9°
Curb weight (lbs.) 3560

PERFORMANCE RATING

On Road
Acceleration . . . . .Good
Passing speed . . . . .Good
Steering Response . . . . .Excellent
Maneuverability . . . . .Excellent
Cornering . . . . .Excellent
Braking . . . . .Excellent
Interior noise . . . . .Fair
Ride . . . . .Smooth-Firm
Seating comfort—Front . . . . .Good
   Rear .Fair
Accessibility of dash controls . . . Excellent
Entry/Exit height to ground . . . . . . .Good
Glove box size . . . . .Fair
Instrument readability . . . . .Good
Head room . . . . .Excellent
Seat belt location . . . . .Fair

Off Road
Traction in soft,
   sandy or muddy soil . . . . .Good
Hillclimbing characteristics . . . . .Good
Rollover angle stability
   (center of gravity) . . . . .Fair
Suspension load
   without bottoming . . . . Excellent
Turning circle . . . . .Good
Ride . . . . Firm
Tire flotation (stock tires) . . . . .Good
Vehicle control . . . . Excellent
Hi-Range 4WD performance . . . . . . .Good
Lo-Range 4WD performance . . . . Excellent
Accessibility of
   transfer case shifter . . . . .Good
Ease of shifting transfer case . . . . . . .Fair
Steering Response . . . . Excellent
Brake, (clutch) accelerator
   pedal location . . . . .Good
Roll bar installation . . . . .Good
Occupant seating stability . . . . .Good
Close proximity visibility
   over hood . . . . Excellent
Sun visor capability . . . . .Good
Headlight illumination for
   off road driving . . . . .Good
Storage capacity (camping gear etc.) Excellent
Fuel tank filler accessibility
   (for funnels etc.) . . . . .Fair
Low gear lugging capability . . . . . . .Good
Brakes/Compression
   downhill capability . . . . .Good
Ease of access to spare tire . . . . . . Excellent

Fuel Consumption
On Road . . . . .12.1 to 14.5 mpg.
(Normal driving—highway and surface streets)
Off Road . . . . .10.8 to 12.0 mpg.

Accessories and Options
Air conditioning effectiveness . . . . N.A.
Heater/Defroster effectiveness . . . . . .Good
Windshield Wiper/
   Washer effectiveness . . . . .Good
Wiper area covered . . . . .Good
Horn (Loudness) . . . . .Excellent
Dash lighting . . . . .Excellent
Interior lighting . . . . .Good
Door handles
   (operation and location) . . . . . . Excellent
Door locks . . . . .Good
Hood latch . . . . .Good
Jack/Lug wrench location . . . . .Fair

the Jeep CJ-5, where you get considerable extra heat under the driver's seat. The Bronco floorboards stay relatively cool. Acceleration and performance were good, both on and off road. Passing speeds were good, too. The V-8 was never sluggish or unresponsive.

HANDLING, STEERING, STOPPING
With the newly modified front suspension, ride characteristics were immediately noticeable as being improved. Even on the street, the front end seemed much stronger, with firmer control. When we took the Bronco off road into some really choppy terrain, the suspension changes got even noticeably better. In places where we had taken Broncos previously on road tests and

had the front end bottom out, all that was gone. Ride was still not harsh, yet the bottoming out was gone. Only on a couple of abnormal jumps where the Bronco was pushed beyond normal expectancy, did it manage to bottom.

Handling and steering performances were also excellent. For a bobtail, the Bronco corners quite flat and smooth.

With new front disc brakes, we found another area that was considerably improved. We noticed an improvement immediately when crossing a stream bed. After emerging from hub deep water, we experienced no brake fade whatsoever. Full braking capabilities were still there, without needing to ride the brake pedal for a drying out period. At the test track, during high speed

brake stops, we noticed no pulling to either side.

COMFORT, CONVENIENCE, OPTIONS
Our test truck was prepared for Ford at Bill Stroppe and Son in Long Beach, California. Bill visited Dick Cepek and had Dick mount a set of Armstrong Norseman tires on white spokers. The Norseman tires were much more capable in our off roading than the stock street tires that came with the vehicle.

Included with the Bronco was Ford's Ranger Package, which lists for an extra $634. We don't know how many people are driving their Broncos off road all the time, but the Ranger package makes for a comfortable interior, with carpeting, etc. It makes a nice touch if your Bronco is your only vehicle.

We also got a vehicle with an auxiliary tank. This option (with skid plate) should be on every Bronco buyer's list. It is an additional $50, but well worth it because of the small size of the stock tank.

SUMMING UP
If you don't mind having a catalytic converter and the necessity of buying unleaded gas, the '76 Bronco is a great, comfortable, mid-sized bobtail. With the front suspension changes for '76 and the addition of disc brakes, the Bronco is really competitive with any other 4x4 on the market. The 302 V-8 is just the right size for this vehicle. With options kept at a minimum, the '76 Bronco is also quite competitive price-wise. Test one and see for yourself.   □

This is fuel tank switch for sending units; fuel line switch-over control is under driver seat. Ford should combine the two into one control as Chevy does.

Unleaded gas is price you must pay for having catalytic converter.

Armstrong Norsemans were mounted for Bill Stroppe by Dick Cepek. Test truck had locking hubs as option.

Bronco transfer case shifter is patterned so you can't shift from 2-high into 4-high accidentally.

Easy to read speedo is surrounded by gauges for fuel, oil pressure, amps and temp.

FORD BRONCO 1966-1980

GROWING UP
IN A HURRY
By John Jelinek

Picture yourself sitting in a boardroom at the Ford Motor Company plant in Dearborn, Michigan. The year is 1965, and two four-wheel drive bobtails have virtually cornered the off-road vehicle market. The Jeep has been around since the day after dirt was invented, and International Harvester produces an excellent 4x4, the Scout, in a converted tractor plant. As one of Ford's corporate luminaries, you want a slice of the action. To get it, your engineering folks have developed a short-wheelbased vehicle that suspiciously resembles the Scout; you wonder, how will the public respond?

STAGE ONE
THE BOBTAIL

When the first Ford Bronco rolled off the assembly line in late 1965 (and hit the streets in early '66), there was little left to guesswork. Ford played it safe and built a pseudo-Scout; it worked and the public responded. The original Bronco powertrain offering was a 170cid 6-cylinder engine that was long on torque and low on excitement in the top end. The chassis was a basic ladder frame with a separate steel body bolted on; the suspension featured coil springs in front (new to 4x4s) and leaves in the rear. The coil springs allowed greater wheel travel and, some feel, led to naming the little bobtail after a bucking bronco. Body styles offered the 1966 buyer a choice between the two-door bobtail Scout replicar and a very, very shortbedded pickup-style option.

Late in the 1966 model year, the Bronco took a bold step into the future with a second engine offering: a 289 V-8. The 200 horsepower V-8 was the first eight optioned in the four-wheel drive market—a trend that immediately took hold in the American marketplace. Initially, the Ford bobtail looked very promising, with a good public response record on its debut. But, as with any new item, there were some shortcomings. Most companies would use later years to work out a new model's rough spots, but Ford chose to let the Bronco stagnate for seven long years, allowing the rest of the four-wheel drive industry to catch up and even surpass Ford's Better Idea. The small changes made in the Bronco during the seven-year drought did little to enhance the general appeal of the vehicle. In

HIGH ROLLERS

1968, the standard 6-cylinder 170 lost five horsepower, when the compression ratio dropped from the original 9.1:1 to 8.7:1. Naturally, this change also affected the torque, but not as seriously as it did the horses. This situation lasted until 1972, when a similar drop in compression (to 8.3:1) knocked the hp rating down below the magic 100 mark—to a stark 97. Another stab at the 170cid six proved to be its undoing in the general marketplace in 1972, as the California (where all good things begin and end) Air Resources Board decreed the 170 too dirty for the California atmosphere. Already shackled with virtually every smog device known to man, the 170 was shelved in favor of the 200cid six, a stronger engine that became standard everywhere in the 1973 season; it featured hydraulic lifters rather than solids, curing the perennial noisiness of the 170.

But the people's choice of engines in the Stage One Bronco was the V-8 mill introduced in the 1968 model, a 302 V-8 that breathed through a 2-barrel carburetor, had an 8.0:1 compression ratio and yielded 130-plus horsepower. Through catalytic converters and other smog devices, the 302 survived as the basic Bronco powerplant until the Stage Two Bronco arrived in 1978.

In 1973, the Stage One Bronco had as close to a banner year as it ever saw, with the addition of an automatic transmission to the option lists and the end of the less-than-successful pickup version. Also new for 1973, a trim package, the Ranger option, brought some real creature comforts to the little bobtail—a swing-away spare tire carrier, front and rear interior carpeting and chrome-plated bumpers. In addition, the Ranger package brought body striping, high-back bucket seats for the front and a vinyl spare tire cover. The same year saw an end to the complaints about the difficulty of low-speed steering—power steering was added. Coupled with the change from the Dana 30 to the Dana 44 front differential (four years earlier), the addition of power steering broadened the Bronco's versatility to include taking the kids to school as well as taking the rough route to the campgrounds. As welcome as the 1973 changes were, the Bronco had lost something in its seven-year standstill, what racers would call a competitive advantage. In 1966 the

Ford Bronco was the state-of-the-art four-wheeler, but seven years later it was a weak sister, light-years behind the Jeep, the Scout and the new kids on the block—the Blazer, Jimmy and Power Wagon.

In the mid-Seventies, the Bronco remained virtually unchanged, with no sheet metal alterations and minimal engineering changes from '74 to '77. The Bronco accomplished far less than covering itself with glory: 1975 saw the elimination of the 6-cylinder engine from the list of Bronco powertrain combinations, and the 302 V-8 became the basic engine, in fact, the only engine available on the bobtail until Stage Two. Also in 1975, Ford succumbed to consumer pressure and popular discontent with the front drum brakes on the Bronco. The next year, Bronco featured front disc brakes as a factory option, and, by the time 1977 rolled around, they became standard, with a power-assist unit as optional equipment. During the same period, Ford engineers were trying desperately to keep ahead of constricting smog control regulations, strapping on a catalytic converter and switching to unleaded fuel in 1975 for California and 1976

Remaining virtually unchanged until 1973, the basic Bronco was the answer for the four-wheeler who wanted a Jeep-like vehicle with the mechanical dependability of Ford.

for the rest of the world. One of the oversights remedied in 1976 Broncos was a very tight and unforgiving fuel-line filter. While fine for street travel, this low-buck item stranded many a Bronco in the dusty and silty areas of the country by plugging up tighter than a snare drum.

The bobtail Bronco was fighting a losing battle against the age-old Jeep for the short wheelbase market; its fumbling, sporadic approach to off-road technology knelled the end of the bobtail line with the 1977 model year. The off-road enthusiast parade had passed the Bronco by, and the 12-year history of Ford's bobtail was about to take a turn for the better.

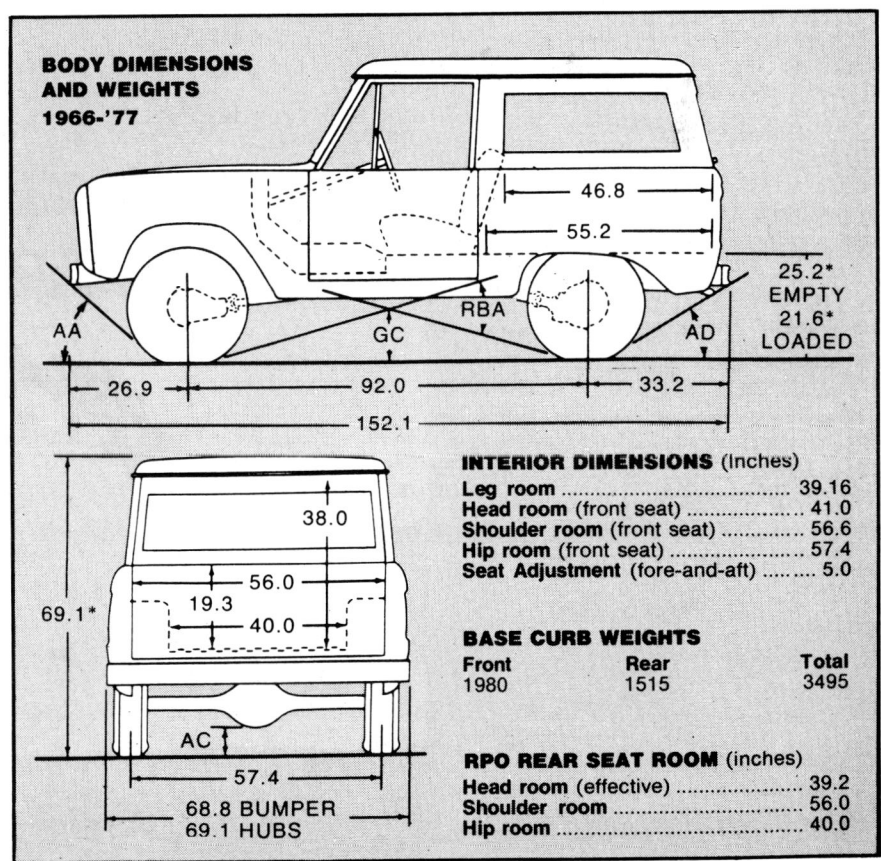

BODY DIMENSIONS AND WEIGHTS 1966-'77

46.8
55.2
25.2* EMPTY
21.6* LOADED
AA
RBA
GC
AD
26.9
92.0
33.2
152.1

38.0
69.1*
56.0
19.3
40.0
AC
57.4
68.8 BUMPER
69.1 HUBS

INTERIOR DIMENSIONS (inches)

Leg room	39.16
Head room (front seat)	41.0
Shoulder room (front seat)	56.6
Hip room (front seat)	57.4
Seat Adjustment (fore-and-aft)	5.0

BASE CURB WEIGHTS

Front	Rear	Total
1980	1515	3495

RPO REAR SEAT ROOM (inches)

Head room (effective)	39.2
Shoulder room	56.0
Hip room	40.0

Plans are afoot to scrap the familiar old Bronco. Even as your eyes scan this page the Ford plant engineers are tooling up to produce its replacement; a larger, Blazer-type vehicle to be called a Bronco. How fitting that our farewell road test is on a super trick Bronco, trimmed to chase a balloon across the United States.

No ordinary looking Bronco, this. Accessorized, painted and outfitted by RVI (Recreational Vehicles, Inc.) of Torrance, California, for the Ford Limited Edition Sail, this Bronco features custom paint, brush guard and even a Smokey type bubble machine on the roof. Underneath it was still stock with 302-cu. in. V-8, automatic transmission, 3.50:1 axle ratios, power steering and power assisted front disc brakes. We picked this bright orange Bronco up at the huge Ford proving grounds in Kingman, Arizona, and took our time getting back to the West Coast, taking it through sand washes in the desert and even heading up the mountains for some snow exercises.

POWERTRAIN AND PERFORMANCE

Ford's once strong 302-cu. in. V-8 has been losing ground to the emission controls each year. For 1977 it can muster only 133 hp at 3600 RPM and 236 lbs.-ft. of torque at 1800 RPM. It brings sadness to our hearts when we remember the Trans-Am racers of the past and the Boss 302 engines that used to produce more than 300 honest horsepower on the street and more than 450 on the race track. Despite the fact that the 302 is no longer a lion, it isn't exactly a pussycat either. The performance has to be described as adequate—it gets the Bronco around without embarrassing the driver.

For 1977 the Bronco features the Ford Dura-Spark type ignition system and silicone spark plug wires. We didn't put enough miles on the Bronco to really strain the ignition system, but we did have some high altitude, below freezing starts which came off without a problem.

Ford's 3-spd. automatic transmission performed well (as they always do) especially in the sand. When the traction gets scarce it's nice to have the torque converter absorbing the engine power in a situation where a manual gearbox and a clutch might just stick you deeper.

Unfortunately there is no choice of axle ratios; Ford has reverted to Henry's color choice theory. "You can have any color you want as long as it's black and

1977 BRONCO
This old friend goes out in style.
Story and photos by Mike Anson

Bronco in full dress balloon chase uniform; custom paint, grille/brush guard, extra lights and even an orange bubble machine on the top. Matching van is shown in the background.

tires. This Bronco, equipped with proper size 10-15LT tires on aluminum alloy wheels, was able to surmount most obstacles, including some really soft snow. We particularly like the size of the Bronco; larger than a Jeep and smaller than a Blazer, because it can get through and over trail hazards and still provide ample seating and storage room.

The short, 92-in. wheelbase makes the Bronco quite maneuverable, even on a twisty and tight trail. In soft dirt the 302 V-8 could break the tires loose for some fun, sliding turns. On the pavement we found this to be the smoothest and most quiet Bronco we have tested; however, part of the quiet must be attributed to the interior package put together by RVI that included carpeting and paneling.

Braking tests revealed that the vacuum assisted front disc/rear drums brake system could haul the 3750-lb. Bronco down from freeway speeds to zero in short order. With the tires inflated to road specs, the Bronco would stop straight and true. After several stops, however, we did experience a bit of fade and had to exert more force on the pedal. We suspect it was the rear drums heating up and it was just a normal amount of fade for such an exhaustive test. Although the front spring rates are higher now for the stock Bronco than in the past, there was still some noticeable brake dive.

Overall we found the handling to be

you can have any gear ratio you want as long as it's 3.54:1 in front and 3.50:1 in the rear. The only option is the addition of Traction-Lok limited slip device in the rear end. These gear ratios present a problem for owners who want to install larger diameter tires; the gear ratios are diluted even more. Desert four wheelers can live with the high gears, those who travel in the mountains will suffer.

RIDE, HANDLING AND BRAKING

The Bronco's ride qualities have been the subject of varying opinions since the day it was introduced. Some say it's too soft, especially in the front, and others claim the ride is too harsh (usually due to pitching on paved roads). In any case, the Bronco's ride has never been called too smooth or too luxurious. Our 1977 machine did seem to be better behaved than the older models.

Off pavement performance was very good and we feel the Formula Desert Dog tires had something to do with that. Perhaps the poor Bronco has been maligned all these years because everybody was testing them with the stock

Ford's 302-cu. in. V-8 powered the Bronco through sand and snow. Strange-looking, flat distributor cap indicates the engine is equipped with the Ford Dura-Spark ignition system.

much better than we remembered it to be and were once again surprised at the agility of the Bronco.

COMFORT, CONVENIENCE, OPTIONS

When was the last time you saw a Bronco interior fitted with woodgrain paneling? This Bronco was treated to a custom interior by RVI, a vehicle conversion firm better known for their van conversions than Bronco treatments.

When Ford needed a group of chase vehicles for their record-setting 19-day, crosscountry balloon trip they went to RVI for the cosmetic treatment and our old friend Bill Stroppe at Bill Stroppe and Son in Long Beach, California, for the engine and chassis modifications. Our test Bronco was not modified by Stroppe, but RVI had done a complete number on the interior and exterior.

First the Bronco was carpeted. RVI usually uses shag carpet, but knowing this Bronco was going to cover some hard ground on the 8000-plus miles it would see chasing Karl Thomas in the hot air balloon, they used the stock-type, cut-pile carpet. Stealing a trick from their van interiors, they added some small woodgrain panels along the rear section. Overhead they installed a sunroof and a gold flecked headliner. A Johnson CB radio and a pair of spotlights, one on each side, completed the interior.

1977 BRONCO
PRICES AND OPTIONS

Base price $5692.05
Ranger package (includes carpeting, vinyl seat covers, vinyl door trim, outside moldings and assorted trim items.) . . . . $ 669.00
Automatic transmission . . . . $ 315.00
Balloon Chase trim package (includes wheels & tires, paint and striping, tire cover, wood-grain interior paneling, grille guard, sunroof, sidepipes and additional lighting—overhead amber light not included.) $1399.00

SPECIFICATIONS

Engine . . . . OHV V-8	Steering Ratio. 17.5:1
Bore & Stroke (ins.) . . . . . . .4.00 x 3.00	Turning diameter (ft.) 34
Displacement (cu. in.) 302	Tire Size . . . .10-15LT Formula Desert Dogs
HP @ RPM . . . . .133 @ 3600	Brakes . . . . .front disc/rear drum
Torque: lbs.-ft @ RPM . . . . . .236 @ 1800	Front Suspension . . . . .live axle, coil springs
Compression Ratio/Fuel 8.4:1	Rear Suspension. . . . . .live axle, leaf springs
Carburetion 2V	Wheelbase (ins.) 92.0
Transmission. . . . . .3-spd. automatic	Overall length (ins.) 152.1
Transfer Case . . . . Dana 20, 2-spd.	Width (ins.) 69.1
Final Drive Ratio (axle ratio) 3.50:1	Height (ins.) 69.1
Steering type . . . . integral power	Front tread width (ins.) 57.4

Rear tread width (ins.) 57.4
Fuel tank capacity (gals.) 14
Auxiliary fuel tank capacity (gals.) 8
Engine oil capacity (qts.). . . . . . .5 w/filter
Ground clearance,
front & rear differential (ins.). . . . 8.4/8.1
Approach angle . . . . 43°
Departure angle . . . . 27°
Curb weight (lbs.). 3750

PERFORMANCE RATING

On Road

Acceleration. . . . . .good
Passing speed . . . . .good
Steering Response. . . . . .very good
Maneuverability. . . . . .very good
Cornering . . . . .very good
Braking. . . . . .good
Interior noise . . . . .very good
Ride .good
Seating comfort—Front . . . . .fair
　　　　　　　　Rear. . . . . .fair
Accessibility of dash controls . . . . .fair
Accessibility of transmission shifter excellent
Entry/Exit height to ground. . . . . . .good
Glovebox size . . . . .good
Instrument readability . . . . .fair
Head room. . . . . .good
Seat belt location . . . . .good

Off Road

Traction in soft,
　sandy or muddy soil. . . . . .very good
Hillclimbing characteristics . . . . .good
Rollover angle stability
　(center of gravity) . . . . .good
Suspension load
　without bottoming . . . . .good
Turning circle . . . . .very good
Ride .good
Tire flotation . . . . .excellent
Vehicle control . . . . .very good
Hi-Range 4WD performance. . . . . . . .good
Lo-Range 4WD performance. . . . .very good
Accessibility of
　transfer case shifter . . . . .good
Ease of shifting transfer case. . . . . . .good
Steering Response. . . . . .very good
Brake, (clutch), accelerator
　pedal location . . . . .good
Roll bar installation. . . . . .N.A.
Occupant seating stability . . . . .good
Close proximity visibility
　over hood. . . . . .good
Sunvisor capability . . . . .good
Headlight illumination for
　off road driving . . . . .good
Storage capacity (camping gear etc.) . . .good
Fuel tank filler accessibility
　(for funnels etc.). . . . . .fair
Low gear lugging capability . . . . . . .good
Brakes/Compression
　downhill capability . . . . .excellent
Ease of access to spare tire. . . . . .excellent

Fuel Consumption

On Road . . . . .13.8 mpg.
(Normal driving—highway and surface streets)
Off Road . . . . .10.2 mpg.

Accessories and Options

Air conditioning effectiveness. . . . . . .N.A.
Heater/Defroster effectiveness. . . . . .good
Windshield Wiper/
　Washer effectiveness. . . . .
Wiper area covered . . . . .good
Horn (Loudness) . . . . .good
Dash lighting. . . . . .good
Interior lighting . . . . .good
Door handles
　(operation and location) . . . . .good
Door locks. . . . . .good
Hood latch. . . . . .good
Jack/Lug wrench location . . . . .fair

Bronco sport interior was comfortable and durable. Power steering made driving through the sand washes much easier. Spotlight handles were located at the lower corner of the windshield.

Fancy headliner and sunroof were part of the cosmetic touches added by RVI.

Outside they sprayed a bright orange base paint and added a yellow and black stripe treatment. A chrome grille/brush guard with Per-Lux fog lamps and Zelmont driving lamps was bolted to the front end. Another pair of Zelmonts were fitted on the top along with a full width Federal bubble machine with orange flasher. We had great fun with the overhead lights—if only we had a siren too. The rear tire cover featured a light bulb to signify Ford's "better idea." The hot air balloon was also decked out to look like a light bulb.

A total of six vehicles received the RVI and Stroppe treatment for the balloon chase: two Broncos, two Ford vans and two Ford pickup trucks—all painted in the same orange with the special trim. After the record was set, Bill Stroppe explained one highway trooper's reaction to this fast moving sextet racing to the site of a balloon landing. "We might have been just a touch over the limit," Stroppe grinned, "and I was in the lead as we crested this hill, too late to 'get under' his radar. He was so astonished to see six custom Fords shooting by he must have forgotten to set the radar. He just watched us drive by."

A fitting farewell for our old friend the Bronco . . .going out in style with custom paint and interior and being driven by Bill Stroppe. ❑

Formula Desert Dog tires, size 10-15LT on aluminum alloy rims really helped the off road handling and traction. Sidepipes shown were just for show; exhaust was stock.

BRONCO VS BRONCO

A DARING COMPARISON OF OLD VERSUS NEW By Steve Campbell

stance, was the last to carry the original body styling, and its standard engine—a 302ci V-8—was the most powerful that had been offered up to that time. The Bronco II, on the other hand, epitomizes Ford's efforts to create a technologically advanced 4x4 that includes a smaller version of the Twin-Traction-Beam front end introduced in 1980 as well as a fuel-conscious V-6 engine that—while delivering nowhere near the guts of the 351- or 400-cubic-inch monsters that became available in 1978—provides more than enough muscle to haul its light package.

It is virtually impossible to find a purely stock '77 4x4 of any make these days, and that seems especially true of the Bronco. Off-roaders treat original-equipment machines as no more than a starting point from which to create a truly worthy vehicle, so the factory rubber and wheels are immediately discarded in favor of larger, more aggressive equip-

Bronco owners always seem to be engaged in a sort of sibling rivalry: The '66 was best, one will say, because it was the first, the simplest and the toughest. Another will point out that the '77 was better, more powerful, tougher. No, a third will comment, the '78 carried even more horsepower, was bigger inside and out and was the toughest of them all. And now, with the downsized Bronco II rolling across the outback, yet another generation adds its own opinion: The littlest pony is the most comfortable, gets the best mileage and is tougher than all the rest. The common element throughout the Bronco's 19-year history is un-

mistakably its durability—its toughness—but so many changes have taken place in the 4x4's workings over the past two decades that we, too, have become intrigued by the question of which bobtail is best. Hence, we decided to initiate an admittedly subjective and informal comparison of old versus new.

After considerable debate around the office, we chose to match the '77 Bronco against the newest model, this year's Bronco II. Although this choice immediately leaves us open to criticism from other year-model owners and fans, we felt that these two players represent the greatest diversification in the Ford sport/utility family while still embodying the most outstanding features of the early and late types. The '77 Bronco, for instance,

ment, and little time is wasted before the suspension has been beefed, the body lifted and the engine reworked. Much of our comparison is therefore the product of memory, research into our archives for impressions set down in road tests performed seven years ago, endless hours spent poring over long-ago-filed specification charts and maintenance manuals and conversations with others who've been acquainted with both the '77 and Ford's newest horse.

One such Bronco buff is Kent Broersma, whose bobtail was featured in our May '84 issue ("Broersma's Bronco"). We chose his machine to graphically represent the older version because the changes he's made, while definitely enhancing the vehicle's performance, re-

BRONCO vs BRONCO

tain the essential look and feel of the original. Additionally, Kent's knowledge of the Bronco line made him an invaluable contributor to our story: He previously owned a '66, is the primary builder of his current '77 and has spent many hours helping with the construction of his brother's '78. His affinity for the early Ford bobtail is unquestionable, and at the conclusion of his time on the test track and over the off-road trails of our photographic expeditions, he had become a staunch believer in the Bronco II as well.

If a completely unbiased observer chanced upon our comparison team while our Broncos were parked side by side, he probably would be struck by how alike the two are in styling. From the beginning, the Bronco favored function over flash, and while the '84 model's lines have been somewhat softened by

slightly more gradual curves in the sheetmetal and wrap-over rear quarter windows, its exterior is no less boxy or sturdy-looking than that of the '77. The older vehicle's hood is a tad longer, and the narrow bubbles over the front fenders have succumbed to a more aerodynamic approach, but the Ford design engineers have retained such basics as wind wings in the passenger compartment glass, flared wheelwells (exaggerated by Bushwacker flares on Broersma's 4x4 but still evident on less-modified '77s) and overhang measurements that remain amazingly close: identical 28.5-inch marks up front and a mere 2.6-inch difference at the rear, with the older model measuring 33.3 inches from wheel center to bumper against the Bronco II's 35.9 inches.

In fact, if a designer in 1977 had been asked to create a then-futuristic rendition of the Bronco, the '84 skin could easily have been the result. In each dimensional category, the two are remarkably close in stock trim. The '77 is slightly taller at 73 inches as opposed to the Bronco II's 69, but the new model is longer at 158.4 inches compared to the '77's 153.8. The earlier Bronco is 69.1 inches wide from fender to fender, and the '84 edition measures only 65 inches. Overall, the '77 isn't really much larger than its downsized heir. (To be fair,

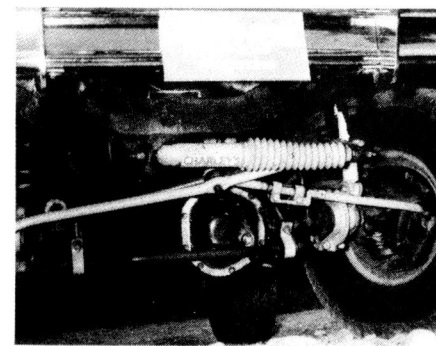

The early Bronco used a live axle located by coil springs up front. It was tough and reliable, but its stiffness lost points when put against the Twin-Traction-Beam front end of the Bronco II. Broersma has obviously done a bit of redesigning on his own.

though, the Bronco didn't become a truly big 4x4 until the fully redesigned '78 version hit the road. Its overall length was 180.3 inches, and it stood 75.5 inches tall and 79.3 inches wide.)

Mechanically, the differences between the '77 and the '84 Bronco II are vast. The '77 utilizes a live axle that sends both half shafts directly into the ring-and-pinion set within a single housing, but it supplants the traditional leaf springs with coils, providing a softer ride and less unsprung weight. The Bronco II, profiting from Ford advances that were introduced in 1980, rides on a Twin-Traction-Beam (TTB) front suspension that lets each forward wheel react independently to bumps and depressions. This system wasn't too impressive in the full-size Bronco because it provided only slightly more travel and compliance than the straight-axle setup with a marginally smaller mass and unsprung weight advantage, but in the Bronco II it's an obvious benefit. Probably because of reworked spring rates, weight ratios and differing component geometry, the TTB works well in the newest, lightest Bronco, giving it a clear advantage over the '77. (Whether it will prove as strong as either the live axle or its bigger TTB predecessor remains to be seen, but we haven't broken one yet, and we've tried harder than most owners might.)

The powertrains in the two Broncos are likewise very dissimilar, due mostly to the engineering philosophies in vogue when they were designed. Only old ladies or extremely foresighted fossil-fuel visionaries went for less than a full house in 1977, which is reflected by the fact that the 302 V-8 was the *only* Bronco engine available that year. In contrast—America having suffered the effects of oil embargoes and ensuing gas-station lines—the Bronco II's fuel-efficient V-6 is the only engine offered this year. Our '84 comparison vehicle's five-speed overdrive transmission further underlines the change in thinking: Its 3.96:1 first to 0.84:1 fifth gear ratios easily outpull the '77 Bronco's C-4 three-speed

With 19 years' worth of Broncos to choose from, our selections for a head-to-head showdown were not easily made. We finally opted for the newest Ford bobtail and the '77 Bronco. Kent Broersma's early version was used to represent the older model because the modifications he's made retain the look and feel of the original. Here, Broersma (right) and Editor Michael Coates debate the relative merits of the two ponies.

Much has changed, but much remains the same. While the '84 Bronco II reflects a move toward smoother body lines, the boxy shape looks as strong and sturdy as that of the '77 Bronco with which we compared it.

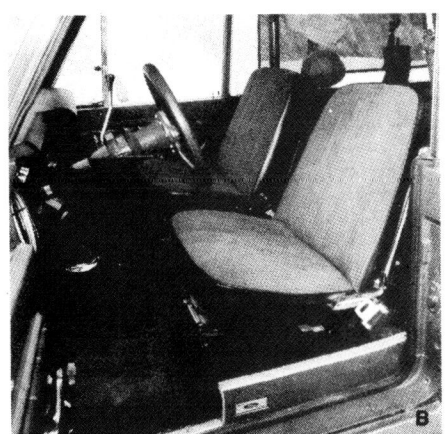

When it came time to compare interiors, the Bronco II (A) won hands down. A better gauge package, greater range of driving positions and all-around comfort were the reasons. Even though Broersma had added a tachometer and new upholstery, the '77 (B) simply wasn't in the same league.

The dragstrip comparison—conducted with our electronic timing equipment—was a closer match than we expected. Broersma's Bronco caught and beat the new version at the top end, but the Bronco II's holeshot from the line kept the margin narrow.

automatic at the bottom end and provide even greater mileage boosts at highway cruising speeds. But even the finest close-ratio gearing can't overcome pure muscle under the hood, although the 400 pounds shaved off of the current model help narrow the gap.

The stock 302 was SAE-rated to deliver 133 horsepower at 3600 rpm and 236 lb-ft of torque at 1800 rpm. The Bronco II's engine comes reasonably close in power with 115 horses at 4600 rpm, but its meager 150 lb-ft of torque at 2600 rpm appears slightly anemic. Yet the '84 version gave its ancestor a reasonable run for the money in our standing quarter-mile dragstrip runs. The '77—Broersma's Bronco, which benefits from an aftermarket camshaft, headers and a reworked ignition system—breezed through in 19.06 seconds at 75.93 mph; the stone-stock Bronco II tripped the timer at 19.84 seconds, though at a vastly slower 65.8 mph. (The relatively narrow margin in time and broader range of speeds can be at least partially explained by yet one more mechanical difference: Broersma's Bronco is driven by 3.50:1 third-member gearing, which was stock in '77; our comparison Bronco II was turning optional 3.73:1 cogs. Combined with the transmission-ratio differences and engine outputs, the results worked out just as they should have: The Bronco II blew the '77 away off the line but was caught and smothered in the middle and high ranges.)

Off-road, the two performed in almost the same way, with the '77 displaying an ultimately insurmountable edge over the sandy terrain we covered. Its automatic tranny and low-end torque pulled it easily through soft stretches where the Bronco II displayed a propensity for wheel hop. On one slippery uphill section, the '84

bobtail's lack of power became particularly evident as the engine lugged and a series of clutch- and throttle-feathering maneuvers were necessary to keep the engine from dying. That slope was eventually overcome by the newer 4x4, but only with a running start. The Bronco II, in fact, went everywhere the '77 did, but driver effort and concentration were called into play to a much greater degree. With the '77 it was a simple case of aim and go.

Both vehicles offered no-nonsense transfer-case operation, but the Bronco II's automatic-locking hubs won a close vote for convenience. (Some off-roaders, regardless of how silly or old-fashioned it might seem, still enjoy the ritual of exiting the cab and stooping to twist the dial. It has something to do, they say, with the whole idea of entering wild country and the feeling of drama that goes with it.) The '84 model's mechanical convenience ends at the hubs, however. Owner maintenance for the new Ford—as with nearly all modern vehicles, foreign and domestic—has been very nearly engineered out of existence. Either special tools or the elasticity of a contortionist is required for even the simplest chores under the Bronco II's hood, while the '77 engine, though also a bit cluttered, at least allows the backyard tinkerer to get a wrench on the spark plugs. Even with the less convenient hubs, then, chalk up another mark for the older version.

The Bronco II's 170ci, V-6 engine (A) is a mass of plumbing, pulleys and wires stuffed into a tiny compartment. Maintenance—even something as basic as changing spark plugs—is a bear. On the other hand, the '77 Bronco's 302ci V-8 (B) is reasonably accessible.

Our Broncos performed off-road just as they had on the dragstrip. The '84 went everywhere the early version did, but it took a little more time to get there.

BRONCO vs BRONCO

An examination of the interiors begins to balance things out however. In stock trim, the '77 Bronco offered few amenities. The fact that it carried door-mounted armrests and a heater were worth noting in an introductory road test published seven years ago. While the author of that article rated the front bucket seats good for their lateral support, he also noted that the rear seat was an extra-cost option. The stock '77 also came up lacking in the dashboard, which featured only a speedometer, rudimentary climate controls and a few idiot lights to monitor engine performance (or destruc-

tion, since that type of indicator comes on only when the engine has entered a state of terminal disarray). Kent Broersma has augmented his instrumentation with a tachometer, and he has installed an aftermarket stereo system and a CB unit. The Bronco II's factory dash, in comparison, includes oil-pressure and water-temperature gauges as well as an ammeter. All that's really missing is a tachometer. The center console carries a warning panel that indicates inoperative tail- and headlamps, brake lights and low fuel and washer-fluid levels. In addition, our comparison '84 was equipped with an overhead-mounted digital clock, a fully adjustable map light and a cruise-control system incorporated into the steering wheel. In this category, the poor '77 was buried under an avalanche of technological improvements. (To get cruise control in 1977, you had to buy a Lincoln Continental Mark IV.)

The seating in the Bronco II isn't the best we've seen in an '84 vehicle, but it provides reasonable support and comfort. It is the split-back rear bench, however, that gives the Bronco II a definitive seating edge. For convenience and function, it is much more advantageous than the older model's fixed seat. Likewise, we found the '84 to be a more comfortable daily driver. Its adjustable steering wheel allowed a fuller range of driving positions, and though the older Bronco was every bit as maneuverable, its solid-axle ride lost points. (It wasn't abusive, but its highway and off-road stiffness weren't really comparable to the smoother cruising we did in the Bronco II.)

Finally, having compiled all our evidence, we settled back to ponder the question once more. Which Bronco *is*

better? Our ultimate consensus—bound to cause controversy—is that new is better than old. In almost every area, the Bronco II's advanced technology and design features proved superior. Even the major exception to those findings—powertrain output—was mitigated by our fuel-economy figures. The '77 Bronco's strong V-8, which made it an easier pony to ride off-road, delivered only 14.6 mpg.

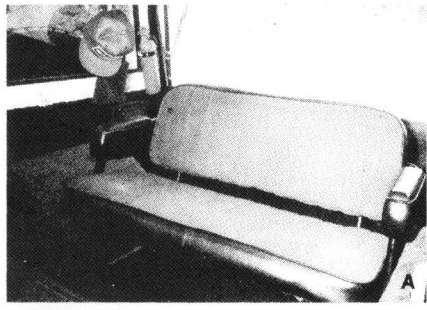

The final blow inside was the rear seating. The early model (A) didn't even come with a rear bench in standard trim, though Broersma's bobtail was equipped with the extra-cost option. In the Bronco II (B), however, the individually folding seat not only came standard but allowed for a full range of cargo and passenger usage.

In the end, our decision was relatively easy, though it's bound to be controversial: The Bronco II came out on top. In only one area—powertrain—did it fall short of mastering its older brother.

Broersma's Bronco was equipped with high-flotation tires and a more powerful engine, so it breezed over our sandy test site with ease. The leaner Bronco II wasn't quite so agile in these conditions, but it was far from being a dog.

4-WHEEL & OFF-ROAD ROAD TEST SPECIFICATIONS 1977 FORD BRONCO

GENERAL:

Vehicle	1977 Ford Bronco
Model	Standard
Base Price	$5260 (in 1977)

ENGINE:

Type	V-8
Displacement (cu in.)	302
Bore & Stroke (in.)	4.00 x 3.00
Compression Ratio	8.4:1
Carburetion	2-barrel
Fuel Requirement	Regular

LIQUID CAPACITIES:

Fuel (gal.)	14.0
Oil (qt)	5.0

TRANSMISSION:

Type	3-speed automatic
Ratios	First: 2.46:1; Second: 1.46:1; Third: 1.00:1; Reverse: 2.18:1

TRANSFER CASE:

Type	2-speed
Low Range Ratio	2.34:1
Hubs	Manual locking

AXLES:

Ratio	3.50:1

BODY & FRAME:

Chassis	Ladder frame
Body	Steel
Cargo Capacity (cu ft)	68.7
Cargo Dimensions (in.)	53.0x54.0x41.5

SUSPENSION:

Front	Live axle/coil spring
Rear	Live axle/leaf spring

STEERING:

Type	Power-assisted recirculating ball
Turns Lock-to-Lock	4.25

BRAKE SYSTEM:

Front	Disc
Rear	Drum

WHEELS:

Type	Steel
Size (in.)	15x5.5

TIRES:

Size	G78x15D

WEIGHT:

Curb Weight (lb)	3860
Advertised GVW (lb)	4900

DIMENSIONS:

Turning Radius (ft)	17.0
Overall Height (in.)	73.0
Minimum Ground Clearance (in.)	7.25
Front/Rear Track (in.)	58.5/57.5
Overall Width (in.)	69.1
Front Overhang (in.)	28.5
Rear Overhang (in.)	33.3
Wheelbase (in.)	92.0
Overall Length (in.)	153.8

ENGINE OUTPUT:

SAE Horsepower	133 hp @ 3600 rpm
SAE Torque	236 lb-ft @ 1800 rpm

MILEAGE:

Actual (mpg)	14.6

ACCELERATION:

0-30 (sec)	4.84
0-40 (sec)	6.82
0-50 (sec)	8.98
0-60 (sec)	12.15
Standing ¼-mile (sec)	19.06 @ 75.93 mph

The Bronco II's V-6 powerplant came home with a respectable 19.6 mpg average.

Obviously, this comparison isn't going to change the minds of too many early Bronco lovers, but the question begged to be answered. Besides, we've been running short of fun letters to read. We're sure to get a few after going out on a limb like this. *4WOR*

4-WHEEL & OFF-ROAD ROAD TEST SPECIFICATIONS 1984 FORD BRONCO II

GENERAL:

Vehicle	Ford Bronco II
Model	Eddie Bauer
Base Price	$12,648

ENGINE:

Type	V-6
Displacement (cu in.)	170
Bore & Stroke (in.)	3.66 x 2.70
Compression Ratio	8.2:1
Carburetion	2-barrel
Fuel Requirement	Unleaded regular

LIQUID CAPACITIES:

Fuel (gal.)	23.0
Oil (qt)	5.0

TRANSMISSION:

Type	5-speed manual
Ratios	First: 3.96:1; Second: 2.08:1; Third: 1.39:1; Fourth: 1.00:1; Fifth: 0.84:1; Reverse: 3.39:1

TRANSFER CASE:

Type	2-speed
Low Range Ratio	2.48:1
Hubs	Automatic locking

AXLES:

Ratio	3.73:1

BODY & FRAME:

Chassis	Ladder frame
Body	Steel
Cargo Capacity (cu ft)	25.6 (seats up); 64.9 (seats down)

SUSPENSION:

Front	Twin-Traction-Beam/coil spring
Rear	Live axle/leaf spring

STEERING:

Type	Power-assisted recirculating ball
Turns Lock-to-Lock	4.0

BRAKE SYSTEM:

Front	Disc
Rear	Drum

WHEELS:

Type	Styled steel
Size (in.)	15x6JJ

TIRES:

Size	P215/75R-15

WEIGHT:

Curb Weight (lb)	3440
Advertised GVW (lb)	4160

DIMENSIONS:

Turning Radius (ft)	16.1
Overall Height (in.)	69.0
Minimum Ground Clearance (in.)	6.2
Front/Rear Track (in.)	56.5/56.5
Overall Width (in.)	65.0
Front Overhang (in.)	28.5
Rear Overhang (in.)	35.9
Wheelbase (in.)	94.0
Overall Length (in.)	158.4

ENGINE OUTPUT:

SAE Horsepower	115 hp @ 4600 rpm
SAE Torque	150 lb-ft @ 2600 rpm

MILEAGE:

Actual (mpg)	19.6

ACCELERATION:

0-30 (sec)	3.82
0-40 (sec)	6.89
0-50 (sec)	10.16
0-60 (sec)	15.26
Standing ¼-mile (sec)	19.84 @ 65.8 mph

CONTINUED FROM PAGE 118

crease in rpm at idle whenever the engine heats up. A vacuum-controlled device on the carb increases engine rpm in order to burn expanded fuel. A Ford engineer indicated that this could be controlled quite simply by rerouting the vacuum tube to a petcock attached to the dashboard. The amount of vacuum could then be controlled from inside the cab. This little rpm-increasing device can be extremely dangerous off-road, especially when you're trying to descend a hill.

One test driver, long associated with Broncos, voiced his dissatisfaction with the new transfer case shift lever. He preferred the earlier T-handle, which he said made shifting much easier. Speedometer error was negligible on the Bronco; the speedo read 28 at 30 mph and was dead-on at 55 mph.

While not the most popular vehicle among the staff (the CJ-7 and Terra pickup vied for this somewhat dubious honor), the Bronco was in the top three. A direct competitor in the marketplace with Jeep's CJ-7 (if Ford does decide to cancel the Bronco, Jeep will reap the rewards), the Bronco is fun to drive both on and off the road. Adding dual shocks up front and maybe a stabilizer bar in the rear would give it cat-like stability. A judicious choice of gearing and tires would improve both hillclimbing and acceleration.

Motoring down the highway in a Bronco is reasonably comfortable; however, at certain speeds the ride gets choppy because the front end pitches up and down. But with a wheelbase of only 92 inches, that's to be expected. Even so, it's not nearly as rough as the ride of an 84-inch Jeep CJ-5.

The Bronco ranks high in water shielding, both for engine and interior. Repeated water dunkings and stream crossings failed to make the engine sputter, the brakes fade or the driver damp.

Ford doesn't recommend towing trailers of more than 2000 pounds. Furthermore, they don't even offer any trailering options. For trailers up to 2000 pounds, the Bronco should be equipped with the 4600-pound GVW package, larger radiator, power steering, G78x15 tires and a frame-mounted hitch.

As a utility vehicle, the Bronco does a good job. For those wanting a weekday commuter car/weekend booniemobile combination, a '73 or newer model is the one to buy. The Bronco is more comfortable than its direct competition and it's got more cargo space as well. ●

CAN AND TIRE HOLDER
Continued from page 80

the corners to keep the carriage head from turning. About 2 inches from the bottom tube on the flat plate, drill and tape a 3/8-inch hole. A 3/8-inch bolt with a washer welded on the head pushing against the tailgate keeps things from flexing in the middle.

Bolt the spare tire up to the rack and the cans to the can holders. Position the can and holder on the rack and mark each side. Remove the holders, tack weld them, and double check everything before welding solid. The cross braces can now be added.

I also used the stock latch by moving it to a new position just between the left side can holder and the spare tire. Large sheet metal screws hold it in place with the stock bolts filling in the old holes.

A new license plate bracket and light has to be purchased, or fabricate one to mount on the bumper and a plate cut to cover the old light hole.

This can-spare tire rack was tested over 1400 miles of Baja roads two days after it was built, and it came through with flying colors. Hope you're as happy with yours as I am with mine. □

During the mid-Sixties, the sport of off-roading was discovered by the American public. Actually, it was rediscovered, since the first motor-driven vehicles were somewhat dirt- and mud-oriented by necessity, and the military later gave us our first taste of four-wheeling with trucks developed to survive adverse conditions.

The new generation of off-roaders found that it could take an appropriately equipped vehicle hunting, fishing or vacationing with the whole family, tackling the rough terrain and hauling all the necessary gear at the same time. It became a family-oriented recreation and a lucrative new market for the automotive manufacturers overnight.

Ford Motor Co. jumped at the chance to get heavily involved and was ready to introduce the "all new" '66 Bronco in the fall of '65 in the form of a fully enclosed, short-wheelbase, truck-like vehicle with a standard six-cylinder or optional V8 engine. It could be purchased either as a two- or four-wheel drive version depending on how serious the buyer was about getting off the pavement. Although sparse by today's standards, the interiors were functional, and the uncarpeted models could be hosed down after an outing.

This terrific little off-roader gave way to a bigger and somewhat plusher version in 1976. This model was based on

BRONCO
BIRTHDAY 22 YEARS OLD AND GOING STRONG

the F-series chassis and offered many more options, especially comfort items for a changing market. The big Bronco was well accepted and was soon selling far more units per year than the early Bronco had during its best years.

During the mid- and late-Seventies' gas crises, Ford pressed ahead with plans for a new down-scaled version of the Bronco to replace the big F-series vehicle, but by the time it was set for introduction, full-size model sales were doing better than ever. Therefore, the company decided to keep both lines as long as there were enough sales to support them. One of the more interesting findings was that there were two completely separate markets. The Bronco II's big sales hadn't affected the F-series Bronco at all!

Today's Broncos, both full- and mid-size, are healthy in terms of sales, and with major refinements being added annually, they've become more durable and effective in an off-road environment. The full-size version now utilizes a small-block port-injected V8 that gives the power of past years' engines but doesn't sacrifice mileage in the process. Its little brother, the Bronco II, is now running an injected V6 rated at 140 horsepower. It also has a new Touch Control option that will let the driver move into four-wheel drive at speed, which is generally when you need it. No one wants to stop on a steep hill to shift the transfer case.

Both Broncos have a tremendous sales record, still holding down the No. One spot for any four-wheel drive utility vehicle in either category. They will no doubt be around for many years to come, servicing the die-hard Ford enthusiast who has grown out of his pickup and into a Bronco as the size of his family increases.

It's hard to believe it has been 22 years since the first model rolled off the assembly line, but at the rate they're going, Broncos should be around for another 20, capturing the imaginations of young adventurers across the United States and getting families in and out of tough places. ●

Tidy classic from a simpler era

BY MATT STONE
PHOTOS BY KIRK WILLIS

Debate continues over what rightly earns the title of "The First Sport-Utility Vehicle." Most will say it was military versions of what we now call a Jeep Wrangler, though the folks at Land Rover may offer another opinion. Chevrolet and GMC make a good case for the 1982 S10 Blazer and Jimmy as being the first "modern era" SUV, as does the still-with-us 1984 Jeep Cherokee. I would say none of this arm-wrestling matters, as the badge is most rightly worn by the covered wagons used by settlers moving West to perfect their homestead claims. Think about it: a vehicle with all the comforts of home, because everything they could carry from their last home was inside. There was seating for the entire family, with a power source and suspension that had to be able to handle all manner of terrain. So in this sense, nothing with an internal combustion engine has any right to the "first" claim anyway. But that is truly another story. ...

By the early 1960s, the first hints of what we now think of as a 2-door SUV were already available. Besides the aforementioned civilian Jeeps, Jeepsters and Land Rovers (the latter being none

136

1973 Ford Bronco

too common in the U.S. at the time), there were Toyota Land Cruisers and perhaps most notably, the International Harvester Scout. The first Scouts appeared in 1961 and cast a pattern that's still valid today: a square-rigged, full-fendered vehicle employing truck chassis and running gear, but in a smaller 2-door package. They were available in convertible, steel-cabbed pickup and station-wagon body configurations.

Power came from a variety of 4-, 6- and 8-cylinder engines, and Scouts could be had with 2- or 4-wheel drive. They quickly became the favorite of forest rangers everywhere.

Ford can hardly be accused of missing a trend in trucking, then or now. Sales of International Scouts and the other entries demonstrated strong growth, at least on a percentage basis, in the early 1960s, and Ford's model

planners correctly hypothesized that the trend would continue. The use of market-research data as a tool for identifying new model design characteristics and features was much less common 30-plus years ago than it is today, but the company's researchers contacted off-roading clubs and thousands of what would now be called "target market buyers" to hear what they wanted and needed in this type of vehicle. Dearborn's entry was internally dubbed U-100. Development began in late 1963, and the Ford Bronco was introduced on October 1, 1965, as a 1966 model.

Like the Scout, Bronco was offered in three body styles, at least initially. There was the Roadster, a Jeep-like open truck with optional top and doors, and the hardtop Wagon, which included the doors and a metal hardtop with side glass. The third model, what we would now look at and call a pickup truck, was named the—you guessed it—Sports Utility. It was a bit unusual in that its bed was actually wider than it was long. The new Ford was dimensionally similar to the Scout as well. With a length of 152.1 in., the Bronco was nearly 2 in. shorter than the Scout, while the Scout's width was just 1.2 in. wider than the Ford's 69.2 in. The biggest difference was the wheelbase, 92.0 in. for the Bronco and 100.0 in. for the Scout. It would be unfair to say the Bronco was a copy, but the similarities are striking.

Ford had plenty of engines in the parts bin, and initially offered a 170-cu-in. inline six as standard equipment. Borrowed from the Falcon, it was rated at 105 bhp, and was available only with a fully synchronized 3-speed manual transmission. Shortly thereafter, the Mustang's 289 V-8 was made optional. At 200 bhp, this engine was rated at nearly double the output of the base six and gave the Bronco much-needed punch and towing power, though it was still only available with a manual transmission, which no doubt cost it some sales.

"Unexpected traction, unexpected action" claimed advertisements about the Bronco's 4-wheel-drive system, certainly an important aspect of its multi-use appeal. Ford didn't skimp in the axle department; out back was the company's nearly indestructible 9-in. third member, a similar version of which can still be found under every NASCAR SuperTruck, and a Dana 30 unit up front (updated to the even-beefier Dana 44 for 1971). The front

hubs were locked in at all times, and manual unlocking hubs were offered as an option.

Dana also provided the 2-speed transfer case, offering 4-wheel Low and 4-wheel High ranges, plus 2-wheel drive. If there's one place where these first-series Broncos really outdid their competition, it was in the suspension department. Ford had finally done away with front leaf springs on its standard pickup models for 1965, and the Bronco was also equipped with a front coil/rear leaf setup. This contributed to a better ride and less suspension vulnerability; those who have ever snapped a front leaf spring on a rock will understand.

"Form follows function" describes the early Bronco's standard interior trim and equipment levels. Anything you didn't sit or step on was painted metal, and much like a Volkswagen, engine functions were monitored by one large, multifunction instrument in front of the driver. It contained the speedometer, odometer, fuel gauge, engine temperature, oil pressure and ammeter. The balance of the switchgear could be recognized from other Ford products. Base price for a '66 Wagon was $2625, and a total of 23,766 Broncos were built that first year.

Beginning in 1967, Ford began offering a variety of option packages designed to increase comfort and sparkle up the Bronco's utilitarian appearance. For example, that year's "Sport" package included things like armrests, wheel covers, a headliner, interior trim upgrades, bright metal trim around the windows, chrome bumpers and a cigarette lighter. Pretty basic stuff from today's perspective, but much appreciated by the Bronco owner of 30 years ago.

It would be impossible to even think

of an early Bronco without mentioning the late Bill Stroppe. Off-road racing was quickly gaining in popularity during the late 1960s, and Ford went to Stroppe, hoping he could give the Bronco a dose of his Carrera Pan-Americana-winning magic, as he had done with factory-sponsored Lincolns a decade and a half earlier. The Long Beach-based Holman and Moody-Stroppe skunk works and race shop helped morph the Bronco into a more-than-capable dirt racer. Drivers like Bill Rush, Pete Torres, Stroppe's son Will and future truck-racing legend Walker Evans rode Broncos to overall and class wins in the Baja 500, Mexican 1000 and Mint 400 enduros.

But no combination says "One Bad Bronco" more than Stroppe himself teaming with Parnelli Jones to drive Big Oly (see story on page 74). Olympia Brewery sponsored this part Bronco, part NASCAR stocker that Jones drove to back-to-back wins in the 1000 in 1971 and 1972, not to mention bagging both the Mint 400 and Baja 500 in '73. Built by Parnelli and Dick Russell, Big Oly featured power steering and an automatic transmission ... fitments practically unheard of on any race car of the era. Bill once described his numerous experiences as navigator/passenger with Jones to me as follows: "He drove like the Devil himself. His right foot only had one position—flat to the floor. He looked straight ahead, relaxed and concentrating on going as fast as we could. There were only three things that could hap-

pen—we would win, we could break or we would die."

Stroppe also offered his own line of performance parts, as well as what may have been one of the first "tuner SUVs," the Stroppe Bronco. Equipped with a winch, big wheels and tires, a raised suspension, more chrome, special identification and other goodies, it was *the* Bronco to have. I know. My boyhood buddy Stephen got a maroon one with dual glasspacks—as a present—from his parents. I was jealous. Still am. ...

Ford would continue developing the Bronco, upgrading standard equipment and offering more options over the years. Smaller units were replaced by 200-cu.-in. sixes and 302-cu.-in. V-8s. The Roadster was dropped after 1968, and the pickup model bowed out after the 1972 model year. Two appeal-broadening options made their appearance for 1973, perhaps inspired by the suc-

cess of Big Oly: power steering and a C-4 3-speed automatic transmission.

Our Salon feature Bronco, belonging to Hemet, California, firefighter Brian Altizer, is one such equipped 1973 model. Altizer is only its second owner, purchasing the Sequoia Brown Metallic wagon from the proverbial little old lady, whose husband had passed away. "It needed a substantial cosmetic restoration," comments Altizer, "but the mechanicals are basically

original, as is much of the interior." This particular Bronco features the Ranger package, which includes additional chrome trim, two-tone paint and interior comforts such as the houndstooth cloth-seat inserts. While most Bronco owners have modified their trucks with the latest off-road suspension hardware and highly modified 302 or 351 V-8s, Brian and his brother Mike, whom he credits with much of the restoration work, took great pains to keep it as original as possible. Altizer is no stranger to these first-series Broncos. Besides this sub-47,000-mile example, he and girlfriend Cathey also own a '70 and a '71, which see daily use.

In yet another variation of the Ford versus Chevy battle, the Bow-Tie gang responded with their own such rig, the Blazer, in 1970. Rather than being a purpose-built vehicle with its own body like the Bronco, the Blazer was a short-wheelbase iteration of Chevrolet's full-size pickup truck. It proved to be the right formula, at least for the time: by 1972, Blazer was out-selling Bronco by a 2-to-1 margin (44,266 vs 21,892). The trend continued, and by 1976 the spread was 5-to-1, the Bronco selling 13,325 units and the Blazer nearly 75,000. If imitation is the sincerest form of flattery, then Ford flattered Chevrolet by moving the Bronco to its large-truck platform for 1978. Sales jumped to 77,917 that year, and broke 100,000 in 1979. The era of the classic Bronco had come to an end.

But gone is not forgotten, as these trucks have garnered a nearly cult-like following today. As Ford was bringing the Expedition to market just a bit more than 30 years after that first, tidy Bronco was born, many wondered why Ford chose to call its new full-size, 4-door SUV by a new name, while letting the Bronco badge ride off into the sunset after the 1996 model year. Thankfully, the Ford marketeers realized that the Expedition was indeed something completely different, and wisely chose not to brand-mismanage the more historic nameplate. You only need look at Brian Altizer's Bronco to understand why. 🚚